THE BEGINNING

The Story of the Early Days of Christianity

Dr. Dino J. Pedrone

WESTBOW
PRESS®
A DIVISION OF THOMAS NELSON
& ZONDERVAN

WestBow Press books may be ordered through booksellers or by contacting:

WestBow Press
A Division of Thomas Nelson & Zondervan
1663 Liberty Drive
Bloomington, IN 47403
www.westbowpress.com
1 (866) 928-1240

ISBN: 978-1-9736-6061-3 (sc)
ISBN: 978-1-9736-6062-0 (hc)
ISBN: 978-1-9736-6060-6 (e)

Library of Congress Control Number: 2019904641

Print information available on the last page.

WestBow Press rev. date: 05/01/2019

Thanks

I wish to thank the following people who dedicated themselves to making this book possible:

Corey Adams...An assistant who loves Christ and the work God has given him to do. Thank you, Corey, for your faithfulness to and organization of this project.

Rosina Brandon.....Rosina is an amazing Christian lady. Despite illness she faithfully labored with the text and editorial work until it was finished. Your dedication is an example to all of us. Thank you, Rosina, and thanks to your husband, Emerson, who was so willing to give yours and his time for this Project.

Adam Pedrone...One editor looked at your illustrations and simply said 'Amazing'. They are amazing. Thank you for giving your God given gift of art to the project. The illustrations help tell the story of the early days of Christianity.

Roberta 'Bobbi' Pedrone...You are a woman of God and to my amazement God has allowed me to have you as my wife for over one half a century. Your insight, advice, recommendation accompanied with wit and wisdom go a long way in making this project, we believe, a blessing to many.

Introduction

It was my nineteenth trip to Israel. Our beautiful Mercedes bus was traveling along a strip of road by the Sea of Galilee. The sea is a very humble, small lake alongside the city of Tiberias. It is not a large lake. The body of water is 53 kilometers in circumference, 21 kilometers long, and approximately 13 kilometers wide. The maximum depth is 43 meters. A humble lake and yet it was here that Jesus of Nazareth devoted so much time in His public ministry.

If Jesus is truly God in the flesh, an obvious question comes to mind. Why did Jesus spend so much time here and not in the religious, political capital of Jerusalem? There are at least three obvious reasons.

The first is a prophetic reason. The prophet Isaiah states God would honor Galilee with the Messiah's presence. (Isaiah 9:1-2). This area was looked at with distain because Gentiles also occupied the community. The gospel of Matthew explains Jesus' ministry here in the following way. "… *that it might be fulfilled which was spoken by Isaiah the prophet, saying: the land of Zebulun and the land of Nephtali, By the way of the sea, beyond the Jordon, Galilee of the Gentiles: the people who sat in darkness have seen a great light, And upon those who sat in the region and shadow of death spring up Light has dawned"* (Matthew 4:14-16). Matthew reminds us that 700 years before the Messiah, Jesus would arrive and the light of salvation would light the Gentile world. It was here that Jesus began calling His disciples and one by one they left what they were doing to 'follow Christ'.

That thought leads to the second reason Jesus went to Galilee. It was here that he would gather a small group of citizens to carry on the work after His death. In just three years the training was done. These disciples were located in Capernaum. Peter, Andrew, James, and John were two sets of brothers. Fisherman by trade they were beckoned by Jesus. Here in the common community of Capernaum Jesus selects these four fisherman, adds the tax collector, Matthew, and they are told by the Master the goal was to be fishers of men. Jesus chose a total of twelve followers.

The third reason was also chosen because of the universality of the area. The good news of the gospel states that Jesus of Nazareth would live, die, be buried and rise again. Jesus would minister to all people. Jesus would spend much time in what some called the "Galilee of the Gentiles".

Capernaum was a fishing village with a population of 1,500 during the time of the Hasmoneons. Today there is a Byzantine Church some conjecture contains the remains of the home of Peter. The dynasty lasted a few years beyond 100 BC with the installation of King Herod in 37 B.C. ending their reign. When Jesus was born Herod the Great was the Roman vassal king. He was ruthless, wicked, and arbitrary, yet he erected incredible building projects such as the city of David, Massada, and Caesarea.

It was here that Jesus commences His amazing ministry. The family of Jesus leave Nazareth, go to Bethlehem, and eventually arrive in Egypt to escape the murderous tactics of Herod's killing all male infants two and under. Upon arriving in the area of the Sea of Galilee, Jesus is baptized by John the Baptist (Matthew 3), is tempted by Satan (Matthew 4), and then begins calling these disciples.

Jesus' fame spreads from this place. Even though we have listed three obvious reasons why his ministry starts here, it seems to make little sense.

As we ride along on our journey we will shortly arrive at our hotel for a large Israeli buffet to be followed by a restful sleep.

My Jewish friend, Edan Geva, our licensed tour guide from EinGev Jordan Valley shares a simple, yet most profound thought. "One man from the peasant class of his time speaks to other people of the peasant class of their time, on a nine mile strip of beach, and the entire world has changed. This is so statistically impossible that the only logical conclusion is 'the hand of God'". Fascinating words by my Jewish friend.

Early Jewish and Christian literature gives a vivid portrayal of Christianity. From Galilee to Jerusalem, the most diligent of followers eventually saw Jesus ascend into heaven. The four gospel accounts present the story of his life recognizing that many details are not recorded in the sacred text. "And truly Jesus did many other signs in the presence of His disciples, which are not written in this book; but these are written that you may believe that Jesus is the Christ, the Son of God, and that believing you may have life in His name" (John 20:30-31).

The great question is this. Will Christianity survive when the leader is gone? Today Christians claim over 30 percent of the world's population. Christianity is the majority religion in most places of the world with North and South America, Australia, and some African areas leading the way. How is it possible that a man who spent his early ministry in the small communities of the Sea of Galilee be recognized as God in the flesh?

The book of Acts, the fifth book of the New Testament tells the story. It is this author's desire to track the story and to emphasize as my guide said, "This is the hand of God".

We arrived at our motel. We will observe the story of Galilee on this trip. Our book, however, will tell the story of the early days of Christianity... How it all began.

Will this faith last? The book of Acts gives two reliable reasons pointing to longevity. The first is the resurrection of Jesus Christ. He is not dead! The second is the arrival of the Holy Spirit. The Holy Spirit through the Bible gives us all we need to continue the Christian legacy.

Contents

CHAPTER

1

The Story of Christianity
The Elements
(Acts 1:1-11)

The former treatise have I made, O Theophilus, of all that Jesus began both to do and teach, Until the day in which he was taken up, after that he through the Holy Ghost had given commandments unto the apostles whom he had chosen: To whom also he shewed himself alive after his passion by many infallible proofs, being seen of them forty days, and speaking of the things pertaining to the kingdom of God: And, being assembled together with them, commanded them that they should not depart from Jerusalem, but wait for the promise of the Father, which, saith he, ye have heard of me. For John truly baptized with water; but ye shall be baptized with the Holy Ghost not many days hence. When they therefore were come together, they asked of him, saying, Lord, wilt thou at this time restore again the kingdom to Israel? And he said unto them, It is not for you to know the times or the seasons, which the Father hath put in his own power. But ye shall receive power, after that the Holy Ghost is come upon you: and ye shall be witnesses unto me both in Jerusalem, and in all Judaea, and in Samaria, and unto the uttermost part of the earth. And when he had spoken these things, while they beheld, he was taken up; and a cloud received him out of their sight. And while they looked stedfastly toward heaven as he went up, behold, two men stood by them in white apparel; Which also said, Ye men of Galilee, why stand ye gazing up into heaven? this same Jesus, which is taken up from you into heaven, shall so come in like manner as ye have seen him go into heaven (Acts 1:1-11 KJV).

The work of Jesus Christ was finished. He died, was buried, and rose again. A key Biblical term is redemption. Redemption means "to buy back." In Christian theology the word (Greek: *apolutrosis*) speaks of the deliverance from our sins. The word in the Old Testament Scripture refers to a metaphor of releasing or setting free from bondage. There must be a payment. There are legal terms concerning the substitution of an animal and for the deliverance of a person, a family's possession or property. The word therefore means to buy back. The person accomplishing this is a redeemer. In the New Testament there are two Greek words that are used to convey this truth. "The concept of redemption is nevertheless conveyed in the New Testament by the terms *agorazo* and *lyo* Word Groups."[1] These terms refer to a marketplace transaction. Jesus went into the marketplace of sinners and by His blood cleansed and wiped away every sin. " ... *knowing that you were not redeemed with corruptible things, like silver or gold, from your aimless conduct received by tradition from your fathers, but with the precious blood of Christ, as of a lamb without blemish and without spot. He indeed was foreordained before the foundation of the world, but was manifest in these last times for you who through Him believe in God, who raised Him from the dead and gave Him glory, so that your faith and hope are in God"* (Peter 1:18-21). Christ acted obediently to go to the cross and with the payment of His blood appeased the wrath of God and set all believing sinners free. The work of redemption is done.

The book of Acts, which is the foundation of the story of Christianity, does, however, have unfinished business. It is the business of evangelism. In a little over 30 years the work of Jesus Christ is finished. Now the unfinished work of evangelism continues. The book of Acts tells the beginning story.

Acts is the second volume of Luke's writings. The book of Acts tells the story of the beginnings of the church. It begins with the story of Jesus in His passion. It then proceeds with the ascension of our Lord and the arrival of the Holy Spirit on the day of Pentecost. The book is obviously not the full story of Christianity nor does it cover all the history at that time of the church recorded in Acts.

The book presents two apostles who are very active. The first is Peter. The second is Saul of Tarsus or Paul. More than half of the book records the evangelistic efforts of Paul. The church begins to grow from Jerusalem and eventually to the Gentile world. Christianity grew out of Judaism. It is important to appreciate the Biblical, Jewish roots of the Christian faith.

The key to understanding the book is the arrival and role of the Holy Spirit as He leads, guides, strengthens, and teaches the church to spread out into evangelism. The book is often named The Acts of the Apostles or The Acts of the Holy Spirit. Both are accurate. Perhaps we could call the title: The Acts of the Holy Spirit through the Apostles.

In the first eleven verses of the book there are at least six interesting elements. These elements establish the foundational story of Christianity that is recorded in the rest of the book.

The Past   A Message

"*The former account I made, O Theophilus, of all that Jesus began both to do and teach,*" (Acts 1:1). Theophilus was a person of high rank. He may have been the highest ranking man in the community. "In the community Theophilus is the name or honorary title of the person to whom the gospel of Luke and the Acts are addressed."[2] " *... it seemed good to me also, having had perfect understanding of all things from the very first, to write to you an orderly account, most excellent Theophilus,*" (Luke 1:3) The name means "friend of God". (Theos means God and philos means friend).

"*... until the day in which He was taken up, after He through the Holy Spirit had given commandments to the apostles whom He had chosen*" (Acts 1:2) Four times in this chapter the Scripture teaches that Jesus was taken up. This speaks to the ascension "*Now when He had spoken these things, while they watched, He was taken up, and a cloud received Him out of their sight*" (Acts 1:9); " *... who also said, 'Men of Galilee, why do you stand gazing up into heaven? This same Jesus, who was taken up from you into heaven, will so come in like manner as you saw Him go into heaven'*" (Acts 1:11); " *... beginning from the baptism of John to that day when He was taken up from us, one of these must become a witness with us of His resurrection*" (Acts 1:22). Jesus ascended up. Where did He go? To heaven. What is he doing there? He is seated at the right hand of God. Scripture

~ 3 ~

often emphasis this truth. *"If You are the Christ, tell us."* But He said to them, *'If I tell you, you will by no means believe. And if I also ask you, you will by no means answer Me or let Me go. Hereafter the Son of Man will sit on the right hand of the power of God.'"* (Luke 22: 67-69) *" ... which He worked in Christ when He raised Him from the dead and seated Him at His right hand in the heavenly places"* (Ephesians 1:20). *" ... looking unto Jesus, the author and finisher of our faith, who for the joy that was set before Him endured the cross, despising the shame, and has sat down at the right hand of the throne of God."* (Hebrews 12:2) Here are three passages that teach Jesus is seated at the right hand of God.

The Bible teaches Jesus is God. In the declaration of Jesus' birth, He is *"God with us"* (Matthew 1:23) Jesus is spoken of as the true God. *"And we know that the Son of God has come and has given us an understanding, that we may know Him who is true: and we are in Him who is true, in His Son Jesus Christ. This is the true God and eternal life"* (I John 5:20). God the Father called the Son, God. *"But to the Son He says: 'Your throne O God, is forever and ever; a scepter of righteousness is the scepter of your kingdom'"* (Hebrews 1:8). Thomas recognized Jesus as God. *"And Thomas answered and said to Him, 'My Lord and my God!'"* (John 20:28).

The right hand of God speaks of the power of God. Jesus spoke often of the power that God had given Him. *"And Jesus came and spoke to them, saying, 'All authority has been given to Me in heaven and on earth'"* (Matthew 28:18). *"So then, after the Lord had spoken to them, He was received up into heaven, and sat down at the right hand of God"* (Mark 16:19). *"God is Spirit, and those who worship Him must worship in spirit and truth."* (John 4:24). Jesus said that some people would see him at the right hand of God. *"Jesus said 'I am. And you will see the Son of Man sitting at the right hand of the Power, and coming with the clouds of heaven'"* (Mark 14:62). *"Jesus said to him, 'It is as you said, Nevertheless, I say to you, hereafter you will see the Son of Man sitting at the right hand of the Power, and coming on the clouds of heaven'"* (Matthew 26:64). Stephen, the churches first martyr, saw Jesus at the right hand of God. *"When they heard these things they were cut to the heart, and they gnashed at him with their teeth. But he, being full of the Holy Spirit, gazed into heaven and saw the glory of God, and Jesus standing at the right hand of God, and said, 'Look! I see the heavens opened and the Son of Man standing at the right hand of God:'"* (Acts 7:54-56). It's interesting that no one has seen the Father. (John 1:18); *"And the Father Himself, who sent Me, has testified of Me. You* have neither heard His voice at any time, nor seen His form." (John 5:37). Jesus is God in the flesh. "And without controversy great is the mystery of godliness: God was manifested in the flesh, Justified in the Spirit, Seen by angels, Preached among the Gentiles, Believed on in the world, Received up in glory" (I Timothy 3:16).

Whatever honor and respect belong to God the Father should be granted to the Son. The power of God is always at work. At the right hand of God refers to the omnipresence, omniscience, and omnipotence of God. It's a metaphor speaking of Jesus' authority.

Note this marvelous Scripture in Ephesians. " ... which He worked in Christ when He raised Him from the dead and seated Him at His right hand in the heavenly places, far above all principality and power and might and dominion, and every name that is named, not only in this age but also in that which is to come. And He put all things under His feet, and gave Him to be head over all things to the church, which is His body, the fullness of Him who fills all in all" (Ephesians 1:20-23). The fact that Jesus is sitting is a reminder to us that the work of God in redemption is done.

"... until the day in which He was taken up, after He through the Holy Spirit had given commandments to the apostles whom He had chosen" (Acts 1:2). The unity of the Godhead is found throughout the Acts. Jesus was God, yet He was empowered by the Holy Spirit. The work of the third person of the Trinity is mentioned here. "And the angel answered and said to her, 'The Holy Spirit will come upon you, and the power of the Highest will overshadow you; therefore, also, that Holy One who is to be born will be called the Son of God'" (Luke 1:35). It was the Holy Spirit working in Mary when God the Son became a man named Jesus Christ. Jesus was human. He had a human mother. Jesus spoke of Himself as being anointed by God. "The Spirit of the Lord GOD is upon Me, Because the LORD has anointed Me To preach good tidings to the poor; He has sent Me to heal the brokenhearted, To proclaim liberty to the captives, And the opening of the prison to those who are bound; (Isaiah 61:1).

"Likewise when Jesus spoke in the synagogue in Nazareth he said, 'The Spirit of the LORD is upon Me ... '" (Luke 4:18). When Jesus was baptized in the Jordan River, the Holy Ghost "descended in bodily shape like a dove" (Luke 3:22). Luke 4:14 records that " ... Jesus returned in the power of the Spirit into Galilee ..." Jesus was led of the Spirit into the wilderness. (Luke 4:1).

As we embark on the story of Christianity, we need to give total credence to the doctrine of the Trinity. There is God the Father, God the Son, and God the Holy Spirit. This truth is all through Scripture. Interestingly, the Holy Spirit often is left out or beyond our discussion. Notice, however, these thoughts. Jesus lived, served and journeyed as a human being. He is truly the Son of Man. He is also God. He's the God-man. 100% God. 100% man. Yet he had the leading of the Holy Spirit just as believers do. You and I are completely dependent on the Holy Spirit. If Jesus was anointed to serve, how much more we need to be anointed to service.

The Passion – The Proof

"... to whom He also presented Himself alive after His suffering by many infallible proofs, being seen by them during forty days and speaking of the things pertaining to the kingdom of God. And being assembled together with them, He commanded them not to depart from Jerusalem, but to wait for the Promise of the Father, 'which,' He said, 'you have heard from Me" (Acts 1:3-4).

The evidence of Jesus Christ's redemptive work is overwhelming. After the resurrection Jesus appeared for forty days. For example: On resurrection morning at an early hour, several women came to the tomb to complete the customs of burial. They are surprised to see the tomb empty. Mary of Magdela runs to the apostles. Peter and John sense her concerns. While the women were still at the tomb they were surprised to hear an angel explain that Jesus had risen and their task is to go and tell the brethren. *"So they went out quickly and fled from the tomb, for they trembled and were amazed. And they said nothing to anyone, for they were afraid"* (Mark 16:8). With fear and joy they leave to go to the apostles. *"So they went out quickly from the tomb with fear and great joy, and ran to bring His disciples word"* (Matthew 28:8). *"Then they returned from the tomb and told all these things to the eleven and to all the rest"* (Luke 24:9). In the meantime Peter and John go to the empty tomb. John believes. *"Then the other disciple, who came to the tomb first, went in also; and he saw and believed"* (John 20:8). Peter goes in and sees the handkerchief that had been around Jesus' head lying there by itself. It was customary in our Lord's day that when royalty ate a meal, they would occasionally step out from the banquet a few minutes to rest. If the napkin was neatly folded, it meant he would return. If it was wadded up and placed aside, it meant that the person was through. Peter sees the folded napkin. He knows the custom. Is it possible that Peter knew that Jesus had risen from the grave, but in his backslidden state he may have felt there would be no place for him in the kingdom?

When the other women spoke to the disciples it did not seem that the disciples believed their word. *"Then they returned from the tomb and told all these things to the eleven and to all the rest. It was Mary Magdalene, Joanna, Mary the mother of James, and the other women with them, who told these things to the apostles. And their words seemed to them like idle tales, and they did not believe them"* (Luke 24:9-11).

Mary of Magdela returns to the tomb. She is heartbroken. She looks in the tomb. Jesus approaches behind her. One of the most beautiful conversations take place.

Now when she had said this, she turned around and saw Jesus standing there, and did not know that it was Jesus. Jesus said to her, 'Woman, why are you weeping? Whom are you seeking?'" She, supposing Him to be the gardener, said to Him, 'Sir, if You have carried Him away, tell me where You have laid Him, and I will take Him away.'" Jesus said to her, "Mary!" She turned and said to Him, 'Rabboni!'" (which is to say, Teacher). Jesus said to her, 'Do not cling to Me, for I have not yet ascended to My Father; but go to My brethren and say to them, 'I am ascending to My Father and your Father, and to My God and your God.'" Mary Magdalene came and told the disciples that she had seen the Lord, and that He had spoken these things to her" (John 20:14-18). Jesus sends Mary to the apostles.

Later that day, there are two followers of Jesus walking to Emmaus.

Now behold, two of them were traveling that same day to a village called Emmaus, which was seven miles from Jerusalem. And they talked together of all these things which had happened. So it was, while they conversed and reasoned, that Jesus Himself drew near and went with them. But their eyes were restrained, so that they did not know Him. And He said to them, 'What kind of conversation is this that you have with one another as you walk and are sad? Then the one whose name was Cleopas answered and said to Him, 'Are You the only stranger in Jerusalem, and have You not known the things which happened there in these days?' And He said to them, 'What things?' So they said to Him, 'The things concerning Jesus of Nazareth, who was a Prophet mighty in deed and word before God and all the people, and how the chief priests and our rulers delivered Him to be condemned to death, and crucified Him. But we were hoping that it was He who was going to redeem Israel. Indeed, besides all this, today is the third day since these things happened. Yes, and certain women of our company, who arrived at the tomb early, astonished us. When they did not find His body, they came saying that they had also seen a vision of angels who said He was alive. And certain of those who were with us went to the tomb and found it just as the women had said; but Him they did not see.' Then He said to them, 'O foolish ones, and slow of heart to believe in all that the prophets have spoken! Ought not the Christ to have suffered these things and to enter into His glory? And beginning at Moses and all the Prophets, He expounded to them in all the Scriptures the things concerning Himself. Then they drew near to the village where they were going, and He indicated that He would have gone farther. But they constrained Him, saying, 'Abide with us, for it is toward evening, and the day is far spent. And He went in to stay with them. Now it came to pass, as He sat at the table with them, that He took bread, blessed and broke it, and gave it to them. Then their eyes were opened and they knew Him; and He vanished from their sight. And they said to one another, 'Did not our heart burn within us while He talked with us on the road, and while He opened the Scriptures to us?' So they rose up that very hour and returned to Jerusalem, and found the eleven and those who were with them gathered together, saying, 'The Lord is risen indeed, and has appeared to Simon! And they told about the things that had happened on the road, and how He was known to them in the breaking of bread (Luke 24:13-35)

What an amazing story! They return to Jerusalem to inform the eleven. Jesus then appears to the apostles. He opens the Word of God to them. *"Then, the same day at evening, being the first day of the week, when the doors were shut where the disciples were assembled, for fear of the Jews, Jesus came and stood in the midst, and said to them, 'Peace be with you."* When

He had said this, He showed them His hands and His side. Then the disciples were glad when they saw the Lord. So Jesus said to them again. 'Peace to you! As the Father has sent Me, I also send you." And when He had said this, He breathed on them and said to them, 'Receive the Holy Spirit. If you forgive the sins of any, they are forgiven them; if you retain the sins of any, they are retained" (John 20:19-23). Only God can forgive sins. Jesus, being God, can forgive sins. He is not communicating any power to the disciples. In the two previous verses Jesus says, *'Peace be with you! As the Father sent me, so I am sending you."* He then breathed on them saying, *'Receive the Holy Spirit."* He sent them away to preach the gospel. As Jesus is about to leave the world He will give them the Holy Spirit. We, as witnesses, are to proclaim the same message. The small group is commissioned by the Lord.

Questions settle in. Perhaps Jesus appeared to individuals but there is no Biblical account of his meeting people over the next week. Thomas missed the previous Sunday evening meeting. When informed that Jesus appeared, he refused to accept its validity.

A week later Jesus appears to the eleven with Thomas present. Jesus tells him to look at his hands and put his hands into his side. Jesus has the scars from his episode on the cross. Thomas response is magnificent. "My Lord" (Kurios-Lord, master) "My God" (theos-God of mankind).

There is now instruction to take the 60 mile journey north to Galilee. *"Then Jesus said to them, 'Do not be afraid. Go and tell My brethren to go to Galilee, and there they will see Me"* (Matthew 28:10). *'But go, tell His disciples—and Peter—that He is going before you into Galilee; there you will see Him, as He said to you"* (Mark 16:7). John writes, *'And truly Jesus did many other signs in the presence of His disciples, which are not written in this book; but these are written that you may believe that Jesus is the Christ, the Son of God, and that believing you may have life in His name"* (John 20:30-37). Perhaps things that occurred on their journey were part of what John addresses here.

The apostles arrive at the Sea of Galilee and they are fishing in the morning. Jesus calls to them. It's on this occasion that Jesus and Peter have a lengthy discussion. (John 21:1-19).

The apostle Paul records that Jesus appeared to 500 brethren at one time. (1Corinthians 15:6). There is no indication when this happened or where it occurred. I do wish I had been there! How about you?

Jesus appears to James. *"After that He was seen by James, then by all the apostles"* (1 Corinthians 15:7).

It would seem that Jesus certainly had other appearances. They are not recorded in the Holy Scriptures.

"Then the eleven disciples went away into Galilee, to the mountain which Jesus had appointed for them. When they saw Him, they worshiped Him; but some doubted. And Jesus came and spoke to them, saying, 'All authority has been given to Me in heaven and on earth. Go therefore and make disciples of all the nations, baptizing them in the name of the Father and of the Son and of the Holy Spirit, teaching them to observe all things that I have commanded you; and lo, I am with you always, even to the end of the age. Amen'" (Matthew 28:16-20).

Later He appeared to the eleven as they sat at the table; and He rebuked their unbelief and hardness of heart, because they did not believe those who had seen Him after He had risen. And He said to them, 'Go into all the world and preach the gospel to every creature. He who believes and is baptized will be saved; but he who does not believe will be condemned" (Mark 16:14-16). Jesus gives the Great Commission. ("Go … Evangelize … Disciple!") It was during this period Jesus instructed the disciples to stay in Jerusalem and wait for the coming of the Holy Spirit.

Jesus goes close to Bethany, gives them final instructions, and ascends into heaven. *"And He led them out as far as Bethany, and He lifted up His hands and blessed them. Now it came to pass, while He blessed them, that He was parted from them and carried up into heaven. And they worshiped Him, and returned to Jerusalem with great joy, and were continually in the temple praising and blessing God. Amen"* (Luke 24:50-53).

The Promise – A Helper Is Coming

"… for John truly baptized with water, but you shall be baptized with the Holy Spirit not many days from now" (Acts 1:5).

Believers baptism is identifying with Christ's death, burial and resurrection. However, prior to this ordinance Jewish believers used baptism for a ritual. It was considered to be a cleansing as a ceremony for Gentiles. John the Baptist took this and applied it to Jews. John claimed his baptism was of repentance. *'I indeed baptize you with water unto repentance, but He who is coming after me is mightier than I, whose sandals I am not worthy to carry. He will baptize you with the Holy Spirit and fire"* (Matthew 3:11). *"Then Paul said, 'John indeed baptized with a baptism of repentance, saying to the people that they should believe on Him who would come after him, that is, on Christ Jesus*" (Acts 19:4). This baptism then is a cleansing of one's mind. It speaks to a new direction. His baptism demonstrates a recognition of turning from sin with a desire to look forward to the coming of the Messiah. John was stern. He even reminded the most religious of people to repent. *But when he saw many of the Pharisees and Sadducees coming to his baptism, he said to them, 'Brood of vipers! Who warned you to flee from the wrath to come? Therefore bear fruits worthy of repentance*" (Matthew 3:7-8). A new kingdom is coming. A new era is about to dawn.

Christian baptism today is a picture of Christ's death, burial and resurrection and it points us to the gospel. The gospel is the good news of what Jesus has done.

Jesus tells his followers in 1 Corinthians they will be baptized by the Holy Spirit. A further explanation of this is recorded in *"For by one Spirit we were all baptized into one body—whether Jews or Greeks, whether slaves or free—and have all been made to drink into one Spirit."* (1 Corinthians 12:13). People from all walks of life, regardless of their past, or whether they are from the rich heritage of Judaism or the Gentile world can all be placed into the body of Christ. This is a spiritual baptism. It is about to happen! This body includes many believers. *"For in fact the body is not one member but many"* (1 Corinthians 12:14).

The time is coming, Jesus says – Get ready for it!

Amazingly, the apostles miss the point. They expect something else.

The Potential

"Therefore, when they had come together, they asked Him, saying, 'Lord, will You at this time restore the kingdom to Israel?'" (Acts 1: 6).

This is the disciples' final question prior to the ascension. Here Jesus is connecting an eschatological truth with a glowing reality. The apostles' desire would be to receive the Holy Spirit, and then their connection would be that the kingdom would be Jewish in nature and a social/political kingdom would be established.

Later the apostle Peter provides great insight. *"Of this salvation the prophets have inquired and searched carefully, who prophesied of the grace that would come to you, searching what, or what manner of time, the Spirit of Christ who was in them was indicating when He testified beforehand the sufferings of Christ and the glories that would follow. To them it was revealed that, not to themselves, but to us they were ministering the things which now have been reported to you through those who have preached the gospel to you by the Holy Spirit sent from heaven—things which angels desire to look into"* (1 Peter 1:10-12). The Old Testament prophets wrote about grace and the Holy Spirit. Perhaps they were not sure of what they were writing. They wrote of a suffering Messiah and the glory that would follow. We live in a unique period of time. Some call it the age of grace. The Old Testament writers apparently did not see this period. For over 2000 years Jesus, through the Holy Spirit, is calling believers who are a part of the body (church) of Christ. Jesus tells the disciples here that the timing is on the Father's calendar, not theirs! *"Then the kingdom and dominion, And the greatness of the kingdoms under the whole heaven, Shall be given to the people, the saints of the Most High. His kingdom is an everlasting kingdom, And all dominions shall serve and obey Him"* (Daniel 7:27). The Bible is a progressive revelation. God unveiled His person and plan gradually. The apostles' confusion is understandable. God's timetable is His, not ours.

The Power – The Martyrs

The timing of Jesus first coming was predictable. Mary knew she had the Messiah in her womb. (Luke 1:26-37). The familiar injunction came from the angel Gabriel. *"For with God nothing shall be impossible"* (Luke 1:37). Elizabeth knew when the Messiah would be born. The proclamation from her lips emphasized the birth of Jesus, the Messiah. *"Blessed are you among women, and blessed is the fruit of your womb"* (Luke 1:42).

The ancient Simeon, a just and devout man, was waiting for the coming of the Messiah. *"And behold, there was a man in Jerusalem whose name was Simeon, and this man was just and devout, waiting for the Consolation of Israel, and the Holy Spirit was upon him. And it had been revealed to him by the Holy Spirit that he would not see death before he had seen the Lord's Christ"* (Luke 2:25-26). When Mary and Joseph brought the baby Jesus to him, he wrapped his arms around the infant proclaiming *'Lord, now you are letting your servant depart in peace according to your word; For my eyes have seen your salvation which You have prepared before the face of all peoples, A light to bring revelation to the Gentiles, and the glory of Your people Israel"* (Luke 2:29-32).

Anna, a prophetess of the tribe of Asher and daughter of Phanuel, was 84 years old and had been looking for redemption in Jerusalem. She saw Jesus and told all who would listen of the redemption that had come to Jerusalem. (Luke 2:36-38). In the seven-week prophecy of Daniel, the addition of the years leads to the timing of Jesus birth and eventual march into Jerusalem on what is traditionally called Palm Sunday. (Daniel 9:24-27). The coming of Jesus the first time was predictable as to time. His second return ... Only the Father God knows.

Jesus tells the disciples their responsibility. A new power is about to come. He tells the disciples they will receive this power. The word power here is *dunamis*. It literally means dynamite. It is not dynamite as we sometimes characterize it! The word is translated in the Old Testament as *heyil* and can mean power of a host. The Greek word speaks to miraculous power! The word is used in Luke 5:17, referring to the power of the Lord to heal people. There is another word in the Greek Language. It is *exousia* and it is translated as authority. In Matthew 7:28, 29 we find crowds were amazed at Jesus since he taught with *exousia*. The *dunamis* is the power of God in the message delivered while the exousia is the resultant authority of the message.

The Holy Spirit, the third person of the Trinity, will be given. He is not just mystical or mysterious. He is the one Jesus promised. *'If you love Me, keep My commandments. And I will pray the Father, and He will give you another Helper, that He may abide with you forever—"* (John 14:15-16). *"Nevertheless I tell you the truth. It is to your advantage that I go away; for if I do not go away, the Helper will not come to you; but if I depart, I will send Him to you. And when He has come, He will convict the world of sin, and of righteousness, and of judgment: of sin, because they do not believe in Me; of righteousness, because I go to My Father and you see Me no more; of judgment, because the ruler of this world is judged. 'I still have many things to say to you, but you cannot bear them now. However, when He, the Spirit of truth, has come, He will guide you into all truth; for He will not speak on His own authority, but whatever He hears He will speak; and He will tell you things to come. He will glorify Me, for He will take of what is Mine and declare it to you. All things that the Father has are Mine. Therefore I said that He will take of Mine and declare it to you"* (John 16:7-15). Both *dunamis* or *exousia* are from the Holy Spirit.

Dynamite as we know it today was invented by Alfred Nobel. Nobel was a Swedish chemist, engineer and businessman who invented other explosives as well as dynamite. He's also well known as the founder of the Nobel prizes. The *dunamis* of Acts 1:8 has nothing to do with Nobel's dynamite other than the word perhaps comes from this Greek term.

The purpose of this *dunamis* is that we may be witnesses. In Acts 1:7

Jesus identifies the word authority. *"And you are witnesses of these things"* (Luke 24:48). This is a continuation of Luke's teaching in Luke. The word for witness is translated in English as martyr. The word means 'my witnesses' or 'my martyrs'. The witnessing appears two-fold. First, it is the record of both the teachings and work of Jesus (Acts 1:1). Secondly, it speaks of the purpose of God which is to present God's Son, Jesus Christ of Nazareth, as the Savior to humankind.

In Acts 1:8 this message of Jesus ('witnesses to Me'") would begin in Jerusalem. The Rabbinical teachers distinguished Jerusalem from the rest of Judea. "Jewish scholar, Alfred Edersheim points out that this is a proof of intimate acquaintance with the Rabbinical phraseology of the time."[3]

The geographic locations are Jerusalem, then Judea, Samaria, and the rest of the world. The word *both* in Acts 1:8 refers to at the same time! As a ministry begins in its Jerusalem (home base), it spreads to Judea (wider base), Samaria (people groups) and the uttermost parts of the world (world). This is the command for worldwide missions.

Many verses abound on the call to being witnesses. *"This Jesus God has raised up, of which we are all witnesses"* (Acts 2:32); *"And with great power the apostles gave witness to the resurrection of the Lord Jesus. And great grace was upon them all"* (4:33); *"And we are His witnesses to these things, and so also is the Holy Spirit whom God has given to those who obey Him"* (5:32); *"And we are witnesses of all things which He did both in the land of the Jews and in Jerusalem, whom they killed by hanging on a tree. Him God raised up on the third day, and showed Him openly, not to all the people, but to witnesses chosen before by God, even to us who ate and drank with Him after He arose from the dead"* (10:39-41); *"For you will be His witness to all men of what you have seen and heard"* (22:15). *"And you also will bear witness, because you have been with Me from the beginning"* (John 15:27). *"Sing to the LORD a new song, And His praise from the ends of the earth, You who go down to the sea, and all that is in it, You coastlands and you inhabitants of them!"* (Isaiah 42:10).

The Prospect – Ascension and Return

Now when He had spoken these things, while they watched, He was taken up, and a cloud received Him out of their sight. And while they looked steadfastly toward heaven as He went up, behold, two men stood by them in white apparel, who also said, 'Men of Galilee, why do you stand gazing up into heaven? This same Jesus, who was taken up from you into heaven, will so come in like manner as you saw Him go into heaven' (Acts 1: 9-11).

It is rather interesting and remarkable that the ascension of Jesus Christ is not recorded in either the gospel of Matthew or the gospel of John. It is recorded in Mark and Luke. Peter speaks to it in Acts 2:33. *"Therefore being exalted to the right hand of God, and having received from the Father the promise of the Holy Spirit, He poured out this which you now see and hear"* (Acts 2:33). Peter addresses it also in Acts 3:31 *" ... he, foreseeing this, spoke concerning the resurrection of the Christ, that His soul was not left in Hades, nor did His flesh see corruption".* *"This Jesus God has raised up, of which we are all witnesses."* *... whom heaven must receive until the times of restoration of all things, which God has spoken by the mouth of all His holy prophets since the world began"* (Acts 3:21). The apostle Paul writes of the ascension several times. *" ... which He worked in Christ when He raised Him from the dead and seated Him at His right hand in the heavenly place"* (Ephesians 1:20). *"And without controversy great is the mystery of godliness: God was manifested in the flesh, Justified in the Spirit, Seen by angels, Preached among the Gentiles, Believed on in the world, Received up in glory"* (I Timothy 3:16).

In the Old Testament there was the Shekinah Glory that filled the Temple.

... so that the priests could not continue ministering because of the cloud; for the glory of the LORD filled the house of the LORD.'" Then Solomon spoke: 'The LORD said He would dwell in the dark cloud. I have surely built You an exalted house, And a place for You to dwell in forever.'" Then the king turned around and blessed the whole assembly of Israel, while all the assembly of Israel was standing. And he said: 'Blessed be the LORD God of Israel, who spoke with His mouth to my father David, and with His hand has fulfilled it, saying, 'Since the day that I brought My people Israel out of Egypt, I have chosen no city from any tribe of Israel in which to build a house, that My name might be there; but I chose David to be over My people Israel' (I Kings 8:11-16). *'In the year that King Uzziah died, I saw the Lord sitting on a throne, high and lifted up, and the train of His robe filled the temple. Above it stood seraphim; each one had six wings: with two he covered his face, with two he covered his feet, and with two he flew. And one cried to another and*

said: 'Holy, holy, holy is the LORD of hosts; The whole earth is full of His glory!' And the posts of the door were shaken by the voice of him who cried out, and the house was filled with smoke (Isaiah 6:1-4).

Here in the ascension we find a cloud. Perhaps it was the Shekinah cloud of the Old Testament teaching.

The Luke account tells us that Jesus raised his hands and blessed His followers. "And He led them out as far as Bethany, and He lifted up His hands and blessed them. Now it came to pass, while He blessed them, that He was parted from them and carried up into heaven. And they worshiped Him, and returned to Jerusalem with great joy, and were continually in the temple praising and blessing God. Amen" (Luke 24: 50-53). The followers of our Lord had their eyes fixed on Jesus. They, with great earnestness, were about to see the event that would finalize the past few days. Their Lord died, was buried, rose again, and now was ascending before their eyes.

Two angels appear. The angelic messengers give a statement that would undoubtedly be written on the minds of the apostles for years to come. Although the angels appeared as men, the text clearly states they were angels.

The white apparel is emblematic of the wholesome and holy nature of these beings.

What did the disciples think? They are gazing into heaven as Jesus goes up. Perhaps they are entertaining the thought that He will come right back. Perhaps they also were awe struck and bewilderment had closed their lips from comment.

The words of the angelic messengers explain to the apostles what just happened. The Jesus who went up will come back in like manner. How did He go up? In a cloud? Yes. In His body? Yes. "For the Son of Man will come in the glory of His Father with His angels, and then He will reward each according to his works" (Matthew 16:27). Jesus will come in the glory of His Father. Perhaps this will be a greater cloud than that of the Old Testament Shekinah. "When all the children of Israel saw how the fire came down, and the glory of the LORD on the temple, they bowed their faces to the ground on the pavement, and worshiped and praised the LORD, saying: 'For He is good, For His mercy endures forever" (2 Chronicles 7:3). " ... who alone has immortality, dwelling in unapproachable light, whom no man has seen or can see, to whom be honor and everlasting power. Amen" (1 Timothy 6:16). Perhaps at His return there will be a magnificent light that is overwhelming. Now Jesus body has no blood. He gave it on the cross.

" ... *but with the precious blood of Christ, as of a lamb without blemish and without spot. He indeed was foreordained before the foundation of the world, but was manifest in these last times for you*" (1 Peter 1:19-20). "*In Him we have redemption through His blood, the forgiveness of sins, according to the riches of His grace*" (Ephesians 1:7). At the resurrection we will have the same kind of body. In this brilliant and illustrious observance, our Lord left the earth. The promise is clear. He is coming back.

Questions

1. What work of Jesus Christ is finished? What were the events that finished it?
2. What work of Christ isn't finished? What is needed to finish this work?
3. Who are the key apostles spoken of often in the book of Acts?

For Discussion

1. How was Jesus empowered by the Holy Spirit? How does this apply to all Christians?
2. What are the two types of power discussed in this chapter?
3. What does Jesus mean when He says, 'It's not for you to know the times or seasons which the Father hath put in His authority'?

2

The Story of Christianity
The Choices

(Acts 1:12-26)

Then returned they unto Jerusalem from the mount called Olivet, which is from Jerusalem a sabbath day's journey. And when they were come in, they went up into an upper room, where abode both Peter, and James, and John, and Andrew, Philip, and Thomas, Bartholomew, and Matthew, James the son of Alphaeus, and Simon Zelotes, and Judas the brother of James. These all continued with one accord in prayer and supplication, with the women, and Mary the mother of Jesus, and with his brethren. And in those days Peter stood up in the midst of the disciples, and said, (the number of names together were about an hundred and twenty,) Men and brethren, this scripture must needs have been fulfilled, which the Holy Ghost by the mouth of David spake before concerning Judas, which was guide to them that took Jesus. For he was numbered with us, and had obtained part of this ministry. Now this man purchased a field with the reward of iniquity; and falling headlong, he burst asunder in the midst, and all his bowels gushed out. And it was known unto all the dwellers at Jerusalem; insomuch as that field is called in their proper tongue, Aceldama, that is to say, The field of blood. For it is written in the book of Psalms, Let his habitation be desolate, and let no man dwell therein: and his bishoprick let another take. Wherefore of these men which have companied with us all the time that the Lord Jesus went in and out among us, Beginning from the baptism of John, unto that same day that he was taken up from us, must one be ordained to be a witness with us of his resurrection. And they appointed two, Joseph called Barsabas, who was surnamed Justus, and Matthias. And they prayed, and said, Thou, Lord, which knowest the hearts of all men, shew whether of these two thou hast chosen, That he may take part of this ministry and apostleship, from which Judas by transgression fell, that he might go to his own place. And they gave forth their lots; and the lot fell upon Matthias; and he was numbered with the eleven apostles (Acts 1:12-26 KJV).

The declaration of Jesus had been given (1:9-11). Now the followers wait. We are the sum total of the decisions we make. In this passage of Scripture, we notice four decisions. Decisions are critical to make in life. These decisions are called choices.

In verse 12 the followers of Christ return to Jerusalem from the Mount of Olives. The Kidron Valley is to the west. The Mount of Olives is 400 feet above the Kidron floor and 200 feet higher than Jerusalem. Their journey is a Sabbath's day journey. This was the maximum distance one was permitted to travel on the Sabbath under rabbinical law. It amounts to around three-fourths of a mile. It is the distance of 2000 cubits a Jew could travel on the Sabbath from the walled limits of a city.

Luke's Gospel teaches ' ... *and were continually in the temple praising and blessing God"* (Luke 24:53). Things were about to change.

The Choice of Harmony

Peter

One does not have to look too far to find disharmony in the body of Christ. The issue that seems to harmonize believers is trouble and then the body of Christ is often disbursed forcing evangelism. Here we have about 120 believers. It is not a large group! Verse 13 identifies them as being in the upper room where verse 15 identifies the once backslidden

Peter assuming a God given rule of leadership. However, the emphasis is on Judas and Peter. *"For it is not an enemy who reproaches me; Then I could bear it. Nor is it one who hates me who has exalted himself against me; Then I could hide from him. But it was you, a man my equal, My companion and my acquaintance. We took sweet counsel together, And walked to the house of God in the throng. Let death seize them; Let them go down alive into hell, For wickedness is in their dwellings and among them"* (Psalm 55:12-15). *"Even my own familiar friend in whom I trusted, Who ate my bread, Has lifted up his heel against me"* (Psalm 41:9)

Here was an example of disloyalty to its maximum. Have you ever had a friend turn on you? Jesus Christ, our Lord, understands all of this. Judas, one of the twelve, was a traitor of the worst sense.

On the other hand it is interesting to notice that Peter assumes leadership. Peter denied the Lord and assumed his life was over.

> *Now Peter sat outside in the courtyard. And a servant girl came to him, saying, 'You also were with Jesus of Galilee.' But he denied it before them all, saying, 'I do not know what you are saying.' And when he had gone out to the gateway, another girl saw him and said to those who were there, 'This fellow also was with Jesus of Nazareth.' But again he denied with an oath, 'I do not know the Man!' And a little later those who stood by came up and said to Peter, 'Surely you also are one of them, for your speech betrays you.' Then he began to curse and swear, saying, 'I do not know the Man!' Immediately a rooster crowed. And Peter remembered the word of Jesus who had said to him, 'Before the rooster crows, you will deny Me three times.' So he went out and wept bitterly'* (Matthew 26:69-75).

The term bitterly refers to near convulsions coming out of the depth of his spirit. I am sure he felt his ministry was ended. In one of Jesus' post resurrection appearances he appeared at the Sea of Tiberias. After an exhausting night of fishing the disciples caught nothing. Jesus stood on the shore watching them (John 21:1-14). He asked them how the fishing was going and the disciples, not realizing it was Jesus, responded in the negative. Jesus command was, *'Cast the net on the right side of the boat, and you will find some.'* They did and were not able to draw in the net. John said to Peter,

'It is the Lord.' Putting on his outer garment Peter plunged into the Sea and swam to the shore. The other disciples came dragging the net in their little boat. Jesus prayed and blessed the food. This was the third time that Jesus had appeared with His disciples in a post-resurrection appearance. This time was about to change the direction of Peter's life. Peter, once a braggadocios man, was different now. His life faced unmitigated failure. He was unsure of himself. '*Simon, son of Jonah, do you love more than these,*' the Lord asked. The term for love is unconditional love. Peter, do you love me more than fishing? Do you love me more than these disciples? Peter, do you really love me? Peter, unsure of himself answers, '*Lord, You know I admire You!*' Jesus said it so simply, '*Feed My Sheep!*' Years later Peter would write to the under-shepherds, "*Shepherd the flock of God which is among you, serving as overseers, not by compulsion but willingly, not for dishonest gain but eagerly,*" (1 Peter 5:2). Perhaps, as Peter wrote, he remembered this moment. Then Jesus asks a second time the same question. With sorrow Peters responds the same way. Jesus says 'Tend (shepherd) my sheep.' On the third occasion Jesus changes the word and says, '*Do you love me?*' He changes the request to friendship. Peter is grieved. The difference that will shortly change Peter forever will be that the Holy Spirit will come on him (Acts 2). It will not be just Peter serving the Lord, but the Holy Spirit living through Peter.

It has always been somewhat comical to me to find that Peter then asks about John. "*Then Peter, turning around, saw the disciple whom Jesus loved following, who also had leaned on His breast at the supper, and said, 'Lord, who is the one who betrays You?*" Peter, seeing him, said to Jesus, '*But Lord, what about this man?*" Jesus said to him, '*If I will that he remain till I come, what is that to you? You follow Me*" (John 21:20-22).

Jesus told him to mind his own business and "follow me." God sovereignly raises up leadership. From this early conversation by the Sea of Galilee the mighty church of Jesus Christ would be raised up! The backslidden, now repentant Peter, would lead the way.

Choice of Individual Rights
Judas Iscariot

The first thing out of Peter's mouth was extremely negative. In the world of popular preaching that emphasis "make everybody feel good" the apostle Peter goes negative in first post resurrection message. The subject of Judas is brought up! It is a very sad commentary. The story of hypocrisy and the eventual suicide of Judas is saddening.

The future of the twelve apostles was spectacular! Jesus told those who followed Him, 'that in the regeneration, when the Son of Man sits on the throne of His glory, you who have followed Me will also sit on twelve thrones, judging the twelve tribes of Israel" (Matthew 19:28). Not Judas. He lost the privilege. Jesus was in a conversation with some of His disciples and said, 'there are some of you who do not believe' (John 6:36). In our Lord's high priestly prayer He spoke of Judas as the son of the lost one, the son of perdition (John 17:12). Peter would later write the gospel is for whoever will. "The Lord is not slack concerning His promise, as some count slackness, but is longsuffering toward us, not willing that any should perish but that all should come to repentance" (2 Peter 3:9). Could Judas accept the Savior he was with three years? Yes! Jesus who is omniscient clearly calls him the son of the lost one. The all wise knowing God knew the plan.

Notice three things that Judas did.

First, he guided the opposition: 'Men and brethren, this Scripture had to be fulfilled, which the Holy Spirit spoke before by the mouth of David concerning Judas, who became a guide to those who arrested Jesus ..." (Acts 1:16).

It was Judas who went to the sworn enemies of our Lord and guided them to where Jesus was. " ... and Judas, who betrayed Him, also stood with them" (John 18:5). Disloyalty in a church, company, family, or any organization is hard to accept. It is the sin of Absalom against his father. Here it is Judas sinning against the Lord.

His second issue is that he put financial gain ahead of principle. He was a part of the twelve. He was recognized as being one of the followers of Jesus. Yet, for thirty pieces of silver he betrayed the Son of God. Mark's gospel records Judas' words to the Sanhedrin. ' ... whomever I kiss, He is the One; seize Him and lead Him away safely" (Mark 14:44). As Judas comes into the Garden of Gethsemane he says, 'Rabbi, Rabbi,' and kisses the Lord. The gospel of Matthew further records that the chief priests counted out the thirty pieces of silver (Matthew 26:15).

One can only conjecture the life of Judas prior to this event. Had Jesus offended him? One incident would perhaps describe his outlook. When Mary of Bethany used her very costly oil of spikenard to anoint the feet of Jesus and then used her long flowing hair to wipe His feet as an act of worship it revealed something about her. Three times in Scripture she is seen as worshipping at Jesus' feet. Jesus had been telling His disciples over and over again that He would die and rise again. The disciples did not get it. It appears they wanted a social, political Kingdom established. Even after His resurrection they asked Him, 'Lord, will You at this time restore the Kingdom to Israel" (Acts 1:6).

Mary, however, had learned something. The perfume for the anointing of Jesus' feet cost about a year's wages and her deed was an act of worship, understanding Jesus would be buried. If one is to be buried, they must die! Judas Iscariot described in this passage as Simon's son, objects and says, 'Why was this fragrant oil not sold for three hundred denarii and given to the poor?' This he said, not that he cared for the poor, but because he was a thief, and had the money box; and he used to take what was put in it" (John 12:5-6). Jesus' full response is clear, 'Let her alone; she has kept this for the day of My burial. For the poor you have with you always, but Me you do not have always'" (John 12:7-8).

The third thing Judas did was to be too close to the world. The teaching that Christians are in the world, but not of the world needs to be carefully observed. A balance needs to be key. The balance is that we in love can develop a relationship with many, but our faith needs to be growing and we need to be closer to Jesus than the world. When Judas Iscariot went to the Chief Priests, his conversation seems very familiar, ' ... what are you willing to give me if I deliver Him to you?' When they count out thirty pieces of silver, Judas set out to find the opportunity to betray Him. The Chief Priest had been seeking to take Jesus by trickery (Matthew 14:1). They made a political decision to let Jesus go because of the feast that would cause an uproar by the people. So, a familiar friend would provide the opportunity. His name is Judas Iscariot.

The opportunities to fall into sin are everywhere! A strong life built upon the Word of God through time in the Scriptures, prayer, and involvement in a good local church will strengthen the life of the Christian. Judas chose his individual rights!

There are eight interesting facts concerning what happened to Judas. First he lost fellowship with his friends. In Peter's sermon he states clearly ' ... he was numbered with us ... ' (Acts 1:17). Here he was in a position that, perhaps, many others wanted. The comradery and fellowship he experienced with the other eleven was now gone. He would always be known as the "traitor".

Additionally, he lost his part in the ministry. When someone is to serve the Lord and had the opportunity, then sees it given to another, it is a most heart wrenching situation.

Thirdly, he lost his money. Judas was remorseful. The effect of Jesus' life began to haunt him. He returns to the priests and elders and *proclaims* ' ... *I have sinned by betraying innocent blood* ... ' (Matthew 27:4). He threw down the thirty pieces of silver and went out and hanged himself. The chief priests took the funds and decided it was not lawful to put the money into the treasury, because blood was shed. This made it blood money. They consulted together and bought a piece of property to bury strangers in. The name of the property was called The Field of Blood. Jeremiah the prophet predicted this.

> And Jeremiah said, 'The word of the LORD came to me, saying, 'Behold, Hanamel the son of Shallum your uncle will come to you, saying, 'Buy my field which is in Anathoth, for the right of redemption is yours to buy it.' Then Hanamel my uncle's son came to me in the court of the prison according to the word of the LORD, and said to me, 'Please buy my field that is in Anathoth, which is in the country of Benjamin; for the right of inheritance is yours, and the redemption yours; buy it for yourself. Then I knew that this was the word of the LORD. So I bought the field from Hanamel, the son of my uncle who was in Anathoth, and weighed out to him the money—seventeen shekels of silver' (Jeremiah 32:6-9)

The passage in Acts seems to indicate that Judas had a part in the purchase. "Now this man purchased a field with the wages of iniquity; and falling headlong, he burst open in the middle and all his entrails gushed out" (Acts 1:18). In the account in Matthew, Judas died by hanging himself. Luke, a physician writes in the Acts describing a graphic picture of the death of Judas. Perhaps the reason for ordering these events has a two-fold meaning. First, we need to grasp the words of Scripture. If someone has fallen and their internal organs were disposed it would not than be because of hanging. In the second place, when a person falls they do not usually burst their internal organs. The passages must be coupled together. It seems to this writer that Judas' body was hanging in the Jerusalem sun and the bacteria in his body caused the breakdown of his internal organs. A process known as tissue decomposition takes place. It is possible his skin broke and the internal organs began to spill out.

What we have here are two descriptions. One is given by a medical doctor.

"Then he threw down the pieces of silver in the temple and departed, and went and hanged himself" (Matthew 27:5). *"Now this man purchased a field with the wages of iniquity; and falling headlong, he burst open in the middle and all his entrails gushed out"* (Acts 1:18).

There is no contradiction here. There are two different ways to look at the same issue.

A Potter's field for burial was a common grave. It was a field of clay with much pottery. Unruly, poor, criminals, and the indigent were placed here.

A fourth issue that happened to Judas is that he lost his place with the twelve. There are eleven names listed in the symbolic Upper Room of Apostles. One is missing. That is Judas. We often read of the lost returning. The prodigal came home. The lost sheep was found. The missing coin was returned. Judas, however, lost his place. It must be hard to lose such a prominent position.

Judas also lost his reputation. This is the Potter's Field, the Valley of Hinnom. It is the traditional site of his burial. Few mothers, if any, have any interest in naming their children Judas Iscariot. Iscariot identifies him with a town in the tribe of Judah, Kerioth.

The betrayer lost his position " ... let another take his office" (Acts 1:20). This is one of the saddest commentaries of life. Judas had a position. He had an office. Imagine to be named one of the twelve! What an honor. Through his deceit and disloyalty he loses it all.

His place was taken by another. Two men were placed as it were on a ballot through the process of drawing lots, and one would be chosen. Joseph called Barsabas, also known as Justus is considered. He was probably a disciple that was a good choice, but perhaps he was not as well known or underappreciated. All of us at one time or another have been passed over or perhaps underappreciated. The other was Matthias. We know little of him. He died in A.D. 80.

The final thing that happened to Judas is that he would always be viewed as a fallen man.

It is important that we always guard our names. Two interesting thoughts about my name. My last name is now Pedrone. It was Pedoni. Pedoni means pedestrian in Italian. The traditional story in my family is that my Uncle Tony (all Italians have many Uncle Tony's in their families) came through Ellis Island and changed our name from Pedoni (pedestrian) to Pedrone, which means boss or landowner. However, the most important issue was my father reminding me to protect our family name. Good advice.

Peter had failures, but came back with a great testimony. Judas Iscariot will always be remembered as *"the son of perdition"* (the lost one).

The Choice of Talking with God
Prayer

"These all continued with one accord in prayer and supplication, with the women and Mary the mother of Jesus, and with His brothers" (Acts 1:14)*"And they prayed and said, 'You, O Lord, who know the hearts of all, show which of these two You have chosen'"* (Acts 1:24).

Verse 14 speaks of the church being of one accord. In our study in Acts 2 we will discuss the root of this word. For now we notice that the early Christians were in prayer. The meaning of this passage describes that the people meant frequently as a group. Some of the most blessed experiences of life are when we gather as a group to pray. It may be a life group or a Sunday School class. It may be a few people who join together at lunch at work who pray together. The thought here is that the people were steadfast and carried on with their desire to pray. They stuck together knowing that the promise of the Holy Spirit was about to be fulfilled.

The promise of the Spirit's coming is originally from the Father. *'Behold, I send the Promise of My Father upon you; but tarry in the city of Jerusalem until you are endued with power from on high'"* (Luke 24:49). *"And being assembled together with them, He commanded them not to depart from Jerusalem, but to wait for the Promise of the Father, 'which,' He said, 'you have heard from Me'"* (Acts 1:4). Jesus uses the term Father to remind his followers that this promise was made before Jesus came. *'And I will pray the Father, and He will give you another Helper, that He may abide with you forever, But the Helper, the Holy Spirit, whom the Father will send in My name, He will teach you all things, and bring to your remembrance all things that I said to you'"* (John 14:16, 26). *'But when the Helper comes, whom I shall send to you from the Father, the Spirit of truth who proceeds from the Father, He will testify of Me'"* (John 15:26). *'And in that day you will ask Me nothing. Most assuredly, I say to you, whatever you ask the Father in My name He will give you. I came forth from the Father and have come into the world. Again, I leave the world and go to the Father'"* (John 16:23, 28).

The Holy Spirit first occurs in Genesis 1:2, *"The earth was without form, and void; and darkness was on the face of the deep. And the Spirit of God was hovering over the face of the waters."* Throughout the Old Testament there is an emphasis on the Holy Spirit. *"But there is a spirit in man, And the breath of the Almighty gives him understanding"* (Job 32:8). *'Do not cast me away from Your presence, And do not take Your Holy Spirit from me'"* (Psalm 51:11). As we proceed through Acts 2 we will see His unique arrival in a new light.

There is emphasis here on the women. Mary, the mother of our Lord was there. It was Mary who told the people at the wedding reception to obey Jesus and do whatever He asks (John 2). It was Mary who saw her resurrected Son ascend into Heaven. Now Mary is here. Shortly she will go to live at John's house, but not yet! She is present when the Comforter is about to come.

Notice the brethren are here. We are not sure who this includes, but it is possible there were some who previously did not believe in Jesus. Some of Jesus' own brothers did not believe in Him. *"For even His brothers did not believe in Him"* (John 7:5). These certainly included the family of Jesus and it appears they made a decision to follow Christ closer to His death.

The word *supplication* means to *humbly plead*. When one is to entreat someone strongly for a favor it is a supplication. Here the followers of Jesus are humbly pleading.

In verse 24, chapter 21, there is an attitude of seriousness from the followers of Christ in choosing a man to replace Joseph as one of the original twelve. The prayer was united. The blessing of the Holy Spirit seemed evident even prior to His arrival. Notice that the followers of Jesus had not been commanded to pray, but to wait. Despite this they prayed.

"To take part in this ministry and apostleship from which Judas by transgression fell, that he might go to his own place" (Acts 1:25). The Apostle Peter states the qualifications for the apostle to be named. The apostle must be one who had been with Jesus' disciples and had witnessed the resurrection and ascension of our Lord Jesus Christ. *"Beginning from the baptism of John to that day when He was taken up from us, one of these must become a witness with us of His resurrection"* (Acts 1:22). The two candidates are chosen. There is Joseph Barsabas (Justus: Roman name) and Matthias. Neither one is listed again in Scripture. Some traditions identify Matthias as a missionary to Ethiopia.

The decision is made through the choice of the casting of lots. The names are placed on a stone. They are then put into a container. The container is shaken and then turned over until the stone comes out. This process was used for years in Israel. *"You shall therefore survey the land in seven parts and bring the survey here to me, that I may cast lots for you here before the Lord our God"* (Joshua 18:6). "The lot is cast into the lap, but its every decision is from the Lord" (Proverbs 16:33). Casting of lots in this day was considered to be a method that would reveal the will of God. It was not considered a random act.

Prayer is crucial to Christians. The amazing concept of talking to God is truly breath taking. Today, make sure you spend some time talking to God.

Decision Number Four
A Leader

There are many who question the validity of Mattias as an apostle. The reason for this is the life and ministry of Saul of Tarsus who became the missionary, theologian, and statesman, Paul the apostle. Paul said he was an apostle *'born out of due time"* (1 Corinthians 15:8).

I have no conclusive evidence on this issue, however, Mattias is not mentioned again in the New Testament. It is true that Paul was more prominent than Mattias, however, he was more prominent than the Apostle Peter. A good discussion would be whose name will be written on the foundation with the other apostles? Will it be Paul or Mattias? I think Mattias. How about you?

Decisions are important in life. We all make them. There are many decisions that are key to our Christian lives. A decision is a conclusion after there has been consideration. I encourage you to bathe in prayer your decisions.

Questions

1. What are the four choices this chapter deals with?
2. What were the eight things Judas lost?
3. What are the two types of preaching mentioned in this chapter?

For Discussion

1. What are lessons you have learned from your prayer life?

3

The Story of Christianity
Welcome to a New Lasting Friend

(Acts 2:1-13)

And when the day of Pentecost was fully come, they were all with one accord in one place. And suddenly there came a sound from heaven as of a rushing mighty wind, and it filled all the house where they were sitting. And there appeared unto them cloven tongues like as of fire, and it sat upon each of them. And they were all filled with the Holy Ghost, and began to speak with other tongues, as the Spirit gave them utterance. And there were dwelling at Jerusalem Jews, devout men, out of every nation under heaven. Now when this was noised abroad, the multitude came together, and were confounded, because that every man heard them speak in his own language. And they were all amazed and marvelled, saying one to another, Behold, are not all these which speak Galilaeans? And how hear we every man in our own tongue, wherein we were born? Parthians, and Medes, and Elamites, and the dwellers in Mesopotamia, and in Judaea, and Cappadocia, in Pontus, and Asia, Phrygia, and Pamphylia, in Egypt, and in the parts of Libya about Cyrene, and strangers of Rome, Jews and proselytes, Cretes and Arabians, we do hear them speak in our tongues the wonderful works of God. And they were all amazed, and were in doubt, saying

one to another, What meaneth this? Others mocking said,
These men are full of new wine.(Acts 2:1-13 KJV).

A cts 2 is a turning point in God's Kingdom. The book begins with the ascension of Jesus Christ. The second chapter records the giving of the Holy Spirit. The occasion was the day of Pentecost. From this chapter on the book focuses on the new lasting friend, the Holy Spirit. It commences with the early days of the church, and continues with the early ministry of the apostles, then specially Peter and finally Paul. Christianity rises out of Judaism and the roots of the early church are Jewish. The church eventually would be for all who believe. One of the major teachings from this chapter is the work of God the Holy Spirit.

In chapter one the apostles are told to wait until the Holy Spirit comes. In chapter two of Acts the followers of Christ know the Holy Spirit has come. In chapter one the disciples are engaged and equipped. In chapter two they are empowered. In chapter one the apostles hold back. In chapter two they are sent forth. In chapter one the Savior ascends. In chapter two the Spirit descends.

Jesus predicted the coming of the Holy Spirit. On the last great day of the Feast of Tabernacles Jesus said, 'If anyone thirsts, let him come to Me and drink. He who believes in Me, as the Scripture has said, out of his heart will flow rivers of living water'" (John 7:37-38). The Scripture clearly states that the Holy Spirit had not been given because Jesus had not been glorified (John 7:39). Jesus spoke of the Helper coming. 'If you love Me, keep My commandments. And I will pray the Father, and He will give you another Helper, that He may abide with you forever— the Spirit of truth, whom the world cannot receive, because it neither sees Him nor knows Him; but you know Him, for He dwells with you and will be in you. I will not leave you orphans; I will come to you'" (John 14:15-18). The work of the Holy Spirit was defined by Jesus. 'He will glorify Me, for He will take of what is Mine and declare it to you. All things that the Father has are Mine. Therefore I said that He will take of Mine and declare it to you'" (John 16:14-15).

The moment has arrived. The Holy Spirit has come.

The Event

"When the Day of Pentecost had fully come, they were all with one accord in one place" (Acts 2:1).

The Holy Spirit comes on the day of Pentecost. It is interesting to note that the Holy Spirit did not come because people prayed, tarried, or met conditions. The Spirit's arrival was linked to the pattern of certain feasts. The feast of the Passover (Pesach) is a reminder (commemoration) of the Jewish liberation from slavery in Egypt. The leadership of Moses and eventually Joshua is a very important celebration for Jewish people. The celebration begins on the fifteenth day of Nisan in the Hebrew calendar. The Feast of Unleavened Bread follows Passover and lasts seven days. Matzah is the Hebrew word for Unleavened Bread. It is a reminder of how God miraculously led the children of Israel to freedom. It was at this feast when Jesus astounded the teachers in the temple. *"His parents went to Jerusalem every year at the Feast of the Passover. And when He was twelve years old, they went up to Jerusalem according to the custom of the feast. When they had finished the days, as they returned, the Boy Jesus lingered behind in Jerusalem. And Joseph and His mother did not know it; but supposing Him to have been in the company, they went a day's journey, and sought Him among their relatives and acquaintances. So when they did not find Him, they returned to Jerusalem, seeking Him. Now so it was that after three days they found Him in the temple, sitting in the midst of the teachers, both listening to them and asking them questions"* (Luke 2:41-46).

Unleavened bread was a necessity at this event. Leavened bread has baking yeast, baking powder, or soda. This will cause the dough to bubble and rise. Unleavened bread is however a flatbread that looks like a cracker.

Pentecost is a Jewish festival. It is a harvest festival that is called Shavuot. For Christians this is a special day. For Jewish followers this holiday was held fifty days after Passover.

It is interesting to note the unity of the people. Seldom is there a generation that is as united as this group seemed to be. The Greek work is *homothymadon*. It means oneness or one mind or passion. The background of this word is beautiful. It is a compound of two separate words. One means "rush along" and a second means "unison or togetherness." Somewhere in my past I remember a speaker likening the word to instruments at a concert harmonizing together. When one goes to the concert the various orchestra members warmup and there is chaos. But when the conductor takes his place on his stand and raises his hands into the air there is silence. He then brings his hands down and the beautiful sound of harmony is blended in pitch, tone, volume, and unity under the direction of the master and produces a concert that is capable of touching numerous emotions and energies in the listeners.

Now it is obvious that Christians do not agree with various issues of theology, forms of worship, and even ways to fellowship. There is, however, something that draws us together. Our one accord in passion and thought is Jesus Christ. God's people need to be humble followers of the King of kings understanding He is Lord. Being in one accord is not agreeing on every issue! This term is found several times. Note some of them: *"These all continued with one accord in prayer and supplication, with the women and Mary the mother of Jesus, and with His brothers"* (Acts 1:14). *"So continuing daily with one accord in the temple, and breaking bread from house to house, they ate their food with gladness and simplicity of heart"* (Acts 2:46). *"So when they heard that, they raised their voice to God with one accord and said: "Lord, You are God, who made heaven and earth and the sea, and all that is in them"* (Acts 4:24). *"And through the hands of the apostles many signs and wonders were done among the people. And they were all with one accord in Solomon's Porch"* (Acts 5:12). *" … it seemed good to us, being assembled with one accord, to send chosen men to you with our beloved Barnabas and Paul"* (Acts 15:25).

"And suddenly there came a sound from heaven, as of a rushing mighty wind, and it filled the whole house where they were sitting. Then there appeared to them divided tongues, as of fire, and one sat upon each of them" (Acts 2:2-3)

The word "suddenly" means unexpectedly. An event like no other was taking place. Notice a sound comes from heaven. The Greek word for heaven here is describing the sky; heaven as the abode of God. It implies happiness, eternity, or from the sky. What is about to happen is from God! The sound is "as of a" violent or rushing mighty wind. This does not say it is a wind, but like it. It is supernatural for it comes from heaven. The residents of the house sensed what was taking place. The house here seems to be the same place where the disciples were gathered in Acts 1. It is not clear, however, that this is the case. Some believe the people were in the temple, but the Greek word that is used, oikos, is normally translated as private house. This is a miraculous event and as is so often with miracles they seem to exceed all possibilities. Where do 3000 people fit?

The noise was not wind, but sounded like it. The sight was not fire, but resembled it. The fire seemed to resemble the presence of God.

Other Scripture indicates fire associated with God's presence. *"And the Angel of the Lord appeared to him in a flame of fire from the midst of a bush. So he looked, and behold, the bush was burning with fire, but the bush was not consumed"* (Exodus 3:2). *"Now Mount Sinai was completely in smoke, because the Lord descended upon it in fire. Its smoke ascended like the smoke of a furnace, and the whole mountain quaked greatly"* (Exodus 19:18).

The Evidence

The word "filled" here is a word that is used five times in Acts:

"And they were all filled with the Holy Spirit and began to speak with other tongues, as the Spirit gave them utterance" (Acts 2:4). *"Then Peter, filled with the Holy Spirit, said to them, 'Rulers of the people and elders of Israel … '"* (Acts 4:8). *"And when they had prayed, the place where they were assembled together was shaken; and they were all filled with the Holy Spirit, and they spoke the word of God with boldness"* (Acts 4:31). *"And Ananias went his way and entered the house; and laying his hands on him he said, 'Brother Saul, the Lord Jesus, who appeared to you on the road as you came, has sent me that you may receive your sight and be filled with the Holy Spirit'"* (Acts 9:17). *"And many who had believed came confessing and telling their deeds"* (Acts 19:18).

The term is the aorist form of the Greek word pletho. It speaks of empowerment. In Acts 13:52 he uses another form (verb) pleroo for filled. Notice that the people began to speak with other languages (tongues). Notice that *"the Spirit gave them utterance"* (Acts 2:4).

The term utterance is best defined as impassioned utterances. It is interesting to note that the hearers heard the Word of God in their own languages. *"And when this sound occurred, the multitude came together, and were confused, because everyone heard them speak in his own language"* (Acts 2:6). On the day of Pentecost it seems to me the languages spoken were understood by the hearers in their dialects. The people that had gathered were from all over the Roman Empire. As the new Friend, the Holy Spirit, arrived the people heard the miraculous gospel through a miraculous means – the word in their languages!

To be filled with the Spirit is to consciously practice the presence of Christ. This evidence is possible when we have a mind saturated by the Word of Christ.

The Effect

And there were dwelling in Jerusalem Jews, devout men, from every nation under heaven. And when this sound occurred, the multitude came together, and were confused, because everyone heard them speak in his own language. Then they were all amazed and marveled, saying to one another, 'Look, are not all these who speak Galileans? And how is it that we hear, each in our own language in which we were born? Parthians and Medes and Elamites, those dwelling in Mesopotamia, Judea and Cappadocia, Pontus and Asia, Phrygia and Pamphylia, Egypt and the parts of Libya adjoining Cyrene, visitors from Rome, both Jews and proselytes, Cretans and Arabs—we hear them speaking in our own tongues the wonderful works of God' (Acts 2:5-11)

The first effect is that the Galileans spoke the truth. "They answered and said to him, 'Are you also from Galilee? Search and look, for no prophet has arisen out of Galilee'" (John 7:52). The Galileans were the most unlikely individuals to be proclaiming God's Word. Each of us need to be solid in our growth in Christ and the effect will surprise all of us.

Notice the nations that are mentioned here. The Parthians are considered to be from modern Iran. They were bitter enemies of Rome and were never really conquered by the Roman Empire. The Medes were the Parthian Empire. The Elamites are now in southwestern Iran. Residents in Mesopotamia are between the Tigris and Euphrates Rivers. Cappadocia, Pontus, Asia, Phrygia and Pamphylia are all regions in Asia Minor where there was a large Jewish population. Libya joining Cyrene west of Egypt on the African Coast. In Rome there were many Jews and Greek proselytes. Cretans are the residents of the island of Crete on the southern coast of Greece. The Arabs were living in the kingdom of Nabataean Arab. The message is the wonderful works of God.

Questions

1. The tongues in Acts were _____.
2. What is the one thing that draws Christians together?
3. What does the word unexpectantly mean?

For Discussion

1. How has the Holy Spirit been directing your life?
2. When did you first realize that God the Holy Spirit was working in your life?

4

The Story of Christianity
The Makeup of a Christian Fellowship
(Acts 2:14-47)

*But Peter, standing up with the eleven, lifted up his voice,
and said unto them, Ye men of Judaea, and all ye that dwell
at Jerusalem, be this known unto you, and hearken to my
words: For these are not drunken, as ye suppose, seeing
it is but the third hour of the day. But this is that which
was spoken by the prophet Joel; And it shall come to pass
in the last days, saith God, I will pour out of my Spirit
upon all flesh: and your sons and your daughters shall
prophesy, and your young men shall see visions, and your
old men shall dream dreams: And on my servants and on
my handmaidens I will pour out in those days of my Spirit;
and they shall prophesy: And I will shew wonders in heaven
above, and signs in the earth beneath; blood, and fire, and
vapour of smoke: The sun shall be turned into darkness, and
the moon into blood, before the great and notable day of the
Lord come: And it shall come to pass, that whosoever shall
call on the name of the Lord shall be saved. Ye men of Israel,
hear these words; Jesus of Nazareth, a man approved of
God among you by miracles and wonders and signs, which
God did by him in the midst of you, as ye yourselves also
know: Him, being delivered by the determinate counsel and*

*foreknowledge of God, ye have taken, and by wicked hands
have crucified and slain: Whom God hath raised up, having
loosed the pains of death: because it was not possible that
he should be holden of it. For David speaketh concerning
him, I foresaw the Lord always before my face, for he is on
my right hand, that I should not be moved: Therefore did
my heart rejoice, and my tongue was glad; moreover also
my flesh shall rest in hope: Because thou wilt not leave my
soul in hell, neither wilt thou suffer thine Holy One to see
corruption. Thou hast made known to me the ways of life;
thou shalt make me full of joy with thy countenance. Men
and brethren, let me freely speak unto you of the patriarch
David, that he is both dead and buried, and his sepulchre
is with us unto this day. Therefore being a prophet, and
knowing that God had sworn with an oath to him, that of
the fruit of his loins, according to the flesh, he would raise
up Christ to sit on his throne; He seeing this before spake of
the resurrection of Christ, that his soul was not left in hell,
neither his flesh did see corruption. This Jesus hath God
raised up, whereof we all are witnesses. Therefore being by
the right hand of God exalted, and having received of the
Father the promise of the Holy Ghost, he hath shed forth
this, which ye now see and hear. For David is not ascended
into the heavens: but he saith himself, The Lord said unto
my Lord, Sit thou on my right hand, Until I make thy
foes thy footstool. Therefore let all the house of Israel know
assuredly, that God hath made the same Jesus, whom ye
have crucified, both Lord and Christ. Now when they heard
this, they were pricked in their heart, and said unto Peter
and to the rest of the apostles, Men and brethren, what
shall we do? Then Peter said unto them, Repent, and be
baptized every one of you in the name of Jesus Christ for
the remission of sins, and ye shall receive the gift of the Holy
Ghost. For the promise is unto you, and to your children,
and to all that are afar off, even as many as the Lord our
God shall call. And with many other words did he testify
and exhort, saying, Save yourselves from this untoward
generation. Then they that gladly received his word were*

baptized: and the same day there were added unto them about three thousand souls. And they continued stedfastly in the apostles' doctrine and fellowship, and in breaking of bread, and in prayers. And fear came upon every soul: and many wonders and signs were done by the apostles. And all that believed were together, and had all things common; And sold their possessions and goods, and parted them to all men, as every man had need. And they, continuing daily with one accord in the temple, and breaking bread from house to house, did eat their meat with gladness and singleness of heart, Praising God, and having favour with all the people. And the Lord added to the church daily such as should be saved. (Acts 2:14-47 KJV).

For 25 years I pastored a wonderful congregation in Chambersburg, Pennsylvania. My wife and I raised our children there. I remember coming home one day and to see a drawing of a horse on a piece of paper lying on the dining room table. I asked my wife about the drawing and she told me one of our son's was the artist. I was shocked. I had a Picasso on my hands! I called him in the kitchen and explained to him that the drawing was magnificent. He looked at me with surprise and told me how easy the drawing was. He then went to one of our shelves in the library, pulled out a book, and showed me the same horse. He had traced it!

When I approach this section of Scripture I so often think of that story! If we could trace Acts 2:14-47 onto our churches it would be terrific. Here is the standard for our churches.

The individuals who observed the amazing work of God questioned what this outpouring could mean. The response by the mockers is that the people who were telling the wonderful works of God were inebriated. Here comes Peter. He is now the leader. He is not just a titular leader, but rather a man of God with apostolic authority. One of the great messages in the book of Acts is to be delivered.

The Message   We Are in the Last Days

Peter observes the time of the day is at 9 a.m. It would appear odd that people would be drunk at this hour. Peter draws his listeners back to an earlier day.

> *And it shall come to pass afterward That I will pour out My Spirit on all flesh; Your sons and your daughters shall prophesy, Your old men shall dream dreams, Your young men shall see visions. And also on My menservants and on My maid servants I will pour out My Spirit in those days. And I will show wonders in the heavens and in the earth: Blood and fire and pillars of smoke. The sun shall be turned into darkness, And the moon into blood, Before the coming of the great and awesome day of the LORD. And it shall come to pass That whoever calls on the name of the LORD Shall be saved. For in Mount Zion and in Jerusalem there shall be deliverance, As the LORD has said, Among the remnant whom the LORD calls* (Joel 2:28-32).

In Peter's message he has connected the prophet Joel's message about the Holy Spirit with the beginning of the church that is portrayed by the coming of the third person of the Trinity in a unique way. In the Old Testament the Holy Spirit gave power to some individuals for a period of time. The book of Joel was placed into the canon of Scripture somewhere in a prexilic time. Perhaps the year would be somewhere between 610 – 585 B.C.

The promise is that the Holy Spirit would come in a unique way. Peter quotes from Joel that the Spirit would be on all flesh. These words are spoken to the people of Judah and the dwellers in Jerusalem. He writes to those who are followers of God who are looking for the Messiah. The followers of Jesus were the 120 gathered in the upper room. The mockers were those who did not believe.

A large crowd was gathering for the festivities of the Day of Pentecost. Many spoke in various dialects, but all heard in their own languages. They heard about the wonderful works of God.

Notice the young men and women will prophesy. This is a term that speaks of proclaiming the Word of God.

I am a preacher. I have the opportunity to speak in numerous places. I am often asked if I am used to it. Does the excitement leave? Questionnaires expect my answer to be no. However, I must confess that every time I preach, I do it with a sense of fear and there is never a time I speak that I do not ask God for His anointing in my life. There are times when I have preached and found a listener has heard something from God that I never mentioned. This is the Holy Spirit applying God's Word as He wills.

Joel writes, and Peter proclaims, 'Your old men will dream dreams.' As people grow older it is easy to lose enthusiasm for life. When the Holy Spirit is on an older person there can be a new zeal and zest for life. The dreams here seem to speak of the future. Perhaps the desire for heaven or of blessing grandchildren, or even starting a new chapter in their life is the dream.

The message continues with ' ... your young men shall see visions.' A vision of what God has for them is vital and a vision of the future. I spent a large part of my life in Christian education. It has been such a blessing to see God's power in the lives of many youth who have gone forward to serve Him.

Beginning in verse 17 and going through verse 21 we have the heart of the prophecy. He begins by describing the 'last days'. The last days are a reference to the coming of the Messiah. Remember the Old Testament prophets did not see the age of grace that would begin on the day of Pentecost. The Old Testament prophets saw the king coming and establishing a kingdom. So the Jewish last days began here, 2000 years ago. God is graciously calling out His people, including the Gentiles, and He is chastising Israel for unbelief. The context here is Jewish. The pouring out of the Spirit will prophetically be fulfilled in the age of the kingdom.

In verse 19 there is a description of the events of the return of the Messiah. *'I will show wonders in heaven above And signs in the earth beneath: Blood and fire and vapor of smoke'"* (2:19)

Verse 20 describes the sun and the moon. *"Immediately after the tribulation of those days the sun will be darkened, and the moon will not give its light; the stars will fall from heaven, and the powers of the heavens will be shaken"* (Matthew 24:29). The question is "how does one escape this awful day of the Lord"? What is the escape? *"For then there will be great tribulation, such as has not been since the beginning of the world until this time, no, nor ever shall be"* (Matthew 24:21). This is the gospel message. Call on the name of the Lord!

Are we in the Last Days? "Little children, it is the last hour" (I John 2:18). " *... in those last days spoken unto us by His Son"* (Hebrews 1:2). We are closer to the last days than ever before. Jesus is coming!

We Have Compelling Evidence   (Acts 2:22-36)

Men of Israel, hear these words: Jesus of Nazareth, a Man attested by God to you by miracles, wonders, and signs which God did through Him in your midst, as you yourselves also know—Him, being delivered by the determined purpose and foreknowledge of God, you have taken by lawless hands, have crucified, and put to death; whom God raised up, having loosed the pains of death, because it was not possible that He should be held by it. For David says concerning Him: I foresaw the LORD always before my face, For He is at my right hand, that I may not be shaken. Therefore my heart rejoiced, and my tongue was glad; Moreover my flesh also will rest in hope. For You will not leave my soul in Hades, Nor will You allow Your Holy One to see corruption. You have made known to me the ways of life; You will make me full of joy in Your presence. Men and brethren, let me speak freely to you of the patriarch David, that he is both dead and buried, and his tomb is with us to this day. Therefore, being a prophet, and knowing that God had sworn with an oath to him that of the fruit of his body, according to the flesh, He would raise up the Christ to sit on his throne, he, foreseeing this, spoke concerning the resurrection of the Christ, that His soul was not left in Hades, nor did His flesh see corruption. This Jesus God has raised up, of which we are all witnesses. Therefore being exalted to the right hand of God, and having received from the Father the promise of the Holy Spirit, He poured out this which you now see and hear. "For David did not ascend into the heavens, but he says himself: 'The LORD said to my Lord, 'Sit at My right hand, Till I make Your enemies Your footstool. Therefore let all the house of Israel know assuredly that God has made this Jesus, whom you crucified, both Lord and Christ' (Acts 2: 22-36).

The evidence of the coming of the Holy Spirit and that we are in the last days begins with the life of Jesus Christ. Peter boldly challenges the Israelites to two truths. First, God has worked miracles by Jesus. Jesus came in the flesh. The word miracle here is the same Greek word *dunamis* that is used in Acts 1:8.

There can be no question of His Messiahship. The works and signs were known by all. The Greek word sign is *semeiou*, referring to pointing to Christ. Jesus is God. He is Messiah.

The second evidence is Christ's death. In beautiful harmony, the Scripture draws together the eternal purpose and foreknowledge of God with the human hatred of Jesus, putting Him to death. The four canonical gospels give a description of the death of Jesus Christ. Crucifixion was an ancient Roman practice. Six trials led to His death. These were by Jewish leaders and the last were by Romans. Jesus went through the terrible beating and was mocked. He was taken to the place of a skull. The Savior was separated from His Father. Please note, this was heaven's plan. He died to satisfy the Holy nature of God. This was mankind's plan. They thought he was gone now forever.

The third evidence is the glorious resurrection of Jesus Christ. This is the theme of the apostolic message – Jesus has risen from the grave. The birth pangs of verse 24 speak of His agony. Death was powerless to hold Him. *"Inasmuch then as the children have partaken of flesh and blood, He Himself likewise shared in the same, that through death He might destroy him who had the power of death, that is, the devil"* (Hebrews 2:14).

"For David says concerning Him: 'I foresaw the LORD always before my face, For He is at my right hand, that I may not be shaken'" (Acts 2:25). Peter made good use of the Old Testament Scriptures. He has quoted Joel. Now he quotes from (Psalm 16: 8-11). *"I have set the LORD always before me; Because He is at my right hand I shall not be moved. Therefore my heart is glad, and my glory rejoices; My flesh also will rest in hope. For You will not leave my soul in Sheol, Nor will You allow Your Holy One to see corruption. You will show me the path of life; In Your presence is fullness of joy; At Your right hand are pleasures forevermore"*.

Psalm 16 is a chapter about the Messiah.

(a) Jesus is forecasted as a trusted God. (Psalm 16:1),
(b) The Mediator that all followers believe in, (Psalms 16: 2, 3) and
(c) God who will not accept those who reject Him. (Psalm 16:4).
He is also portrayed as one satisfied with His followers (Psalm 16: 5,6) and one who knows that Almighty God supports them (Psalm 16:7) An incredible prophecy is then given on the resurrection.

There are some scholars who view this Psalm was at the time on the delivery of the promise made by Nathan to David. *"Now You have been pleased to bless the house of Your servant, that it may continue before You forever; for You have blessed it, O LORD, and it shall be blessed forever* (1 Chronicles 17:27). "This was … The probable occasion when Psalm 16 was written."[4] The date is over 1,000 years before Christ. (1044 B.C.) Peter wisely quotes from this Psalm in what will be his most famous message.

Contextually it appears that the Psalmist uses his own life, and yet the passage appears prophetic and therefore Peter uses it in his message. In verse 10 Sheol is mentioned. David would not be abandoned in Sheol, but the fact is that one would not be kept there. The fact that Peter uses this phraseology means that there is another one coming after David. The Bible is the inspired Word of God and part of its uniqueness is how God connects the Old with the New.

Now let's notice an important thought in this section. *"Therefore my heart rejoiced, and my tongue was glad; Moreover my flesh also will rest in hope. For You will not leave my soul in Hades, Nor will You allow Your Holy One to see corruption"* (vv 26, 27).

The word 'hades' is an interesting study. Here the Psalmist is quoted by Peter using the word hades. "Hades was a general term among the Greek writers, by which they exposed this state and this Hades was *tartarus* to the wicked, and *Elysium* to the good."[5]

I have never felt comfortable talking about hell. There are many vivid portraits of hell in Scripture. For those who deny its existence or torment, a metaphorical approach to Scripture must be followed. In my judgment, if a metaphorical approach is used it must then apply to the totality of Scripture. My approach to Scripture has always been one of a literal interpretation unless the text is otherwise stated. Although I do not pretend to have all the answers, I do believe this to be an accurate understanding of Scripture. These are tough passages. Careful, thoughtful prayer needs to be applied to hell. I would advise that the Scripture speak for itself before we add our own commentary. Notice the following passages.

> *Then He will also say to those on the left hand, 'Depart from Me, you cursed, into the everlasting fire prepared for the devil and his angels: And these will go away into everlasting punishment, but the righteous into eternal life"* (Matthew 25:41, 46). *'If your hand causes you to sin, cut it off. It is better for you to enter into life maimed, rather than having two hands, to go to hell, into the fire that shall never be quenched—'* (Mark 9:43). *'And anyone not found written in the Book of Life was cast into the lake of fire."* (Revelation 20:15). *' ... he himself shall also drink of the wine of the wrath of God, which is poured out full strength into the cup of His indignation. He shall be tormented with fire and brimstone in the presence of the holy angels and in the presence of the Lamb. And the smoke of their torment ascends forever and ever; and they have no rest day or night, who worship the beast and his image, and whoever*

receives the mark of his name.' (Revelation 14:10-11). 'Do not marvel at this; for the hour is coming in which all who are in the graves will hear His voice' … and come forth-those who have done good, to the resurrection of life, and those who have done evil, to the resurrection of condemnation.' (John 5:28-29). *'Then the king said to the servants, 'Bind him hand and foot, take him away, and cast him into outer darkness; there will be weeping and gnashing of teeth'* (Matthew 22:13). *'But the sons of the kingdom will be cast out into outer darkness. There will be weeping and gnashing of teeth'* (Matthew 8:12). *' … and will cast them into the furnace of fire. There will be wailing and gnashing of teeth ' … and cast them into the furnace of fire; There will be wailing and gnashing of teeth'* (Matthew 13:42, 50). *' … where 'Their worm does not die And the fire is not quenched. For everyone will be seasoned with fire, and every sacrifice will be seasoned with salt'*(Mark 9:48-49). *'And being in torments in Hades, he lifted up his eyes and saw Abraham afar off, and Lazarus in his bosom. Then he cried and said, 'Father Abraham, have mercy on me, and send Lazarus that he may dip the tip of his finger in water and cool my tongue; for I am tormented in this flame'* (Luke 16:23-24). *'And do not fear those who kill the body but cannot kill the soul. But rather fear Him who is able to destroy both soul and body in hell'* (Matthew 10:28).

There are many terms to describe hell. Sheol is an Old Testament word that describes the grave. "Sheol is translated "hell" thirty-one times and "pit" three times."[6] In Jesus teaching about the rich man and Lazarus, the description is that they went to a place called "paradise" (Luke 23:43). It is also called "Abraham's bosom" which is evidently a part of paradise. The rich man could not escape his torment. For those who teach that Jesus was not speaking about torment, I would ask the question, "What on earth is he trying to say?"

The rich man is punished in Hades. This is burning, separation, loneliness, misery and thirst. If this story is a parable, as some good Bible scholars teach, one must answer the question "What is Jesus saying here? What is He trying to teach? If it wasn't hell and its torment, then what is it?"

Another term that is used is Gehenna. During the reign of King the nation of Israel participated in worship of a false god name, Molech. Ahaz ordered human sacrifice and actually sacrificed his own son. *"And he sacrificed and burned incense on the high places, on the hills, and under every green tree"* (2 Chronicles 28:4). The idol actually was portrayed with open arms. A fire would be started and a child would be sacrificed in his arms. When Josiah reigned he stopped the murder and sacrilege. *"And he defiled Topheth, which is in the Valley of the Son of Hinnom, that no man might make his son or his daughter pass through the fire to Molech"* (2 Kings 23:10). The valley then became the garbage dump of Jerusalem. Jesus used this term as a graphic illustration of our eternal life of separation. It was a place of fire and fumes. *"But I say to you that whoever is angry with his brother without a cause shall be in danger of the judgment. And whoever says to his brother, 'Raca!' shall be in danger of the council. But whoever says, 'You fool!' shall be in danger of hell fire"* (Matthew 5:22). *"But I have a greater witness than John's; for the works which the Father has given Me to finish—the very works that I do—bear witness of Me, that the Father has sent Me"* (John 5:36).

Another descriptive term is a Lake of Fire. *"And anyone not found written in the Book of Life was cast into the lake of fire"* (Revelation 20:15). This description is accompanied with the term "The second death." Death is defined as a separation. It is not an annihilation. Physical death is when the soul separates from the body. *"So we are always confident, knowing that while we are at home in the body we are absent from the Lord"* (2 Corinthians 5:6). Spiritual death is separation from God.

God is a God of eternity. Scripture describes eternity as just that … Eternal. The Old Testament Hebrew word is *olam* and the New Testament Greek word is *aiónios.* "Hell lasts as long as the duration of God."[7]

My advice to those who are debating the existence of hell is this. This is not a subject to be wrong on. If there is no hell of torment, you must decide what is the fate of the unrighteous, and you will need to prove your point without the metaphorical approach. The metaphorical approach will make Scripture a hodgepodge of very interesting philosophical ideas. Also consider this. If there is no hell as Jesus described … why on earth did He suffer as He did?

The quotation in this passage from David does not refer to Israel's former king. It refers to Jesus. David was buried. This person would not see corruption. David writes this is a state of happiness. Jesus was to go to the region of the dead. This seems to be the implication here. The hope that is referred to in verse 26 is a confident expectation.

The term Holy One speaks of one who is devoted to others. This term is often used of Jesus. " ... *saying, 'Let us alone! What have we to do with You, Jesus of Nazareth? Did You come to destroy us? I know who You are— the Holy One of God'"* (Mark 1:24). *"But you denied the Holy One and the Just, and asked for a murderer to be granted to you"* (Acts 3:14). *"And the angel answered and said to her, 'The Holy Spirit will come upon you, and the power of the Highest will overshadow you; therefore, also, that Holy One who is to be born will be called the Son of God"* (Luke 1:35). This Holy One would not see the ways of corruption. Corruption was a term that referred to the grave. The Psalmist wrote centuries prior that this Holy One would not be confined to a grave.

There is great debate on whether Jesus went to hell to experience our suffering. I take the position He did experience our hell, but many well-known scholars, preachers, and teachers do not. For example, British Evangelist, John Wesley wrote "But it does not appear that our Lord went into hell. His soul, when it was separated from the body, did not go thither, but to paradise."[8] The meaning is, *"Thou wilt not leave my soul in its separate state, nor suffer my body to be corrupted"* (Luke 23:43).

Verse 28 reminds us that the Messiah fully knew He would rise again. His message to the disciples was very clear. They did not really get the message until Jesus rose again from the dead and the message changed them, when the Holy Spirit came. The resurrection was Jesus' joy and it needs to be our joy. He is risen and believers shall reign with Him forever. During the agony of Jesus death He knew the resurrection was coming. We will one day be with Him forever in an eternal and happy state.

The Fourth evidence is the exaltation of Christ. (Acts 2:29-36). At the beginning of Peter's sermon he addresses *"Men of Judah"* (Acts 2:14). He then addresses *"Men of Israel"* (Acts 2:22). Now he says *"Men and Brethren."* Secondly, it appears he addresses a more specific Jewish audience. Finally, he defers to the whole group. He is ready to drive home the importance of this day and the exaltation of Jesus Christ over all.

Peter goes back to quoting from David. He states that David is a patriarch. He states that the Israelite king died and is buried. His tomb is visible to those who want to see it. David somehow had divine understanding that another one, greater than this beloved king, would come. Peter exalts Jesus properly because He has risen from the grave. Amidst numerous witnesses, God raised Jesus from the dead. The teaching of the Trinity is clear. *"This Jesus God has raised up, of which we are all witnesses. Therefore being exalted to the right hand of God, and having received from the Father the promise of the Holy Spirit, He poured out this which you now see and hear"* (vv. 32-33). Amazingly, Israel's king wrote *"They said to my lord, sit at my right hand."*

The Holman Bible translation has two words that are translated Lord. "The Hebrew Bible has two words commonly translated "Lord" in English. By distinguishing the two, readers will see a key Messianic thread running into the New Testament … This passage is the most quoted text from "the Hebrew Bible in the entire New Testament – More than Isaiah 53 or Psalm 22."[9]

The word Lord in the New Testament (kurios) means master. Hundreds of times the word is used, most often referring to Jeshua (Jesus). From a traditional standpoint there are English Bibles that print "the Lord". (YHVH) is the name of God in the Old Testament Hebrew text. Jesus is often called "Lord Jesus" or "Lord Jesus Christ". One day everyone will "confess that Jesus (Yeshua) is Lord, to the glory of God the Father" (Philippians 2:10-11).

The word Lord in Psalm 110 is Adonai in the Hebrew text. It means sovereign, master, lord. It is a term used for human males. Sarah called Abraham her lord and David calls Saul his lord.

There are a number of times Adonai is used for God. *"Three times in the year all your males shall appear before the Lord GOD"* (Exodus 23:17). *"Out of the mouth of babes and nursing infants You have ordained strength, Because of Your enemies, That You may silence the enemy and the avenger"* (Psalm 8:2). Oh, give thanks to the Lord of lords! For His mercy endures forever"* (Psalm 136:3).

In the passage in Psalm 110 the word Adonai could refer to David or others who would follow. According to Peter's sermon this is fulfilled when the Lord says to my Lord 'Sit at my Right.' The Lord has a royal status with the initiator. This would appear to be God saying to God, or the Father saying to the Son, or God the Father speaking to the Son and saying sit at my right hand. Peter's emphasis is that the Lord has risen from the grave and he uses Old Testament passages as further evidences.

Peter continues with the remarkable statement to the "house of Israel". This Christ has been appointed by God as Lord (master) and Christ (Messiah).

The response by the people is reflected by the term "pricked" or "cut". The verb is only used here in the New Testament. The meaning is a compunction referring to a deep and very painful emotion. It is like saying "what have we done and how do we correct it?" It appears that the people were contrite and ready to hear the solution!

This is a day of transition. This is, in fact, remarkable. It is the day of new beginnings. Peter clearly states that the hearers are recipients of a promise. *"For the promise to you and to your children and to all who are afar off"* (Acts 2:38).

Peter now speaks of repentance and baptism. When Christians think of the gospel, the immediate reference is to the good news that Jesus died, was buried and rose again. For the people in those early days of Christianity there were different concepts of the gospel. Good News in the first century was a pronouncement. A new ruler would ascend to the throne and this was good news because the propaganda was, this would be a time of peace and safety. The new ruler was here.

Now the word baptism also had different concepts. The Israelites looked backward to Moses leading the people towards the Promised Land. Moses, more so than David, is pictured as the leader of Israel in this context. The people viewed their captivity back to the days in Egypt. God had promised land to Abraham and there was frustration in the fact they could not control this rather small parcel of ground. People looked at, not just individual sins, but at national sins. As John the Baptist proclaimed repentance and baptism, it was more than just an individual mandate. It was for the nation. John's announcement was that the exile would end and a new era was beginning. Jesus requested that John the Baptist baptize Him. *"It came to pass in those days that Jesus came from Nazareth of Galilee, and was baptized by John in the Jordan. And immediately, coming up from the water, He saw the heavens parting and the Spirit descending upon Him like a dove. Then a voice came from heaven, 'You are My beloved Son, in whom I am well pleased"* (John 1: 9-11). Jesus is now here. The disciples keep asking Jesus questions about the arrival of the kingdom.

The kingdom is fourfold. First, it is spiritual. One must be 'born again' (John 3) to enter the kingdom. Second, it is moral as described by the beatitudes. (Matthew 5:1-12). Third, it is literal. Jesus will reign on the earth. (Revelation 20). Finally, it is eternal. *"And at the end of the time I, Nebuchadnezzar, lifted my eyes to heaven, and my understanding returned to me; and I blessed the Most High and praised and honored Him who lives forever: For His dominion is an everlasting dominion, And His kingdom is from generation to generation"* (Daniel 4:34).

The word repentance is our acknowledgment of wrong doings. It is a change of both mind and heart. It is recognizing humanity's lostness and Jesus' salvation.

In Acts 2:38 we are faced with an individual mandate – Be saved! Be baptized! This baptism is a beginning of recognizing that the immersion into the water and the coming out identifies the person with the death, burial and resurrection of Jesus.

The Life of the Fellowship of the Church   (Acts 2:41-47)

> *Then those who gladly received his word were baptized; and that day about three thousand souls were added to them. And they continued steadfastly in the apostles' doctrine and fellowship, in the breaking of bread, and in prayers. Then fear came upon every soul, and many wonders and signs were done through the apostles. Now all who believed were together, and had all things in common, common, and sold their possessions and goods, and divided them among all, as anyone had need. So continuing daily with one accord in the temple, and breaking bread from house to house, they ate their food with gladness and simplicity of heart, praising God and having favor with all the people. And the Lord added to the church daily those who were being saved* (Acts 2: 41-47)

I mentioned earlier the drawing of my son's horse, which I eventually found out was actually traced. Here in Acts 2:41-47 we have the great passage of Scripture that describes what the early church's life was like.

The early church had important elements.

First there was preaching. There are at least 19 sermons in Acts. Peter preaches 7 sermons (chapters 1,2,3,4,5, 10,11). Stephen, the deacon, preaches one, (chapter 7). James preaches one (Acts 15). Paul preached 15 (twice in 13 & 14, one in 17, 21,22,23, 24, twice in 25 & 26, one in 28) (This does not include Philip in Acts 8. Approximately 25% of Acts is preaching. History reminds us of great preachers. Augustine, Luther, Calvin, Zwingli, Knox, Whitfield, Wesley, Edwards, Graham, Evans, Criswell, and the list goes on of mighty preachers. I have met wonderful preachers in small communities that powerfully preach. Urban communities are also blessed with such preachers.

The Greek word for preach comes from the word kērýssō. It means to proclaim, declare, announce, or to speak out as a spoken message like a herald. The word is found over 60 times in the New Testament. The early church had Peter. Acts 1 and 2 are highlighted by Peter's preaching. Peter proclaims here 'Be saved from this perverse generation."

A second Greek word that describes preaching is evangelize – *evaggelizo*. The word carries with it the idea of evangelizing.

It is key to understand that to grow a congregation both spiritually and numerically there needs to be teaching. The Didache was the teaching of the early apostles in the church.

One of the most important roles in a church is a teaching pastor. In Ephesians 4:11 there is a list of gifts given to the church. One of these gifts is listed as Pastor and teacher. The concept here is that the term is pastor teacher. The English word, and, is the Greek word *kai* which can be translated 'even'. So the pastor is … pastor even the teacher. Strong shepherding teaching is needed.

Verse 41 speaks of those who gladly received His word. The term for baptism here refers to those identifying with Christ. They were baptized into the body of Christ. Salvation is God's free gift. Baptism now becomes one of identity with Jesus.

I pastored two churches over a forty year period. I was thrilled to see the thousands baptized over those years. The excitement that is generated with new converts is breathtaking. Here in Acts 2 there were three thousand added to the body. Notice there were those who received His Word. What was the Word? It was the message of the resurrection! Now remember this is the theme of the apostolic message. Jesus is risen. The people who gathered there were specifically the many who arrived for the celebration of the day of Pentecost. Earlier we listed the many nations and dialects that had come. There were many Jews who were anticipating the coming of the Messiah who were in this group. They were Old Testament saints who by faith were looking for their deliverer. What an amazing demonstration of God's new era!

Notice in verse 42 that they continued steadfastly in the apostles' doctrine. The word doctrine refers to teaching. The word apostle can perhaps be best defined as one 'who was sent out'. The Apostles Doctrine is correct and truthful because it refers to the scriptures. In Acts 17 we are introduced to the Bereans who examined the accuracy of what was being taught. All beliefs need to be examined by the Word of God!

The early believers had fellowship. The word means community. Other than our earthly family connected through DNA or adoption, this particular relationship is of primary importance. The word fellowship is a term found in Greco-Roman literature. It was a term that expressed the commitment and care of a marital relationship. It is interesting to notice that these early believers shared their lives together. The "breaking of bread" could refer to the Lord's Table or perhaps a meal by the church members together. I have found in traveling and preaching in numerous churches that a fellowship can bond people quickly together. The two on the road to Emmaus went to their home with the Lord and "broke bread" (Luke 24:35).

The people prayed. The original 120 disciples spent much time in prayer. (Acts 1:14-15). Prayer can be done anytime and anywhere, but it is always special when a group of people pray together.

These four activities are at the heart of a group of believers. They were the study of the apostles' doctrine, fellowship, breaking of bread, and prayer. The believers were in awe. In verse 43 the word fear is the Greek work *phobos* and the term expresses a reaction to God. As unusual events began to unfold, the people were truly in awe and a fresh respect to God was displayed.

The "wonders and signs" is a common term in the early writings. Peter had spoken of this phenomena in verse 22. There is a continual emphasis from Jesus to the work of the Holy Spirit in the lives of the apostles. The risen Savior will continue to do work in the lives through the apostles who have an appointment from God with an authority passed to them through the work of the Holy Spirit and an anointing to accomplish God's work.

Verse forty-four is a remarkable truth. Notice the word "all". All who believed are together, speaking of community. This refers to the teaching of the previous verse. The people saw the remarkable work of God. Note they had all things common. The "all things in common" refers to their pooling together the things that they had. The Greek word for the first 'all' is *pontes* and the second word is *kaponta*. The word "envy" in verse 43 is the same as the first all of verse 44 and it refers to attitude, while the second refers to actions. The idea here seems to be that all people adopted an attitude that caused the people to share the things they had worked hard for. This was not forced on the people by the government, church or the apostles.

Communism is an economic system that is imposed on a group of people for collective ownership of a person's possessions and properties. It is characteristically imposed by the government with the purpose of social changes. The early Christians were sharing willingly as the Holy Spirit gave them direction. This situation does not meet the standard of communism.

As the early Christians saw the community's need, they sold their "possessions and goods" based upon the communal needs. This was a voluntary act by individuals as God gave them direction. Those who had gave to those who had not, because of their faith that was drawn from Jesus and the Holy Spirit.

Verse 46 describes a beautiful scene. Just as the 120 worshipped together in the upper room (Acts 1:14), so the believers were devoted and dedicated to each other based on the recent information that Jesus Christ had risen again. The faith of the early Jews surrounded the temple and these early followers of Jesus the Messiah also had their faith in the resurrection. They gathered at their traditional site of the temple.

The followers of Jesus would go to the temple during the morning and evening hours. Paul, the apostle, would one day rush to the temple for a feast in order that he could talk about Jesus. " ... *but took leave of them, saying, 'I must by all means keep this coming feast in Jerusalem; but I will return again to you, God willing' And he sailed from Ephesus'"*(Acts 18:21). In the early days those who were followers of Jesus visualized Jesus as the promised one who fulfilled the prophecies of the prophets. The future controversy of the Gentiles joining the body would be dealt with later in the book of Acts. How do the Gentiles fit in? Do Jewish people change their traditions and habits? The Jewish followers of Jesus continued to follow the habits and traditions of going to the temple. Remember Jesus taught people in the Temple. The Temple, amongst many things was the place for the Jewish religion to be taught. It also had social overtones to the families of Judaism.

The breaking of bread was part of the fellowship of the people. The sharing of meals together and fellowship was a part of the family of God. The fellowship stemmed from gladness and sincerity.

The sense of joy and gladness resulted in praising God. The concept of praise is a Biblical theme. The Greek word *aineo* is used here. There are often sections of Acts where the word is found. " ... *praising God and having favor with all the people. And the Lord added to the church daily those who were being saved"* (Acts 2:47); *"So he, leaping up, stood and walked and entered the temple with them—walking, leaping, and praising God. And all the people saw him walking and praising God"* (3:8, 9). The people seemed to enjoy each other! One of the keys to enjoying fellowship in the body of Christian life is to show an interest in others. Showing graciousness and interest to others attracts them to us. Perhaps as we enjoy Christ more we will learn to enjoy each other!

Conclusion

In this message by the Apostle Peter and the results that led to this church growing and advancing in God's kingdom. The pattern needs to be followed.

Questions

    1.   What were some of the early practices of the church in Jerusalem?
    2.   How can we apply these practices to our lives?

For Discussion

What practices do you enjoy in your church and why?

5

The Story of Christianity
Healing and Persecution
(Acts 3:1-26)

The early story of Christianity appears idyllic. It is a scene that comes across very pastoral and full of tranquility. There is the outpouring of the Holy Spirit. People understanding the truths in their language. There is a group of followers of Jesus who are enjoying each other in an unprecedented fashion. Chapter 3 begins to change that scene. Persecution is about to come. If this early group of followers are for real they will very swiftly be put to the test. If Christianity is true, persecution will build it.

Now Peter and John went up together into the temple at the hour of prayer, being the ninth hour. And a certain man lame from his mother's womb was carried, whom they laid daily at the gate of the temple which is called Beautiful, to ask alms of them that entered into the temple; Who seeing Peter and John about to go into the temple asked an alms. And Peter, fastening his eyes upon him with John, said, Look on us. And he gave heed unto them, expecting to receive something of them. Then Peter said, Silver and gold have I none; but such as I have give I thee: In the name of Jesus Christ of Nazareth rise up and walk. And he took him by the right hand, and lifted him up: and immediately his feet and ankle bones received strength. And he leaping up stood, and walked, and entered with them into the temple, walking, and leaping, and praising God. And all the people saw him walking and praising God: And they knew that it was he which sat for alms at the Beautiful gate of the temple: and they were filled with wonder and amazement at that which had happened unto him. And as the lame man which was healed held Peter and John, all the people ran together unto them in the porch that is called Solomon's, greatly wondering. And when Peter saw it, he answered unto the people, Ye men of Israel, why marvel ye at this? or why look ye so earnestly on us, as though by our own power or holiness we had made this man to walk? The God of Abraham, and of Isaac, and of Jacob, the God of our fathers, hath glorified his Son Jesus; whom ye delivered up, and denied him in the presence of Pilate, when he was determined to let him go. But ye denied the Holy One and the Just, and desired a murderer to be granted unto you; And killed the Prince of life, whom God hath raised from the dead; whereof we are witnesses. And his name through faith in his name hath made this man strong, whom ye see and know: yea, the faith which is by him hath given him this perfect soundness in the presence of you all. And now, brethren, I wot that through ignorance ye did it, as did also your rulers. But those things, which God before had shewed by the mouth of all his prophets, that Christ should suffer, he hath so fulfilled. Repent ye therefore, and be converted, that your sins may be blotted out, when the times of refreshing shall come from the presence of the Lord. And he shall send Jesus Christ, which before was preached unto you: Whom the heaven must receive until the times of restitution of all things, which God hath spoken by the mouth of all his holy prophets since the world began. For Moses truly said unto the fathers, A prophet shall the Lord your God raise up unto you of your brethren, like unto me; him shall ye hear in all things whatsoever he shall say unto you. And it shall come to pass, that every soul, which will not hear that prophet, shall be destroyed from among the people. Yea, and all the prophets from Samuel and those that follow after, as many as have spoken, have likewise foretold of these days. Ye are the children of the prophets, and of the covenant which God made with our fathers, saying unto Abraham, And in thy seed shall all the kindreds of the earth be blessed. Unto you first God, having raised up his Son Jesus, sent him to bless you, in turning away every one of you from his iniquities. (Acts 3:1-26 KJV).

The Scene   (Acts 3:1-3).

Notice the scene that takes place at 3 o'clock in the afternoon, Peter and John go to the temple to pray. It is the time of prayer. There were certain designated hours for prayer and being loyalists to their Savior, Peter and John go up to pray. Traditional Judaism had set the standard for prayer time at the third (9 a.m.), the sixth (noon) and the ninth hours (3 p.m.).

Peter and John had a close friendship. Together they received the baptism of John. *"He first found his own brother Simon, and said to him, 'We have found the Messiah'" (which is translated, the Christ)"* (John 1:41). They went together to prepare the Passover prior to Jesus' death. *"And He sent Peter and John, saying, 'Go and prepare the Passover for us, that we may eat'"* (Luke 22:8). John took Peter to see the high priest. *"But Peter stood at the door outside. Then the other disciple, who was known to the high priest, went out and spoke to her who kept the door, and brought Peter in"* (John 18:16). They came to the sepulcher together. *"Then Simon Peter came, following him, and went into the tomb; and he saw the linen cloths lying there"* (John 20:6). These are just a few examples of their close relationship.

This begins a remarkable set of miracles that God worked through the apostles.

"… so that they brought the sick out into the streets and laid them on beds and couches, that at least the shadow of Peter passing by might fall on some of them. Also a multitude gathered from the surrounding cities to Jerusalem, bringing sick people and those who were tormented by unclean spirits, and they were all healed" (Acts 5:15,16).

"And the multitudes with one accord heeded the things spoken by Philip, hearing and seeing the miracles which he did. For unclean spirits, crying with a loud voice, came out of many who were possessed; and many who were paralyzed and lame were healed" (Acts 8:6, 7).

"Now God worked unusual miracles by the hands of Paul, so that even handkerchiefs or aprons were brought from his body to the sick, and the diseases left them and the evil spirits went out of them" (Acts 19:11-12)

"*So when this was done, the rest of those on the island who had diseases also came and were healed*" (Acts 28:9).

There are many questions about healing. Is everyone healed? No. "*Erastus stayed in Corinth, but Trophimus I have left in Miletus sick*" (2 Timothy 4:20). Healing is in the Savior. Does God heal today? Yes. Is there a guarantee of our healing? On and on the questions go. The fact is people die. Many die because they aren't healed. Some die instantly through war or accident. But God can and does heal! It really does boil down to His sovereign purpose.

Prayer is such a blessing. If you have someone to pray with, it is such a joy. To know that we pray to a holy God in heaven is a greater joy!

The Sign   (Acts 3:4-10)

And fixing his eyes on him, with John, Peter said, 'Look at us' So he gave them his attention, expecting to receive something from them. Then Peter said, 'Silver and gold I do not have, but what I do have I give you: In the name of Jesus Christ of Nazareth, rise up and walk.' And he took him by the right hand and lifted him up, and immediately his feet and ankle bones received strength. So he, leaping up, stood and walked and entered the temple with them—walking, leaping, and praising God. And all the people saw him walking and praising God. Then they knew that it was he who sat begging alms at the Beautiful Gate of the temple; and they were filled with wonder and amazement at what had happened to him (Acts 3: 4-10).

Here is a lame man from birth who is a beggar. It seems that the apostles are on their way up to the temple and passed by the gate that is called Beautiful. The Beautiful Gate was one of the gates that actually belonged to the Temple. It is not clear today where the gate was located. There are highly acclaimed archeologists who differ in their opinion. My guess is that it may have been what was once called the Double Gate which was located in the southern wall of the Temple Mount. More than likely this was the gate that pilgrims used because of its size and it would appear to be a place for beggars to be. Most worshippers went through this gate to worship.

In Jerusalem today there are 8 gates. They were built by Suleiman the Magnificent, a Turkish Sultan. The Gate of Mercy is no more. The Zion Gate is the Gate of David not far from the traditional site of the king. The Dung Gate gets its name from the refuse dumped nearby. The Gate of Mercy is the Golden Gate or Eastern Gate. It is the gate Messiah will return through. The Lions Gate is named after tigers! It is also spoken of as Stephen's Gate, named after the first martyr of the church. Herod's Gate is called the Flowers Gate and it was not named after Herod. It may refer to a nearby cemetery. The Damascus Gate faces north and is named for the city. The New Gate actually came during the Ottoman Empire. The Jaffa gate was the disembarking gate named for those going to the Jaffa Port.

The lame man most likely suffered many rebuffs, heard ridicule and experienced rejection. In many places of the world there are those who go through dramatic times and beg for a handout. As the case was so often, Peter spoke first. Peter says 'Look at us.'" The man wondered what this would lead to. Perhaps a paper representing cash, a coin, or maybe another rebuff. He expects something. 'So he gave them his attention, expecting to receive something from them'" (vv. 5). There is no faith on this man's part. No message that states, "If you believe you will be healed." He has no reason to believe a healing is coming.

Peter's words were so truthful and yet so painful to this man. 'Silver and gold have I none.'" Peter left all to follow Jesus and wealth was not in his arsenal. Notice that Peter did not say to the man "Such as I have." It would be belittling to the man concerning what he was about to receive. He is not saying I have something less than money. He is saying 'what I have is what this man needs." What God gives us we can share and impart it to others. Here is what he says. 'In the Name of Jesus Christ of Nazareth, rise up and walk.'" "Notice the emphasis on the name. Names are important. Often Christians use Biblical names for their children. In an article from Familia there are 50 Biblical names to give your baby – Their origins and meanings."[10]

An example is as follows:

GIRLS
Abigail
Source: 1 Samuel 25:3
Origin: Hebrew
Meaning: "Father of Exaltation"

Hagar
Source: Genesis 16:1
Origin: Egyptian/Semetic
Meaning: "Foreigner, "The one who escaped," or flight".

Ana/Anna/Hannah
Source: I Samuel 2:1
Origin: Hebrew
Meaning: "Fever" or "Grace"

Claudia
Source: Matthew 27:19
Origin: Latin
Meaning: "Enclosure" or "Haven"

Deborah
Source: Judges 4:4
Origin: Hebrew
Meaning: "Bee"

BOYS

Abel
Source: Genesis 4:2
Origin: Hebrew
Meaning: "Stream"

Abraham
Source: Genesis 1-2
Origin: Hebrew
Meaning: "His Strength"

Adam
Source: Genesis 2:7
Origin: Hebrew
Meaning: "Living Man"

Ben-Hur
Source: I Kings 4:8
Origin: Hebrew
Meaning: "Son of Ur"

Benjamin
Source: Genesis 35:24
Origin: It comes from the Hebrew word "Binyamin"
Meaning: "Son of the Right Hand" or "Beloved"

Felipe
Source: John 1:44
Origin: Greek
Meaning: "He who leans on his military complex"

The point is, every name carries with it a meaning. Often it was descriptive of the person's character.

The name Jesus has a derivation from the Latin Jesus. It is a transliteration of the Greek Jesus. The name was very common in Judea where our Savior was born and lived his earthly life. Jesus is often called the Son of God, while Son of Man refers to his earthly life.

According to Bible Encyclopedia (Web Bible Encyclopedia Home) "there are 956 Names and Titles of God."[11]

For example, God is called Abba, which is a transliteration of the Greek word which means Daddy or Papa. Jesus is spoken of as blessed and only Potentate, meaning he is the Blessed and only Ruler. " ... *which He will manifest in His own time, He who is the blessed and only Potentate, the King of kings and Lord of lords*" (Timothy 6:15). Jesus is spoken of as the "Bright and morning star" (Revelation 22:16).

The name Jesus means Savior or Salvation. In the Old Testament the name occurs often.

In Acts 3 Peter identifies Jesus and states he is from Nazareth which identifies his childhood home. Again, Jesus means Savior. Lord Jesus Christ refers to the master, Savior, who is Messiah (the anointed one). It is interesting that the name of Jesus invokes healing on this man.

In verse 7 Peter takes him by the hand and lifts him up. This was an indication of the sincerity of Peter. He reaches out to extend help. Each follower of Christ needs to do the same thing. We should reach out to help the needy. The man's feet and ankle bones immediately received strength which was an indication of the miraculous power of God. The faith exercised in this miracle was on the apostle's part. The man was passive.

Perhaps Peter was remembering when Jesus lifted up his mother-in-law and she was healed. "*So He came and took her by the hand and lifted her up, and immediately the fever left her. And she served them*" (Mark 1:31). The healing in both cases was because of Jesus.

The writer of Acts is Luke "the beloved physician." "*Luke the beloved physician and Demas greet you*" (Colossians 4:14). These words, found nowhere else in the New Testament like this, appear to be that of a medical doctor.

The man leaps, walks, and enters the temple with Peter and John. He seems to be outwardly and verbally praising God. He has a story to tell. Each of us has a story to tell. We have a journey we are on and our story becomes our testimony. Each testimony is different. Mine is not yours, nor yours mine! It is, however, our story!

The people who were in the temple are amazed at what takes place. This is important. The emphasis here should not be just on the healing. The scene is a human interest story of a much longer narrative. This incident will set up the first account of the early apostles who will be persecuted for their commitment to Jesus of Nazareth. John and Peter will be arrested (Acts 4) and the persecution of the early church will become a major part of the story of Christianity. The preaching of the Word began the movement of the early church, but it was persecution that caused the church to grow and expand, based on the commission that Jesus gave. (Acts 1:8).

The Supplement to the Miracle
(Acts 3: 11-12)

The porch that is called Solomon's was one of two porches. This is the reconstructed temple under King Herod. The porch was on the east side of the temple. It had a roof protecting it from challenging weather. If one went through this porch, they would arrive in an area known as the Court of the Gentiles. Josephus, the Jewish scholar historian, described it " ... there was a porch without the temple, overlooking a deep valley, supporting the walls of four hundred cubits, made of four square stone, very white;

the length of each stone was twenty cubits, and the breadth six; the work of king Solomon, who first founded the temple."[12]

Jesus was here at Hanukkah. *"And Jesus walked in the temple, in Solomon's porch"* (John 10:23). This place evidently was the gathering place for believers. The sedate, stately, ritual of the evening sacrifice was interrupted and there was the observation of joy and praise.

The Servant Who Provided the Miracle
(Acts 3:13a)

Peter preaches. Again, I am overwhelmed at this man who was such a backslidden individual and cursed his ministry was now the spokesman for the believers. He quickly identifies that this miracle has nothing to do with him or John. *"So when Peter saw it, he responded to the people: 'Men of Israel, why do you marvel at this? Or why look so intently at us, as though by our own power or godliness we had made this man walk'"* (Acts 3:12). Peter uses the Hebrew history that would gain attention by citing Abraham, Isaac and Jacob. He identifies God with these three patriarchs. It was of special importance that he show the God of these three had glorified the Servant Jesus. Peter can help us to link Jesus to the Old Testament Servant. *"Behold! My Servant whom I uphold, My Elect One in whom My soul delights! I have put My Spirit upon Him; He will bring forth justice to the Gentiles"* (Isaiah 42:1). *"Behold, My Servant shall deal prudently; He shall be exalted and extolled and be very high"* (Isaiah 52:13). *"He shall see the labor of His soul, and be satisfied. By His knowledge My righteous Servant shall justify many, For He shall bear their iniquities"* (Isaiah 53:11). In acknowledging Him at His baptism and transfiguration, by working through Him the mighty miracles, and for the working of the present miracle of healing which had been called faith in "the name of Jesus of Nazareth."[13] There is an identity that connects Jesus to Jewish theocracy, theology, and history. A servant is God's personal ambassador. Jesus is that ambassador.

The Savior Who is the Theme of the Miracle
(Acts 3: 13b-26)

God the Father has glorified Jesus. He is the Son of God. Peter retells some of the story by mentioning Pontius Pilate. Pilate's determination and desire was to let Jesus go. He wanted to release him.

The word 'denied' in verse fourteen carries with it the idea of repudiated or disowned. Here is this servant who has been approved by God and the people disowned him. I remember traveling to a meeting with my wife to preach on a Sunday. We were housed in a motel room and the next morning we went to a room to eat breakfast. I noticed a man staring at me. As we left breakfast I noticed he followed my wife at a distance towards my car. As I put our suitcase in the car, I was ready to get in the driver's side and he asked if he could talk to me. "Of course," I said, and went and stood at the curbside next to the car. "How can I help you?" He said, "I noticed at breakfast you prayed." I nodded affirmatively. He then said, "Who were you praying to?" "Jesus," I replied. The next words were chilling "Can Jesus help me?" I spent a few minutes with him. He just returned from Iraq and his wife and family left him and he had no friends. My heart ached for him. He was disowned, repudiated, and denied. Jesus had this experience with those who should have followed him.

Peter tells the people at the porch that Jesus is holy. This is the word that means separated to God. The holy one is a Messianic title. Simon Peter said to Jesus on another occasion ' ... *Lord to whom shall we go? You have the words of eternal life. Also we have come to believe and know that you are the Christ, the Son of the Living God*'" (John 6:68-69). The holy one is a Messianic title.

The people ordered an insurrectionist named Barabbas to be released in place of the Holy One. Jesus is identified as the Prince of Life which speaks to the fact that He is the originator, pioneer and author of salvation. "*For both He who sanctifies and those who are being sanctified are all of one, for which reason He is not ashamed to call them brethren*" (Hebrews 2:11).

Verse sixteen carries a powerful truth. His name speaks of the very nature of God. This faith comes through Christ. You see, it is not hard to live the Christian life. It is impossible to live the Christian life. God healed this man and this situation provides the evidence of how the Christian life is lived. Christ must live His life through us to enjoy the Christian life. This man's healing was God's doing. Our salvation that leads to sanctification is Christ living His life through us.

Peter's rebuke is softened in verse seventeen! Perhaps he now recalls his own failures! He does not desire to heap reproach on the people. The Holy One and just reminds us of moral perfection. We are so far removed from that. The nation actually chose a rebel whose hands had blood all over them instead of Jesus. Yet Peter himself denied the Lord. Amazingly,

Christ's goodness and holiness did not affect the jeering crowd when Jesus died.

Peter begins in verse 19 to drive home the purpose of the healing. Here was a man that was lame from birth. He is now healed. What is the point of this? The point is not to heal everyone, although God has the ability to do that. The point is to use this graphic illustration as an impetus to bring people to Christ. Peter drives home four truths.

First he speaks about repentance. In Acts 2:38 the apostle addressed the importance of repentance in his message on the day of Pentecost.

In the Old Testament there is a steady stream of the call to repentance. The message began again in the New Testament as John the Baptist thundered, *'I indeed baptize you with water unto repentance, but He who is coming after me is mightier than I, whose sandals I am not worthy to carry. He will baptize you with the Holy Spirit and fire'"* (Matthew 3:11). Jesus' message on repentance is illustrated when some told him of the Galileans whose blood Pilate had mingled with their sacrifices. In Jesus brief response he says on two different occasions, *'I tell you, no, but unless you repent you will all likewise perish"* (Luke 13: 3, 6). The Greek word *metanoeó* (repentance) does not mean to turn from sin. The word means to change one's mind. If the changing of the mind is sincere, than the actions will also illustrate a change. Note the following passages.

> *Therefore bear fruits worthy of repentance, and do not begin to say to yourselves, 'We have Abraham as our father. For I say to you that God is able to raise up children to Abraham from these stones. And even now the ax is laid to the root of the trees. Therefore every tree which does not bear good fruit is cut down and thrown into the fire.' So the people asked him, saying, 'What shall we do then?' He answered and said to them, 'He who has two tunics, let him give to him who has none; and he who has food, let him do likewise'. Then tax collectors also came to be baptized, and said to him, 'Teacher, what shall we do?' And he said to them, 'Collect no more than what is appointed for you' Likewise the soldiers asked him, saying, 'And what shall we do?' So he said to them, 'Do not intimidate anyone or accuse falsely, and be content with your wages' (Luke 3:8-14). ' ... but declared first to those in Damascus and in Jerusalem,*

and throughout all the region of Judea, and then to the
Gentiles, that they should repent, turn to God, and do works
befitting repentance'. (Acts 26:20).

Peter, in Acts 2 and 3, is calling on the people to change their mind about Jesus. He is calling upon the people to recognize that Jesus is Lord and Christ.

Now salvation is a work of God. Our salvation has nothing to do with our good works. *"For by grace you have been saved through faith, and that not of yourselves; it is the gift of God, not of works, lest anyone should boast"* (Ephesians 2: 8, 9). No one can come to Christ and repent unless God calls and pulls Him. *"No one can come to Me unless the Father who sent Me draws him; and I will raise him up at the last day"* (John 6:44). *"Him God has exalted to His right hand to be Prince and Savior, to give repentance to Israel and forgiveness of sins"* (Acts 5:31). *"When they heard these things they became silent; and they glorified God, saying, 'Then God has also granted to the Gentiles repentance to life'"* (Acts 11:18). In his second epistle Peter writes about God's longsuffering that pulls people to Jesus. Repentance is not a work that earns salvation. When one repents and trusts Christ there will be a change in action that will produce works. *"Therefore bear fruits worthy of repentance"*(Matthew 3:8). When one grasps this truth we can truly shout with praises "Hallelujah, What a Savior!"

In the book of John there are numerous passages of Scripture that simply state to believe in Christ. *"For God so loved the world that He gave His only begotten Son, that whoever believes in Him should not perish but have everlasting life. For God did not send His Son into the world to condemn the world, but that the world through Him might be saved"* (John 3:16, 17). *"He who believes in the Son has everlasting life; and he who does not believe the Son shall not see life, but the wrath of God abides on him"* (John 3:36). The Greek word is translated believe. It comes from the root word *pistis* and is derived from the word meaning to persuade. It appears to me that the concept of repentance is grounded in this word. "The Greek word *pisteuō* means to believe, trust, rely upon, and its related noun is *Pistis* ..." In his gospel, John does not use the words repent, repentance, or faith to describe the way people are saved. He uses believe since the term includes all of these concepts.

The reason all people need to be saved is because of our lostness. We are all lost in need of a Savior. Every single person needs to come to

Christ and be saved. That is why Jesus came to the earth to go through the awful agony that led to the cross. The book of Romans perhaps best describes this issue. Romans chapters 1-3 describe humanities lostness. Romans 1 declares that the wicked world is lost. Romans 1:18-19 describes the problem. In Romans 2 the moral world is lost. The verse that best describes this is verse one. *"Therefore you are inexcusable, O man, whoever you are who judge, for in whatever you judge another you condemn yourself; for you who judge practice the same things"* (Romans 2:1). In Romans 3 the obvious conclusion is found in Romans 3:23. " *... for all have sinned and fall short of the glory of God"* (Romans 3:23). Romans 3:24 declares *"being justified freely by His grace through the redemption that is in Christ Jesus".* Through the work of Christ all who believe can be saved.

Peter then gives the message of eternal value. Jesus is coming again. The listeners would imagine that Peter was thinking, as he did prior to this, of the restoration of Israel. *"Therefore, when they had come together, they asked Him, saying, 'Lord, will You at this time restore the kingdom to Israel'"* (Acts 1:6). There will be a time of restitution that will take place in the future.

> *For behold, I create new heavens and a new earth; And the former shall not be remembered or come to mind'* (Isaiah 65:17). *'Therefore, when they had come together, they asked Him, saying, Lord, will You at this time restore the kingdom to Israel. To the angel of the church of Ephesus write, 'These things says He who holds the seven stars in His right hand, who walks in the midst of the seven golden lampstands: I know your works, your labor, your patience, and that you cannot bear those who are evil. And you have tested those who say they are apostles and are not, and have found them liars; and you have persevered and have patience, and have labored for My name's sake and have not become weary. Nevertheless I have this against you, that you have left your first love. Remember therefore from where you have fallen; repent and do the first works, or else I will come to you quickly and remove your lampstand from its place—unless you repent'* (Revelation 2:1-5).

Peter wrote of this in his second epistle. *"Nevertheless we, according to His promise, look for new heavens and a new earth in which righteousness* dwells" (2 Peter 3:13). Peter references Old Testament events written by the prophets that lead to the truth of the Lord Jesus Christ.

"*Yet now, brethren, I know that you did it in ignorance, as did also your rulers*" (Acts 3:17). Peter states that the prophets wrote about the future coming of Christ, but also "those days" would be the time Peter was in. The return of Christ would actually be in the future. There was a similarity between Jesus and Moses in that they were lawgivers, but Jesus came to fulfill the Law. The prophets of old were to tell the story of a Messiah to come.

The message that was sent has fulfilled the Abrahamic Covenant and the message has in fact been delivered to the Jews first! The Jew should therefore be the first to recognize, repent and give themselves to this Christ.

The great hymn by Horatio Spafford so beautifully describes this work by Christ in the following verse.

> "My sin-Oh the bliss of this glorious thought.
> My sin-not in part but the whole.
> Is nailed to the cross.
> And I bear it no more,
> Praise the Lord, praise the Lord, O my soul."[14]

CHAPTER

6

The Story of Christianity
Evidences of Being With Jesus
(Acts 4:1-13)

And as they spake unto the people, the priests, and the captain of the temple, and the Sadducees, came upon them, Being grieved that they taught the people, and preached through Jesus the resurrection from the dead. And they laid hands on them, and put them in hold unto the next day: for it was now eventide. Howbeit many of them which heard the word believed; and the number of the men was about five thousand. And it came to pass on the morrow, that their rulers, and elders, and scribes, And Annas the high priest, and Caiaphas, and John, and Alexander, and as many as were of the kindred of the high priest, were gathered together at Jerusalem. And when they had set them in the midst, they asked, By what power, or by what name, have ye done this? Then Peter, filled with the Holy Ghost, said unto them, Ye rulers of the people, and elders of Israel, If we this day be examined of the good deed done to the impotent man, by what means he is made whole; Be it known unto you all, and to all the people of Israel, that by the name of Jesus Christ of Nazareth, whom ye crucified, whom God raised from the dead, even by him doth this man stand here before you whole. This is the stone which was set at nought of you

builders, which is become the head of the corner. Neither
is there salvation in any other: for there is none other name
under heaven given among men, whereby we must be saved.
Now when they saw the boldness of Peter and John, and
perceived that they were unlearned and ignorant men, they
marvelled; and they took knowledge of them, that they had
been with Jesus.(Acts 4:1-13 KJV).

T he rulers, elders, scribes, including the high priest Annas, plus
Caiaphas, John, Alexander, and many others of the high priests
gathered at Jerusalem, knew that the followers of Jesus Christ had
been with Jesus.

It was Tertullian, the early church father, who wrote "the blood of the
martyrs is the seed of the church."[15] Tertullian, born in Carthage, notes
numerous foundational truths pleading for Christianity. This is perhaps
the statement he is best known for.

There were at least four sects of Judaism during these days. There were
Pharisees, Zealots, Essenes, and Sadducees. Many of these individuals
were politically powerful, aristocrats, and landowners.

In verse one some of these groups, along with the rulers of the temple
"came upon" the followers of Christ. The term is the Greek word that
speaks to a hostile move. It is important to remember that for centuries
the prophets of Israel spoke about the coming of a Messiah. Most Jewish
people rejected Jesus as Messiah. When Jesus was on the earth the Jewish
people were in bondage to the Roman Empire. The reason for the anger
toward the followers of Christ is that the message of the resurrection was
grieving to them. Jesus had warned about false Messiahs.

Then Jesus went out and departed from the temple, and
His disciples came up to show Him the buildings of the
temple. And Jesus said to them, 'Do you not see all these
things? Assuredly, I say to you, not one stone shall be left
here upon another, that shall not be thrown down.' Now as
He sat on the Mount of Olives, the disciples came to Him
privately, saying, 'Tell us, when will these things be? And
what will be the sign of Your coming, and of the end of the
age?' And Jesus answered and said to them: 'Take heed
that no one deceives you. For many will come in My name,

saying, 'I am the Christ,' and will deceive many. And you will hear of wars and rumors of wars. See that you are not troubled; for all these things must come to pass, but the end is not yet. For nation will rise against nation, and kingdom against kingdom. And there will be famines, pestilences, and earthquakes in various places. All these are the beginning of sorrows. Then they will deliver you up to tribulation and kill you, and you will be hated by all nations for My name's sake. And then many will be offended, will betray one another, and will hate one another. Then many false prophets will rise up and deceive many. And because lawlessness will abound, the love of many will grow cold. But he who endures to the end shall be saved. And this gospel of the kingdom will be preached in all the world as a witness to all the nations, and then the end will come. 'Therefore when you see the 'abomination of desolation,' spoken of by Daniel the prophet, standing in the holy place" (whoever reads, let him understand), then let those who are in Judea flee to the mountains. Let him who is on the housetop not go down to take anything out of his house. And let him who is in the field not go back to get his clothes. But woe to those who are pregnant and to those who are nursing babies in those days! And pray that your flight may not be in winter or on the Sabbath. For then there will be great tribulation, such as has not been since the beginning of the world until this time, no, nor ever shall be. And unless those days were shortened, no flesh would be saved; but for the elect's sake those days will be shortened. "Then if anyone says to you, 'Look, here is the Christ! or 'There!' do not believe it. For false Christs and false prophets will rise and show great signs and wonders to deceive, if possible, even the elect. See, I have told you beforehand. Therefore if they say to you, 'Look, He is in the desert!' do not go out; or 'Look, He is in the inner rooms!' do not believe it. For as the lightning comes from the east and flashes to the west, so also will the coming of the Son of Man be. For wherever the carcass is, there the eagles will be gathered together. Immediately after the tribulation of those days the sun will be darkened, *and the moon will not give its light; the stars will fall from heaven, and the powers of the heavens will be shaken. Then the sign of the Son of Man will appear in heaven, and then all the tribes of the earth will mourn, and they will see the Son of Man coming on the clouds of heaven with power and great glory. And He will send His angels with a great sound of a trumpet, and they will gather together His elect from the four winds, from one end of heaven to the other. Now learn this parable from the fig tree: When its branch has already become tender and puts forth leaves, you know that summer is near. So you also, when you see all these things, know that it is near—at the doors! Assuredly, I say to you, this generation will by no means pass away till all these things take place. Heaven and earth will pass away, but My words will by no means pass away. But of that day and hour no one knows, not even the angels of heaven, but My Father only. But as the days of Noah were, so also will the coming of the Son of Man be. For as in the days before the flood, they were eating and drinking, marrying and giving in marriage, until the day that Noah entered the ark, and did not know until the flood came and took them all away, so also will the coming of the Son of Man be. Then two men will be in the field: one will be taken and the other left. Two women will be grinding at the mill: one will be taken and the other left. Watch therefore, for you do not know what hour your Lord is coming. But know this, that if the master of the house had known what hour the thief would come, he would have watched and not allowed his house to be broken into. Therefore you also be ready, for the Son of Man is coming at an hour you do not expect. Who then is a faithful and wise servant, whom his master made ruler over his household, to give them food in due season? Blessed is that servant whom his master, when he comes, will find so doing. Assuredly, I say to you that he will make him ruler over all his goods. But if that evil servant says in his heart, 'My master is delaying his coming,' and begins to beat his fellow servants, and to eat and drink with the drunkards, the master of that servant will come on a day when he is not looking for him and at an hour that he is not aware of, and will cut him in two and appoint him his portion with the hypocrites. There shall be weeping and gnashing of teeth* (Matthew 24).

This is just one of the numerous writings that speak to the false Messiahs of Jesus' day.

There is Judah the Galilean who is mentioned in Acts 5:37. Josephus, the Jewish historian wrote about Theudes who had people follow him with their possessions to the Jordan River. According to the teacher he asked the Jordan to part, which didn't happen.

Simon Ben-Kosiba was a hero to Jewish followers. Kosiba had several victories. He was declared by a famous rabbi, Rabbi Akiva, as the Messiah. Over time the Jews rejected him. There had been other Messianic leaders.

Jesus posed another problem. The issue before these religious leaders was not just the perfect life of Jesus. The issue was the resurrection. How do people get around that?

The Christian leaders are not imprisoned. This would begin unbelievable persecution against the Christians that would eventually lead to many deaths.

The growth of the church was remarkable. 5,000 men believed. Some commentaries considered this to be a masculine term. If women and children were added, perhaps upwards of 20,000. People believed.

The dilemma facing the opponents of the Christian is this. They may stop the apostles but how can they possible stop the message. Jesus is not welcome as the Messiah. Nevertheless, the issue is how will they deal with the resurrection?

Notice some unique features of the apostles.

A Submissive Spirit   (Acts 4:1-4)

Now as they spoke to the people, the priests, the captain of the temple, and the Sadducees came upon them, being greatly disturbed that they taught the people and preached in Jesus the resurrection from the dead. And they laid hands on them, and put them in custody until the next day, for it was already evening. However, many of those who heard the word believed; and the number of the men came to be about five thousand (Acts 4: 1-4).

The disciples came before these leaders. They offer no resistance. Peter and John are brought before the crowd. The 24 rulers, family heads and tribes gather. The 70 plus of the Sanhedrin gather.

In the Old Testament, the Mosaic Law was very specific. When one claimed a miracle, the basis of the teaching and miracle was examined. The question to be answered was the origination of the miracle. Was it really from God?

> *If there arises among you a prophet or a dreamer of dreams, and he gives you a sign or a wonder, and the sign or the wonder comes to pass, of which he spoke to you, saying, 'Let us go after other gods'—which you have not known—'and let us serve them,' you shall not listen to the words of that prophet or that dreamer of dreams, for the LORD your God is testing you to know whether you love the LORD your God with all your heart and with all your soul. You shall walk after the LORD your God and fear Him, and keep His commandments and obey His voice; you shall serve Him and hold fast to Him. But that prophet or that dreamer of dreams shall be put to death, because he has spoken in order to turn you away from the LORD your God, who brought you out of the land of Egypt and redeemed you from the house of bondage, to entice you from the way in which the LORD your God commanded you to walk. So you shall put away the evil from your midst* (Deuteronomy 13:1-5).

The disciples were submissive. They were ready to present their case of the resurrected Lord.

A Spirit Filling   (Acts 4:8)

"*Then Peter, filled with the Holy Spirit, said to them, "Rulers of the people and elders of Israel*" (4:8).

The disciples' preoccupation was not their defense or self-preservation. Their preoccupation was the glory of God. Peter was told by Jesus about the coming of the Holy Spirit. He preached about the Spirit's filling. Now he practices this amazing truth.

Seizing the Opportunity   (Acts 4: 8-13)

The apostles were submissive to the process. Submission does not mean cowardice. Submission in this case was courage under control. Peter and John are on trial for the benefit of the healing of the sick man. Peter speaks courageously, leaving the outcome to God.

The Christian message is exclusive. Since there is a resurrection, there is only one person to believe in. It is also inclusive. Only those who believe will be saved. Christians, therefore, are considered intolerant.

Here is Peter speaking to the well-educated religious leaders and accusing them of killing Jesus. Peter is uneducated in their eyes. He has not been to the rabbinical schools. He is considered to be an untrained, non-professional theologian with no formal rabbinical training, yet he confronts the religious leaders.

The issue that the religious leaders did not consider is twofold. Peter had learned from the greatest rabbi. This rabbi had written all their Old Testament laws. Secondly, as they would soon admit, Peter and his followers had been with Jesus.

The stone Peter refers to relates back to an Old Testament passage. "*The stone which the builders rejected Has become the chief cornerstone*" (Psalm 118:22). Peter, along with the other apostles, were once questioned by Jesus concerning the Lord's identity. Jesus clearly stated the question and Peter gave the remarkable answer. "*When Jesus came into the region of Caesarea Philippi, He asked His disciples, saying, 'Who do men say that I, the Son of Man, am?'' So they said, 'Some say John the Baptist, some Elijah, and others Jeremiah or one of the prophets.'' He said to them, 'But who do you say that I am?''' Simon Peter answered and said, 'You are the Christ, the Son of the living God.''' Jesus answered and said to him, 'Blessed are you, Simon Bar-Jonah, for flesh and blood has not revealed this to you, but My Father who is in heaven. And I also say to you that you are Peter, and on this rock I will build My church, and the gates of Hades shall not prevail against it*" (Matthew 16:13-18).

The religious leaders hear that Jesus is the chief cornerstone. He upholds and sustains the building. He is a stone of offense. "*Behold, I lay in Zion a stumbling stone and rock of offense, And whoever believes on Him will not be put to shame*" (Romans 9:33). He is a precious cornerstone.

"Behold, I lay in Zion a stumbling stone and rock of offense, And whoever believes on Him will not be put to shame" (1 Peter 2:6). Jew and Gentile will be united in Christ.

The message of salvation can only be found in Christ. *"Nor is there salvation in any other, for there is no other name under heaven given among men by which we must be saved"* (Acts 4:12). There is no other way. Jesus is the only way. The evidence? The resurrection of Jesus Christ is clearly the difference maker!

The boldness of Peter and John was overwhelming and gave evidence. Not schooled in rabbinical law, these men learned this somewhere. The conclusion ... they had been with Jesus! *"Now when they saw the boldness of Peter and John, and perceived that they were uneducated and untrained men, they marveled. And they realized that they had been with Jesus"* (Acts 4:13).

Obeying Their Master
(Acts 4:14-31)

And seeing the man who had been healed standing with them, they could say nothing against it. But when they had commanded them to go aside out of the council, they conferred among themselves, saying, What shall we do to these men? For, indeed, that a notable miracle has been done through them is evident to all who dwell in Jerusalem, and we cannot deny it. But so that it spreads no further among the people, let us severely threaten them, that from now on they speak to no man in this name. So they called them and commanded them not to speak at all nor teach in the name of Jesus. But Peter and John answered and said to them, 'Whether it is right in the sight of God to listen to you more than to God, you judge. For we cannot but speak the things which we have seen and heard' So when they had further threatened them, they let them go, finding no way of punishing them, because of the people, since they all glorified God for what had been done. For the man was over forty years old on whom this miracle of healing had been performed. And being let go, they went to their own companions and reported to all that the chief priests and elders had said to them. So when they heard that, they raised their voice to God with one accord and said: Lord, You are God, who made heaven and earth and the sea, and all that is in them, who by the mouth of Your servant David have said: 'Why did the nations rage, And the people plot vain things? The kings of the earth took their stand, And the rulers were gathered together Against the LORD *and against His Christ. For truly against Your holy Servant Jesus, whom You anointed, both Herod and Pontius Pilate, with the Gentiles and the people of Israel, were gathered together to do whatever Your hand and Your purpose determined before to be done. Now, Lord, look on their threats, and grant to Your servants that with all boldness they may speak Your word, by stretching out Your hand to heal, and that signs and wonders may be done through the name of Your holy Servant Jesus.' And when they had prayed, the place where they were assembled together was shaken; and they were all filled with the Holy Spirit, and they spoke the word of God with boldness* (Acts 4:14-31).

The Sanhedrin are now in an impossible situation. Two things cannot be denied. First, the man is obviously healed. Secondly, Jesus rose from the grave. An interesting observation can be made here. What if the disciples had acquiesced to the Sanhedrin's demand? Could it be possible that church history would be different? Peter's response at an upcoming trial puts it so clearly. " ... *we ought to obey God rather than men*" (Acts. 5:29). Bible scholar, F.F.Bruce, notices and I paraphrase ... It is particularly interesting that (as far as the information goes) the Sanhedrin did not take any serious action to disprove the apostle acts of affirming the resurrection of Jesus Christ.

The Sanhedrin commanded the apostles to cease speaking or teaching in the name of Jesus. Peter's response is full of conviction and integrity. '*For we cannot but speak the things which we have seen and heard*'" (Acts 5:20). The council continued to threaten the followers of Christ, but then let them go. They observed the people bringing glory to God for the healing of the man who was more than forty years old.

The disciples go to their friends and tell the story of what the elders and chief priests did. A symphony of praise was on the lips of these Christians as they gave glory to God for this remarkable event. Obedience to their master brought great joy. The second Psalm is on the hearts of these early Christians. The word for Lord in verse 24 is that of a slave owner. It is used 3 other times. *"But there were also false prophets among the people, even as there will be false teachers among you, who will secretly bring in destructive heresies, even denying the Lord who bought them, and bring on themselves swift destruction"* (2 Peter 2:1). *"For certain men have crept in unnoticed, who long ago were marked out for this condemnation, ungodly men, who turn the grace of our God into lewdness and deny the only Lord God and our Lord Jesus Christ"* (Jude 4). *"And they cried with a loud voice, saying 'How long, O Lord, holy and true, until You judge and avenge our blood on those who dwell on the earth'"* (Revelation 6:10). The common word for Lord is *kurios*. This word is *despaotes*. It refers to the absolute Master of the Universe. In the Greek version of the Old Testament it refers to the angel of Jehovah. In this passage it appears that this may be the earliest record of recognizing the glory of God as the reason for praise. He is the God of creation as well as the director of history.

In verses 29-31 there are three petitions. First, they requested God to look on their hearts and protect the servants of God. Secondly, they requested for strength to speak with boldness the Word of God. And finally, that God would stretch out His hand in order for the people to see God's great works.

The signs and wonders were to give demonstration and verification of the power and reality of the resurrection of Jesus Christ. The constant message of the Acts is the resurrection.

> *Now the multitude of those who believed were of one heart and one soul; neither did anyone say that any of the things he possessed was his own, but they had all things in common. And with great power the apostles gave witness to the resurrection of the Lord Jesus. And great grace was upon them all. Nor was there anyone among them who lacked; for all who were possessors of lands or houses sold them, and brought the proceeds of the things that were sold, and laid them at the apostles' feet; and they distributed to each as anyone had need. And Joses, who was also named Barnabas by the apostles (which is translated Son*

of Encouragement), a Levite of the country of Cyprus, having land, sold it, and brought the money and laid it at the apostles' feet (Acts 4:32-37).

You and I are administrators of what God has provided. If we have been with Jesus it will be revealed by how we live out our faith. Such is seen with the early apostles and followers of Christ. These early Christians were a closely knit group. Trouble and threats often drew them together. There are several obvious items that drew them together. They had remembered what Jesus said and did. Many of these followers remembered Him well. They now had a cause. The proclamation of the resurrection must be trumpeted. *"And with great power the apostles gave witness to the resurrection ..."* (Acts 7:33). With such a strong cause, there was equally strong opposition. The opposition would try to destroy, not just slow down this proclamation. These early Christians were closely knit together with one heart and one mind. The evidence of these was quickly seen in their giving. In these early days of Christianity, the believers gave abundantly of what they owned.

A new personality now steps in the narrative. His name is Joses or Barnabas. His is not of the preaching ministry of Peter. This man would bring to the early believers what every church needs a lot of, and that is encouragement.

When someone walks into a church, what makes it different from a club, political meeting, or a fraternity or sorority? The difference is the presence of the Holy Spirit and the evidence is the message that accompanies God's presence of encouragement.

Barnabus was a prominent Christian disciple. He was a Cypriot Jew (Acts 4:36). The name Joses is usually thought of as a form of Joseph. It appears this is the first name of Barnabus. His name therefore is Joses Barnabus. He would eventually minister with Paul the Apostle in missionary work. He is mentioned as an apostle in Acts 14:14 which appears to refer to Paul and Barnabus, sent out as missionaries. Barnabus had a cousin named Mark. Several historians seem to indicate that this is not John Mark (Acts 2:12) but Mark the evangelist (2 Timothy 4:11). "The opinion that this Mark is a different Mark is found in the writings of Hippolytus of Rome who thought them to be separate people."[16]

The name Barnabus means son of consolation, encouragement and contentment. He is an example of God's choice to teach followers of

Christ about encouragement. Notice two examples from this passage of encouragement.

The early sharing of the saints of God was an example of encouragement. (4:32-33).The congregation was growing. The early believers were preoccupied with ministry to each other. There was an obvious humility stemmed from seeing themselves in relationship to Jesus Christ. Trivial matters seemed insignificant and the reality of the resurrection caused them to have a huge desire to evangelize. When a group of people are so consumed with their mission that they desire everyone else to hear the message it provides ownership.

The early Christians were extremely generous. God's favor revealed for His grace was evident. They shared their economic prosperity. In the history of Christianity, men and women have shared their wealth. A bottom line recognition is that all things come from God. With this concept, giving was simply an extension of what they had received from their Lord. When some had a need, the people were prompted by the Holy Spirit to give and they felt an obligation to use their resources to meet the need. In those early days some sold their property and gave it to the ministry. It literally meant to liquidate capital assets, reduce their own security, and do it with the joy of giving in kingdom work. This was a voluntary move.

In my personal life I have learned this valuable lesson. When my wife and I were newlyweds I went to my home church and became the Director of Christian Education. This was my first fulltime ministry assignment. The church gave me a salary of $60 per week. In the first month our pastor led the church into a stewardship campaign. We were challenged to give a tithe of our income to God's work. After much prayer, my wife, Bobbi, and I decided we would give above the tithe. We decided to give $10 of every check. As a new husband I had not really thought of what it would take to pay our bills. I then decided to develop a budget. My budget revealed we didn't have enough money to pay our $10. My wife reminded me that, tempting as it was, it seemed that God was directing us to stay with the plan and not break down from our commitment. Every week we gave the $10. What a lesson we learned. God knew how to take care of us. There were many times someone would drop food off at our house from their gardens. Often someone would anonymously pick up our check at a restaurant. At the end of the year all of the bills were paid on time and I received a pay increase! Over the many years of ministry we have given hundreds of thousands of dollars away. There were times I felt we were being short changed. I have learned a lesson, and I am constantly learning, nothing could be further from the truth. God owns all and takes care of His people. I can't be foolish and overspend to go beyond my means, but I can't out give God either.

The example of this truth in the early church is this man Barnabus. He had a piece of land, sold it, and brought the money to the apostles' feet. This Levite of Cyprus was a huge example. Barnabus is described in Acts 11:24. *"For he was a good man, full of the Holy Spirit and of faith. And a great many people were added to the Lord"* (Acts 11:24). Barnabus was a faithful, Christ-like example.

Jesus described giving in Luke 6:38. *"Give, and it will be given to you: good measure, pressed down, shaken together, and running over will be put into your bosom. For with the same measure that you use, it will be measured back to you"* (Luke 6:38). Economic blessing is predicated as a heart to give. Why? God owns it all. I encourage you to give. Give to your church. Give to the needy. Balance your checkbook. Pay bills on time. Save for retirement. Pay your mortgage. Give the first gifts to God. He owns it all!

Questions

1. What was Barnabus' greatest contribution?
2. What were the evidences that the apostles had been with Jesus?

For Discussion

1. What are some characteristics in our lives that can reflect we have been with Jesus?

7

The Story of Christianity
What Do You Fear?

(Acts 5:1-11)

But a certain man named Ananias, with Sapphira his wife, sold a possession, And kept back part of the price, his wife also being privy to it, and brought a certain part, and laid it at the apostles' feet. But Peter said, Ananias, why hath Satan filled thine heart to lie to the Holy Ghost, and to keep back part of the price of the land? Whiles it remained, was it not thine own? and after it was sold, was it not in thine own power? why hast thou conceived this thing in thine heart? thou hast not lied unto men, but unto God. And Ananias hearing these words fell down, and gave up the ghost: and great fear came on all them that heard these things. And the young men arose, wound him up, and carried him out, and buried him. And it was about the space of three hours after, when his wife, not knowing what was done, came in. And Peter answered unto her, Tell me whether ye sold the land for so much? And she said, Yea, for so much. Then Peter said unto her, How is it that ye have agreed together to tempt the Spirit of the Lord? behold, the feet of them which have buried thy husband are at the door, and shall carry thee out. Then fell she down straightway at his feet, and yielded up the ghost: and the young men came in, and found her

*dead, and, carrying her forth, buried her by her husband.
And great fear came upon all the church, and upon as many
as heard these things.*(Acts 5:1-11 KJV).

The early church ran into a road block. The sacrificial giving was now blighted by deception. This is very much an example that reminds us of the sin of Achan, recorded in the book of Joshua when he took things that belonged to God.

When there is sin in the camp, the way back is repentance and restitution that will lead to restoration. No such remedy in this narrative.

The Pretense   (Acts 5:1-5)

English professors rightly warn against starting a sentence with a conjunction. This chapter begins, however, with a conjunction "But". It is used because of the contrast in the previous chapter. Chapter four ended with the example of Barnabus and his heartfelt giving. We are introduced to a couple named Ananias and Sapphira. They are members of the early Christian church in the city of Jerusalem.

As the couple observe the generosity of Barnabus, they decide that the respect Joses received should be theirs. In verse two the Scripture emphasizes 'he kept back'. The word means to misappropriate. It is the Greek word *nosphizomai*. It is the same word in the Greek translation of Joshua 7:21 of Achan's sin. The story in Joshua and in Acts is not as much a story of giving, but one of deceit and lying. Eventually, both Ananias and Sapphira agreed to give this possession. Both are implicated in their deception. The keeping back is an indication of defrauding and vanity aimed at minimizing the graciousness of God. It appears that when money takes over as the motivator of life it is possible that integrity may be at stake. Up to this chapter we often read about the glory of God. Here God's glory is minimized.

Peter confronts Ananias directly and correctly. How Peter had knowledge of this is not clear. Perhaps he had the gift of knowledge from God at this moment. (1 Corinthians 12:8). Perhaps the word was out about the deception. Peter knew and confronted Ananias, who may have been expecting praise. No praise was forthcoming.

It is interesting to note that Peter does not accuse Ananias of lying to him, the church, or the apostles. His lying is to the Holy Spirit. In his lying to the Holy Ghost he has sinned directly against God. The Holy Spirit is God. This Scripture clearly connects God and the Holy Spirit as one. The Trinitarian teaching of three in one is clearly scriptural. There are three persons in the Godhead. God the Father, God the Son and God the Holy Spirit. Not three Gods, but three persons in the Godhead. This is the Holy Trinity!

Peter states clearly that the land belonged to Ananias and Sapphira. It was theirs. Giving or keeping it was up to them. The issue was not withholding some of it, but pretending to give "what they did not give". It's to mislead, delude, dupe, to be underhanded. It is the misrepresentation of truth.

Having been in the ministry more than half a century, I have seen deception. It hurts deeply those who are deceived. It is painful. Peter lied about his knowing Jesus at the crucifixion. He knew he was wrong. He wept bitterly which means he wept with agony-like convulsions. Jesus looked at him and he would probably never forget that look. (Luke 22:61). Peter knew the heartache of deception. He repented. He thought his ministry was over. Thank God it wasn't. Ananias shows no sign of repentance.

The episode was so unnecessary. Pride comes into our lives. Satan can influence us. God can influence us. The sin or obedience is up to us.

Ananias is so shocked and overwhelmed. He falls down and dies. Peter did not declare this. He too was probably shocked. No one in the church has the right to call a death sentence on anyone. I have observed, however, that those who try to hurt the church, God knows and will deal with them.

Don't touch the church!

There are those who believe that God dealt too harshly. I find there are times we want God to be what we want Him to be ... Not the God that He is! Frankly speaking, the fact that God delays His righteous justice is a wonder. In this case, Ananias could not live in the environment of the blessing of the church.

It appears to me that Ananias fell over from fear, and perhaps he had a cardiac issue. Regardless of the cause, fear came upon the people. The word here is defined as panic, fear or even terror. This was a shock to the church.

The idea of fear and its biblical meaning has many components. "The fear of the Lord is the beginning of knowledge" (Proverbs 1:7). In the Old Testament the word speaks of the results. For example, when Isaac and Rebekah came into land they were not familiar with, Isaac, like his father, told a half-truth to deceive the men. Isaac did this because he feared the men would kill him and take his wife. When the Egyptian army pursued Isaac they feared the army would overtake them. When Moses came down from Mount Sinai, the people saw the demonstration of thunder and begged Moses to intervene. They feared for their lives!

Fear in the New Testament is usually in the lives of Christians who are out of step with God. *"Therefore, since a promise remains of entering His rest, let us fear lest any of you seem to have come short of it"* (Hebrews 4:1).

In Acts, the story of this couple's death was a warning to the church. This was the results. They did not want this to happen to them!

The Perception   (Acts 5:6)

As fear spread across these early believers, some strong young men came and carried him out to his burial. I am sure the words of the flock were those of concern for themselves. Here is a word to churches and their leaders. Don't try to be what you are not. Don't deceive. It will catch up with you!

The Punishment   (Acts 5:7-10)

In about three hours, Sapphira came in. Evidently she had no idea of the proceedings. Peter confronts her. He lists the price of the land and asks the question. She responds with the same deceptive reply. This ends the short lived and foolish deceit against the Holy Spirit that tests God's patience.

A church, or a person, loses its power when there is an attempt to deception. Truth has a way of surfacing to the top.

The Purging   (Acts 4: 11-13)

Sowing and reaping go hand in hand. Church discipline, when necessary, deters others from sinning. Private sins should be dealt with privately. When there is public sin, there needs to be public dealing of the matter based on a church's practice of discipline. Often the public embarrassment leads to a fear that is healthy for the church.

As I leave writing this chapter our nation is exposing numerous sinful practices of national leaders and entertainers. My heart aches for those who have been offended and for the perpetrators who are guilty and face such embarrassment. It is a message to all of us to refrain from deception.

> *Finally, all of you be of one mind, having compassion for one another; love as brothers, be tenderhearted, be courteous; not returning evil for evil or reviling for reviling, but on the contrary blessing, knowing that you were called to this, that you may inherit a blessing. For He who would love life And see good days, Let him refrain his tongue from evil, And his lips from speaking deceit. Let him turn away from evil and do good;*
>
> *Let him seek peace and pursue it. For the eyes of the LORD are on the righteous, And His ears are open to their prayers; But the face of the LORD is against those who do evil* (1 Peter 3:8-12).

Questions

1. What was the sin of Ananias and Sapphira?
2. Who did they lie to?

For Discussion

1. How, in your estimation, did Peter know when Ananias and Sapphira sinned?

8

The Story of Christianity
What Makes One Worthy?

(Acts 5:12-42)

And by the hands of the apostles were many signs and wonders wrought among the people; (and they were all with one accord in Solomon's porch. And of the rest durst no man join himself to them: but the people magnified them. And believers were the more added to the Lord, multitudes both of men and women.) Insomuch that they brought forth the sick into the streets, and laid them on beds and couches, that at the least the shadow of Peter passing by might overshadow some of them. There came also a multitude out of the cities round about unto Jerusalem, bringing sick folks, and them which were vexed with unclean spirits: and they were healed every one. Then the high priest rose up, and all they that were with him, (which is the sect of the Sadducees,) and were filled with indignation, And laid their hands on the apostles, and put them in the common prison. But the angel of the Lord by night opened the prison doors, and brought them forth, and said, Go, stand and speak in the temple to the people all the words of this life. And when they heard that, they entered into the temple early in the morning, and taught. But the high priest came, and they that were with him, and called the council together, and all the senate of the children of Israel, and sent to the prison to have them brought. But when the officers came, and found them not in the prison, they returned and told, Saying, The prison truly found we shut with all safety, and the keepers standing without before the doors: but when we had opened, we found no man within. Now when the high priest and the captain of the temple and the chief priests heard these things, they doubted of them whereunto this would grow. Then came one and told them, saying, Behold, the men whom ye put in prison are standing in the temple, and teaching the people. Then went the captain with the officers, and brought them without violence: for they feared the people, lest they should have been stoned. And when they had brought them, they set them before the council: and the high priest asked them, Saying, Did not we straitly command you that ye should not teach in this name? and, behold, ye have filled Jerusalem with your doctrine, and intend to bring this man's blood upon us. Then Peter and the other apostles answered and said, We ought to obey God rather than men. The God of our fathers raised up Jesus, whom ye slew and hanged on a tree. Him hath God exalted with his right hand to be a Prince and a Saviour, for to give repentance to Israel, and forgiveness of sins. And we are his witnesses of these things; and so is also the Holy Ghost, whom God hath given to them that obey him. When they heard that, they were cut to the heart, and took counsel to slay them. Then stood there up one in the council, a Pharisee, named Gamaliel, a doctor of the law, had in reputation among all the people, and commanded to put the apostles forth a little space; And said unto them, Ye men of Israel, take heed to yourselves what ye intend to do as touching these men. For before these days rose up Theudas, boasting himself to be somebody; to whom a number of men, about four hundred, joined themselves: who was slain; and all, as many as obeyed him, were scattered, and brought to nought. After this man rose up Judas of Galilee in the days of the taxing, and drew away much people after him: he also perished; and all, even as many as obeyed him, were dispersed. And now I say unto you, Refrain from these men, and let them alone: for if this counsel or this work be of men, it will come to nought: But if it be of God, ye cannot overthrow it; lest haply ye be found even to fight against God. And to him they agreed: and when they had called the apostles, and beaten them, they commanded that they should not speak in the name of Jesus, and let them go. And they departed from the presence of the council, rejoicing that they were counted worthy to suffer shame for his name. And daily in the temple, and in every house, they ceased not to teach and preach Jesus Christ.(Acts 5:12-42 KJV).

What made those early believers worthy before God? The fact is, a holy God cannot look at us with favor unless it is through the resurrected Lord Jesus Christ. The apostles knew this and wanted to please Christ. *"So they departed from the presence of the council, rejoicing that they were counted worthy to suffer shame for His name"* (Acts 5:41). The word means to be "thought or counted worthy".

The early church is booming. Multitudes are added. The word multitude is used more than the word crowd in Scripture. It refers to a throng or a great number. Notice the people are still at Solomon's Porch; the same location of the man who was healed. The power of God is very strong and people want the shadow of Peter to pass over them. The sick and demon possessed came and many were healed. The religious, even some who were fascinated by Peter and the message, would not join the new group. *"Yet none of the rest dared join them, but the people esteemed them highly"* (5:13). The beds here were cots or a small bed, and there were straw mattresses. People from everywhere were coming.

The gospel message will provoke a hostile reaction from a world system that is satanic. The Sanhedrin now are very nervous. This movement would go against their entire religious system. Everything from their positions, religious systems, and theology appeared to be at stake.

The Persecution   (Acts 5:17-28)

"Yes, and all who desire to live godly in Christ Jesus will suffer persecution" (2 Timothy 3:12).

"For what credit is it if, when you are beaten for your faults, you take it

patiently? But when you do good and suffer, if you take it patiently, this is commendable before God" (1 Peter 2:20).

"For it is better, if it is the will of God, to suffer for doing good than for doing evil" (1 Peter 3:17).

The high priest and the sect of the Sadducees are filled with indignation. The word means zeal or envy. Their zeal was against the teaching of the resurrection and envy is against the popularity at this time of the apostles. Sadducees did not believe in resurrection and it was anathema to them to think of Jesus rising from the grave.

The high priest will bring three accusations against the apostle. " ... *saying, 'Did we not strictly command you not to teach in this name? And look, you have filled Jerusalem with your doctrine, and intend to bring this Man's blood on us'"* (Acts 5:28). First there was the accusation that they taught in Jesus name. Then the accusation was that they filled Jerusalem with doctrine. Finally, they accused the disciples of intending to bring "this Man's" blood on us. You'll remember when Pilate claimed innocence of the death of Jesus that the people responded ' ... *His blood be on us and on our children'"* (Matthew 27:25). There was in this day, evidently, a careful avoidance of using the name Jesus. Therefore, the high priest says 'this man'. The religious leadership must have remembered the cry of the people for the blood to be on them. To bring "God's blood" on another signifies guilt on someone for murdering the innocent.

So what caused the unbelievable stir? The apostles are placed in prison. (Acts 5: 18-27). The angel of the Lord opens the prison doors and orders the apostles to go and stand in the temple, then to speak to the people the words of life. What are the words of life? Jesus Christ has risen. The officers came to check on the prisoners in the early hours of the morning and did not find them there. Although the prison was shut securely and the guards were present, there were no apostles. One of the officers saw these new followers of Jesus teaching in the temple and he rushed to tell the captain of the officers. The apostles are then brought to the high priest who delivers his frank and stern warning.

What is the issue? Again, it is the resurrection of Jesus Christ. The disciples are not charged with ignorance. They are charged with malice. The orders of the Sanhedrin were disregarded!

Peter's response was directed by the Holy Spirit. This man who at one time denied the Lord Jesus Christ delivers a brief, potent, and classic message.

The passage says 'Peter and the other apostles'. It appears to me that Peter is representing the others. Peter was now accepted as the spokesman for the group. The apostles' decision was to obey God. Peter does not ridicule nor demean the high priest and his followers. For 3 plus years these disciples were taught by the best. They were taught by Jesus. Jesus called, qualified, and prepared these men to follow him. In Peter's brief speech he credits the response to God. Peter speaks on behalf of the apostles. The disciples must speak in the name of God because it is so deserved by Him they have a duty. They must speak in the name of Jesus!

It is fascinating to again see the emphasis on the resurrection of Jesus Christ. God is given credit for raising Jesus from the dead. The blame for Christ's death Peter places on the religionists he is speaking to. He says Jesus was slain and hung on the cross. Crucifixion in Roman times was usually reserved for slaves, disloyal military, Christians, and opponents to the government. Seldom did it happen to Roman citizens. "In antiquity crucifixion was considered one of the most brutal and shameful modes of death. Probably originating with the Assyrians and Babylonians, it was used systematically by the Persians in the 6th century B.C. Alexander the Great brought it from there to the eastern Mediterranean countries in the 4th century B.C. and the Phoenicians introduced it to Rome in the 3rd century B.C. It was virtually never used in the pro-Hellenic Greece. The Romans perfected crucifixion for 500 years until it was abolished by Constantine I in the 4th century A.D. Crucifixion in Roman times was applied mostly to slaves, disgraced soldiers, Christians, and foreigners-only very rarely to Roman citizens. Death, usually after 6 hours – 4 days, was due to multifactorial pathology after effects of compulsory scourging and maiming. Hemorrhage and dehydration causing hypovolemic shock and pain, but the most important factor was progressive asphyxia caused by impairment of respiratory movement. Death was probably commonly precipitated by cardiac arrest … The attending Roman guards suddenly leave the site after the victim had died …"[17] Among the methods of capital punishment, crucifixion was not in the Jewish courts or penal code. Peter is well aware of the laws, yet he reminds the Jewish leaders of their interference in crucifying Jesus of Nazareth. The procedure in crucifying the Son of God is in keeping with Jewish law. It was the Roman leader, Pontius Pilate, who reluctantly ordered the crucifixion. It is interesting that Peter uses the term "hanged on a tree". "*If a man has committed a sin deserving of death, and he is put to death, and you hang him on a tree, his body shall not remain overnight on the tree, but you shall surely bury him that day, so that you do not defile the land which the LORD your God is giving you as an inheritance; for he who is hanged is accursed of God"* (Deuteronomy 21:22, 23). "The act of putting to death by nailing or binding to a cross. Among the modes of Capital Punishment known to the Jewish penal law, crucifixion is not found; the "hanging" of criminals "on a tree" mentioned in Deuteronomy 21:22 was reported in New Testament times only after lapidation ... A Jewish court could not have passed a sentence of death by crucifixion without violating the Jewish law."[18]

As Peter emphasizes the issue of the cross, he places Jesus as being exalted to the right hand of God, which is a picture of authority. Jesus is spoken of as a Prince and Savior. The word Prince is seldom used of Jesus. It's seen twice in Acts and once in Hebrews. The word means originator, instigator of something new, or beginner. The term refers to the one who takes the lead in everything. He is the instigator and Savior to provide repentance and forgiveness. Jesus possesses salvation and leads the way in redemption.

The deity of Christ is closely declared. This Savior provides forgiveness of sin in and by Him.

Peter states that the apostles are followers of Christ because of seeing the Savior. The word for witness here is mortures (transliteration) from which we receive the English word martyr. The "these things" could refer to anything from the central theme of the resurrection to the giving of Barnabas to the miracles of healing that took place. The record is clear. These disciples saw and believed.

There were several reasons the religious leaders were so upset. First, a message like the one Peter delivered threatened their position. This teaching was new and it was different to their teachings. Second, a resurrection meant that although Jesus was not physically there, he was a threat to the people. Another issue is that exalting Jesus appeared to lessen the view of the God these Israelites worship.

The Scripture states that these followers of the Old Testament law(s) were "cut to the heart". It speaks of a painful emotion. It is a strong uneasiness. The root cause was their guilt. They were missing out on the truth. Jesus of Nazareth was the Messiah. He is the one and only and they are missing out and doubt in them has risen because of their wrongdoing. This "prick of the heart" describes the action of a saw with a lacerating pain.

The Proposition of Gamaliel   (Acts 5:34-39)

God always places the right people in the right place. Attending the conversation was a Pharisee named Gamaliel. Gamaliel is highly respected. He is a doctor of law. This scholar was a leading authority in the first century A.D. He was a member of the Sanhedrin. He was the grandson of a great Jewish teacher, Hillel the Elder. His father was Simeon ben Hillel. He seems to have a lenient approach to the law and had great influence in his day. Gamaliel was a mentor of Saul of Tarsus who became the famous apostle Paul. Paul's recognizing Gamaliel's influence is clearly stated in scripture. *"I am indeed a Jew, born in Tarsus of Cilicia, but brought up in this city at the feet of Gamaliel, taught according to the strictness of our fathers' law, and was zealous toward God as you all are today"* (Acts 22:3). Gamaliel is also mentioned in the writings of Josephus and the Talmud.

Gamaliel gives an answer to the Sanhedrin that will encourage the apostle and literally salvage their lives. He mentions someone named Theudas. He was a Jewish rebel. Somewhere and sometime during this period he led those who followed him in a brief revolution and revolt. He also mentions Judas of Galilee who was a Jewish leader that led the charge against the Romans for the taxes that were imposed by Quirinus.

Gamaliel's point is clear. Theudas and Judas both were short lived in their rebellion. What they did was not of God. Their movements vanished. His recommendation is clear. If these followers of Jesus are false, their movement will fail. If it be of God it doesn't matter what is done to them, God's work will not cease!

The Privilege of the Apostles (Acts 5:40-42)

This whole epistle ends with the unthinkable. The apostles are beaten. The episode began with the healing of the lame man! The consequences of a good deed and marvelous miracle is the beating of the apostles. Without the heeded advice of Gamaliel, the apostles would probably be put to death. The beating is a flogging. Flogging is the act of lashing someone with whips or rods in order to inflict pain, hurt, or harm with the result of putting the victim in line of the desire of the person(s) inflicting the punishment. Jesus predicted this and other similar events.

The word worthy seems to mean that they rejoiced to be counted in the same breath as their Savior, who too experienced a flogging. The demand from the Sanhedrin is to refrain from preaching in Jesus name. Instead the disciples publically went to the temple and to every house teaching and preaching that Jesus is the Christ? They devoted themselves to teaching in Jesus name!

Questions

1. What is the history of crucifixion?
2. Why were the apostles beaten?

For Discussion

1. From your experience, where is persecution taking place in the world and what is the cause?

9

The Story of Christianity Organization of and Persecution Against The Church

(Acts 6:1-15)

And in those days, when the number of the disciples was multiplied, there arose a murmuring of the Grecians against the Hebrews, because their widows were neglected in the daily ministration. Then the twelve called the multitude of the disciples unto them, and said, It is not reason that we should leave the word of God, and serve tables. Wherefore, brethren, look ye out among you seven men of honest report, full of the Holy Ghost and wisdom, whom we may appoint over this business. But we will give ourselves continually to prayer, and to the ministry of the word. And the saying pleased the whole multitude: and they chose Stephen, a man full of faith and of the Holy Ghost, and Philip, and Prochorus, and Nicanor, and Timon, and Parmenas, and Nicolas a proselyte of Antioch: Whom they set before the apostles: and when they had prayed, they laid their hands on them. And the word of God increased; and the number of the disciples multiplied in Jerusalem greatly; and a great company of the priests were obedient to the faith. And Stephen, full of faith and power, did great wonders and miracles among the people. Then there arose certain of the synagogue, which is called the synagogue of the Libertines, and Cyrenians, and Alexandrians, and of them of Cilicia and of Asia, disputing with Stephen. And they were not able to resist the wisdom and the spirit by which he spake. Then they suborned men, which said, We have heard him speak blasphemous words against Moses, and against God. And they stirred up the people, and the elders, and the scribes, and came upon him, and caught him, and brought him to the council, And set up false witnesses, which said, This man ceaseth not to speak blasphemous words against this holy place, and the law: For we have heard him say, that this Jesus of Nazareth shall destroy this place, and shall change the customs which Moses delivered us. And all that sat in the council, looking stedfastly on him, saw his face as it had been the face of an angel.(Acts 6:1-15 KJV).

There are many Christians who hold to the view that the first church began in Jerusalem. The group that began is now highly influential and growing. It appears in the early days of Christianity that the group was not a highly contrived organization or corporation, nor was it a loose community. It is an organism, a form of life, made up of numerous people with various gifts and abilities to process the functions. Better structure is needed to accomplish this goal. Acts 6:1 seems to infer that there was a system in operation to help with daily needs.

A division developed between the Grecians and the Hebrews. The Grecians were Hellenistic who brought the Greek language and culture into their lifestyle. These were Hellenistic Jews who were dispersed and some arrived in the city of Jerusalem. For some reason they are neglected in comparison to the Hebrews. The Hebrews were the natives from the Jewish population. Palestinian Jews were suspicious of the Hellenists because of their Greek culture they brought into their families.

The church is growing. When the church was young and smaller, it was not difficult to stay united. As the church grew there were challenges. Murmuring begins to develop. Murmuring often refers to a low confidential complaining that grows into a problem like a disease to our health. It must be doctored. It must be dealt with.

The early church reflects a desire to help the widows. Paul in his letter to Timothy gives another group of Christians instructions on dealing with widows. The widows prayed for the church and some lived in the church and served there.

The apostles were overwhelmed with this need. The early apostles were to commit themselves first and foremost to the Word of God. The "serving of tables" probably refers to the actual serving of the meals and the raising of the revenues. For the apostles to be sidetracked in these cases would limit their ministry. These persons who are called of God to deliver His Word need to make their teaching the priority of their service in the church. They are actually a gift from God. *"And He Himself gave some to be apostles, some prophets, some evangelists, and some pastors and teachers, for the equipping of the saints for the work of ministry, for the edifying of the body of Christ"* (Ephesians 4:11-12). The spiritual guidance they provide cannot be minimized nor limited.

The decision of the apostles is to look for seven men. They are to be honest and they are to be known for integrity. They need to be filled with the Holy Spirit and wisdom. They will be appointed over the business of taking care of the widows. The goal is to appoint seven men and the results is that the apostles will not take time away from the study of God's Word and prayer.

It is interesting to see the care that is given to the task. All seven men who are chosen have Greek names. The implication is that these were Hellenists. Evidently they accepted some of the Greek culture. Christianity is not about adopting culture. It is about accepting Christ and following Him as a disciple. When our Jewish friends accept Jesus Christ as their Savior and Messiah, there should be no plan to take them from their culture. When Gentiles accept Christ, there should be no desire to make them accept Jewish traditions. Jesus is Lord of all!

How do we know this to be true? The resurrection of Jesus Christ is the evidence of who He claims to be. He's God the Son and the Son of God! When these seven men were chosen, they could easily minister and correct the murmuring because they were one of the Hellenists.

Of the seven, two are influential in Acts ... Stephen and Philip.

"Tradition calls Prochorus, the nephew of Stephen and companion of John the Evangelist, who consecrated him bishop of Nicomedia in Bithynia (modern day Turkey). He was traditionally ascribed the authorship of the apocryphal Acts of John, and was said to have ended his life as a martyr in Antioch in the 1st century."[19]

Tradition seems to provide nothing further about Nicanor of Parmenas. Tradition teaches that Trimon was appointed as bishop of the city of Bostre in Arabia. Again, tradition says he died by crucifixion. Nicholas was a native of Antioch. He was a proselyte from Judaism to Christianity.

Stephen became well known. He did 'great wonders and miracles'. Stephen is mentioned in Acts 11:19 and 22:20. He became the first recorded martyr of the Christian church.

Philip preached and reported a great move of God in Samaria. Miracles took place. He left the work in Samaria. He left the work in Samaria to meet an Ethiopian Eunuch in Gaza. Philip had four daughters who prophesied. (Acts 21).

The word for serve is *diakoneó* (Greek). The Greek word in Acts 6:1 for daily ministration (distribution) is *diakonia*, a cognate noun. Serving tables and preaching are both important. "As John Stott used to say, they are both "ministries", and the only difference between them is that they are different!"[20]

The use of diakonia provides reason for many Bible scholars to point out that these first seven men were the original deacons.

The early church had many who were bringing funds to help develop the ministry. These original seven took over the financial distribution and allowed the apostles to preach and teach God's word by providing the study and prayer time for them.

Elders were eventually appointed (Acts 11:29-32). It would seem that this group was the first deacons. The entire congregation trusted the apostles and accepted their recommendation. A ceremony occurred with the apostles laying hands on these seven.

Laying on of hands is found in the Scripture. Although this is not considered a mandate, it has a symbolism. *"Do not lay hands on anyone hastily, nor share in other people's sins; keep yourself pure"* (1 Timothy 5:22). It appears that the laying on of hands is a sign of connecting a messenger with the truth they will deliver. The laying on of hands has no power in itself. To do this is a human endorsement of God's choice. Great caution should be followed in doing it for an obvious reason. It symbolizes a conferral of authority, especially into a position of leadership and, or responsibility. The Hebrew term carries with it the concept of obligation. The person who receives the laying on of hands feels the pressure signifying the load that will be carried with the obligation. The hand signifies power and the strength that is needed from God to perform the task. These seven have the apostles lay hands on them.

This organizational move prompted the church to grow. "The Word of God increased" (Acts 6:7). This indicates a continual, gradual, spiritual growth. Major change was occurring. A new way was developing. The time for sacrifices had passed away. The Temple rituals were vanishing. *"In that He says, 'A new covenant,'" He has made the first obsolete. Now what is becoming obsolete and growing old is ready to vanish away"* (Hebrews 8:13). Instead of fighting the issue, some of the priests saw the light of the gospel. Perhaps they were weary with the wearisome work of the Temple involving the sacrifices which were never sufficient. The sacrifices of the blood of bulls and goats to abolish sins was never final. *"For it is not possible that the blood of bulls and goats could take away sins"* (Hebrews 10:4). Little is mentioned of how these priests became obedient to their faith, nor if they left their profession. What we do know is that a "great company" began to follow the truth of the Lord Jesus Christ.

Persecution

Opposition against the early church was developing from the Sanhedrin. There were three groups who were in opposition to Stephen. The first group mentioned are the Libertines. These were emancipated Roman Jews. They settled in large numbers and probably had their own synagogue. There are Bible scholars who believe that Stephen came from this group. "From this class, we have seen reason to believe that Stephen had sprung".[21] The Cyrenians were from the north coast of Africa between Carthage and Egypt. "They were conspicuous for the offerings sent to the temple and appealed to Augustus for protection against irregular taxes by which the provincial governors sought to intercept their gifts".[22] The man, Simon, who carried Jesus' cross is mentioned as being from Cyrene. He and his two sons, Alexander and Rufus (Mark 15:21) were probably at one time part of this group.

Outside of Rome and Jerusalem the most influential and largest city of Jewish population was Alexandria. The Greek version of the Old Testament came from Alexandria. The great philosopher and teacher, Philo, lived there.

Cilicia had a group of leading members of the synagogue. This area of Asia mentioned is probably Lydin and Ionia with Ephesus as the capital.

These groups were disputing with Stephen. They were questioning the validity of the truthfulness of Stephen's teachings. The dispute was an angry quarrel. So angry were these religionists that they trumped up false charges with false witnesses over issues of truth. Such is the nature of the human heart when the real truth is presented. These religionists in the name of truth lied and deceived to secure and protect their position.

The accusation is that they claimed Stephen taught that Jesus would destroy the temple and change the customs of Moses. These are trumped up charges and false accusations.

Stephen is stared at by the priests, rulers, scribes, and elders. Many of these had not seen Stephen prior to this time. Honor is on Stephen. Confusion covers the face of the religionists. There was evidently a light that brightened Stephen just as the apostles, felt "worthy to suffer" (Acts 5:41) for their Jesus. Stephen prepares himself for his most challenging hour and the glow of God is on him. In our challenges, our God will never leave us nor forsake us!

Questions

1. What the meaning of diakonia?
2. What is the significance of laying on of hands?

For Discussion

1. In your opinion, what does growth in the church look like based on our study of the book of Acts?

CHAPTER

10

The Story of Christianity
A Message for the Ages

(Acts 7:1-60)

Then said the high priest, Are these things so? And he said, Men, brethren, and fathers, hearken; The God of glory appeared unto our father Abraham, when he was in Mesopotamia, before he dwelt in Charran, And said unto him, Get thee out of thy country, and from thy kindred, and come into the land which I shall shew thee. Then came he out of the land of the Chaldaeans, and dwelt in Charran: and from thence, when his father was dead, he removed him into this land, wherein ye now dwell. And he gave him none inheritance in it, no, not so much as to set his foot on: yet he promised that he would give it to him for a possession, and to his seed after him, when as yet he had no child. And God spake on this wise, That his seed should sojourn in a strange land; and that they should bring them into bondage, and entreat them evil four hundred years. And the nation to whom they shall be in bondage will I judge, said God: and after that shall they come forth, and serve me in this place. And he gave him the covenant of circumcision: and so Abraham begat Isaac, and circumcised him the eighth day; and Isaac begat Jacob; and Jacob begat the twelve patriarchs. And the patriarchs, moved with envy, sold Joseph into Egypt: but God was with him, And delivered him out of all his afflictions, and gave him favour and wisdom in the sight of Pharaoh king of Egypt; and he made him governor over Egypt and all his house. Now there came a dearth over all the land of Egypt and Chanaan, and great affliction: and our fathers found no sustenance. But when Jacob heard that there was corn in Egypt, he sent out our fathers first. And at the second time Joseph was made known to his brethren; and Joseph's kindred was made known unto Pharaoh. Then sent Joseph, and called his father Jacob to him, and all his kindred, threescore and fifteen souls. So Jacob went down into Egypt, and died, he, and our fathers, And were carried over into Sychem, and laid in the sepulchre that Abraham bought for a sum of money of the sons of Emmor the father of Sychem. But when the time of the promise drew nigh, which God had sworn to Abraham, the people grew and multiplied in Egypt, Till another king arose, which knew not Joseph. The same dealt subtilly with our kindred, and evil entreated our fathers, so that they cast out their young children, to the end they might not live. In which time Moses was born, and was exceeding fair, and nourished up in his father's house three months: And when he was cast out, Pharaoh's daughter took him up, and nourished him for her own son. And Moses was learned in all the wisdom of the Egyptians, and was mighty in words and in deeds. And when he was full forty years old, it came into his heart to visit his brethren the children of Israel. And seeing one of them suffer wrong, he defended him, and avenged him that was oppressed, and smote the Egyptian: For he supposed his brethren would have understood how that God by his hand would deliver them: but they understood not. And the next day he shewed himself unto them as they strove, and would have set them at one again, saying, Sirs, ye are brethren; why do ye wrong one to another? But he that did his neighbour wrong thrust him away, saying, Who made thee a ruler and a judge over us? Wilt thou kill me, as thou diddest the Egyptian yesterday? Then fled Moses at this saying, and was a stranger in the land of Madian, where he begat two sons. And when forty years were expired, there appeared to him in the wilderness of mount Sina an angel of the Lord in a flame of fire in a bush. When Moses saw it, he wondered at the sight: and as he drew near to behold it, the voice of the Lord came unto him, Saying, I am the God of thy fathers, the God of Abraham, and the God of Isaac, and the God of Jacob. Then Moses trembled, and durst not behold. Then said the Lord to him, Put off thy shoes from thy feet: for the place where thou standest is holy ground. I have seen, I have seen the affliction of my people which is in Egypt, and I have heard their groaning, and am come down to deliver them. And now come, I will send thee into Egypt. This Moses whom they refused, saying, Who made thee a ruler and a judge? the same did God send to be a ruler and a deliverer by the hand of the angel which appeared to him in the bush. He brought them out, after that he had shewed wonders and signs in the land of Egypt, and in the Red sea, and in the wilderness forty years. This is that Moses, which said unto the children of Israel, A prophet shall the Lord your God raise up unto you of your brethren, like unto me; him shall ye hear. This is he, that was in the church in the wilderness with the angel which spake to him in the mount Sina, and with our fathers: who received the lively oracles to give unto us: To whom our fathers would not obey, but thrust him from them, and in their hearts turned back again into Egypt, Saying unto Aaron, Make us gods to go before us: for as for this Moses, which brought us out of the land of Egypt, we wot not what is become of him. And they made a calf in those days, and offered sacrifice unto the idol, and rejoiced in the works of their own hands. Then God turned, and gave them up to worship the host of heaven; as it is written in the book of the prophets, O ye house of Israel, have ye offered to me slain beasts and sacrifices by the space of forty years in the wilderness? Yea, ye took up the tabernacle of Moloch, and the star of your god Remphan, figures which ye made to worship them: and I will carry you away beyond Babylon. Our fathers had the tabernacle of witness in the wilderness, as he had appointed, speaking unto Moses, that he should

*make it according to the fashion that he had seen. Which
also our fathers that came after brought in with Jesus into
the possession of the Gentiles, whom God drave out before
the face of our fathers, unto the days of David; Who found
favour before God, and desired to find a tabernacle for the
God of Jacob. But Solomon built him an house. Howbeit
the most High dwelleth not in temples made with hands;
as saith the prophet, Heaven is my throne, and earth is my
footstool: what house will ye build me? saith the Lord: or
what is the place of my rest? Hath not my hand made all
these things? Ye stiffnecked and uncircumcised in heart
and ears, ye do always resist the Holy Ghost: as your fathers
did, so do ye. Which of the prophets have not your fathers
persecuted? and they have slain them which shewed before
of the coming of the Just One; of whom ye have been now
the betrayers and murderers: Who have received the law by
the disposition of angels, and have not kept it. When they
heard these things, they were cut to the heart, and they
gnashed on him with their teeth. But he, being full of the
Holy Ghost, looked up stedfastly into heaven, and saw the
glory of God, and Jesus standing on the right hand of God,
And said, Behold, I see the heavens opened, and the Son of
man standing on the right hand of God. Then they cried out
with a loud voice, and stopped their ears, and ran upon him
with one accord, And cast him out of the city, and stoned
him: and the witnesses laid down their clothes at a young
man's feet, whose name was Saul. And they stoned Stephen,
calling upon God, and saying, Lord Jesus, receive my spirit.
And he kneeled down, and cried with a loud voice, Lord,
lay not this sin to their charge. And when he had said this,
he fell asleep.*(Acts 7:1-60 KJV).

Caiaphas, the high priest, asks a simple question. He is about to hear an amazing sermon. I have in my library thousands of books. One of those volumes is the treasury of the World's Greatest Sermons by Warren Wiersbe. There are dozens of great messages by some of the leading preachers covering a long span of time. Jesus preached three messages that are sermons for the ages. One is the Sermon on the Mount. Another, the

Olivet Discourse, while the third is the Upper Room Discourse. Early in this volume I mentioned the fact that the books of Acts contains many sermons.

Although Stephen's sermon is not always listed sometimes in the volumes of great messages, it is in fact an amazing historical and theological presentation of the journey of the Jewish people that would lead to the cross. His sermon would anger the people and cause them to desire his demise! The message is the longest one recorded in the book of Acts. "The text is 'you are doing just as your fathers did.'"[23] Stephen gives a historical synopsis of the nation and their subsequent rejection of the messengers of God.

Abraham   (Acts 7:1-8)

He begins with God's call to Abraham in Mesopotamia. *"Then He said to him, 'I am the* LORD, *who brought you out of Ur of the Chaldeans, to give you this land to inherit it'"* (Genesis 15:7). He went to Haran. *"And Terah took his son Abram and his grandson Lot, the son of Haran, and his daughter-in-law Sarai, his son Abram's wife, and they went out with them from Ur of the Chaldeans to go to the land of Canaan; and they came to Haran and dwelt there So the days of Terah were two hundred and five years, and Terah died in Haran"* (Genesis 11:31-32). Verse seven states that the patriarch Abraham had a wandering existence. He purchased a burial place. Abraham did not possess the land for the promise that included his family. Although Abraham dwelt many years in that land and it was his home, it was not held as his own property.

Faith was the key to Abraham's life. He lived on land promised to him that he did not own and was promised a son which appeared impossible because of the age of both he and Sarah his wife. The promise of the possession was positive. It would belong to Abraham and it was his family that would enjoy the possession.

The sign of the covenant for Abraham would be circumcision. This a rite practiced earlier. This is to be the sign of the Abrahamic Covenant. *"And he received the sign of circumcision, a seal of the righteousness of the faith which he had while still uncircumcised, that he might be the father of all those who believe, though they are uncircumcised, that righteousness might be imputed to them also"* (Romans 4:11). If a Hebrew refused circumcision it was the equivalent of refusing God's covenant.

Joseph   (Acts 7:9-17)

Abraham bought the cave of Machpalah from Ephron the Hittite. The story of Joseph is rehearsed. His brothers sold him into slavery, and he lived a life of rejection and persecution. God's hand was on Joseph and through divine wisdom he decided to save food and when a famine arose, he was trusted like no other one else in the kingdom. Joseph was eventually buried at Shechem. The ground there had been purchased by Jacob from the sons of Hamor.

Moses   (Acts 7: 10-44)

Moses was 80 years old when called of God to lead the children of Israel out of Egypt from a Pharaoh who despised the Hebrew people. Stephen rehearses the story from his birth (7:20) to the condemnation of Moloch (7:43). Moloch was a title that was used by the Canaanites deities. Human sacrifices were offered to Moloch. Remphan was a false deity connected to the planet Saturn. In this discourse Stephen points out that the beloved and well respected Moses stated God would raise up a prophet (7:37). He points out that the people did not listen to Moses, but desired to go back to Egypt (7:39).

Joshua   (Acts 7:45)

Moses was buried on Mt. Nebo. Joshua had been mentored by Moses and would lead the nation into the Promised Land.

David and Solomon   (Acts 7:46-50)

David found favor with God. He was truly the man after God's own heart. The point is made, however, that it was Solomon who built the Temple. The emphasis is made that God does not dwell in man-made buildings. The tabernacle was a testimony to the presence of God. The Tabernacle gave way to the Temple. Stephen then quotes from a passage in Isaiah. 'For all those things My hand has made, And all those things exist,'" Says the LORD. 'But on this one will I look: On him who is poor and of a contrite spirit, And who trembles at My word'" (Isaiah 66:2).

Stephen has carefully and thoroughly presented a case for the religious leaders to hear. David has to wait to develop the Tabernacle. David's son, Solomon, built the Temple that was absolutely magnificent.

It appears that Stephen has presented a case of the nation of Israel to give attention to, based on the nations' history. He has emphasized the theme that these religionists were doing the same as their fathers did. Israel has had many privileges they have rejected and in some cases refused to listen to God.

It appears, as well, that Stephen has a sudden change in his message. The tone appears to be full of rage as he categorically lays the crucifixion and rejection of Jesus Christ on the Sanhedrin. The term "stiffnecked" was familiar. *'Go up to a land flowing with milk and honey; for I will not go up in your midst, lest I consume you on the way, for you are a stiff-necked people.'* *For the* LORD *had said to Moses, 'Say to the children of Israel, 'You are a stiff-necked people. I could come up into your midst in one moment and consume you. Now therefore, take off your ornaments, that I may know what to do to you.'' Then he said, 'If now I have found grace in Your sight, O Lord, let my Lord, I pray, go among us, even though we are a stiff-necked people; and pardon our iniquity and our sin, and take us as Your inheritance'* (Exodus 33:3, 5; 34:9). The word stiffnecked means obstinate. The people were stubborn. He call them "uncircumcised". Uncircumcised in heart referred to those who looked at their privileges as exclusive rights. He continues to emphasize that their fathers had presented the prophets and now the Righteous One, their Messiah, they have rejected. Stephen calls them murderers and betrayers. The Holy Spirit was given as a gift. Now the religionists are resisting Him.

Many Bible teachers sense that the Sanhedrin were murmuring among themselves and therefore Stephen's quick reaction and accusations against them was based on both how their forefathers rejected the prophets and now rejected the Son of God.

The Scripture teaches the people were "cut to the heart". There are eight Greek words that can be rendered cut. This one is the same word used previously in Acts. *"When they heard this, they were furious and plotted to kill them"* (Acts 5:33). The word is Diaprio. *Dia* means asunder and *prio* to know. Metaphorically, it means to be cut to the heart. They were so angry they "gritted their teeth". "They began to gnash their teeth at him (just like a pack of hungry snarling wolves). Stephen knew it meant death for him."[24] Stephen was filled with the Holy Spirit. The theme of the Scriptures is the glory of God. Stephen gazes into heaven and sees the glory of God. Jesus stands to welcome Stephen home. He stands to recognize and witness one of the choice servants. *"Also I say to you, whoever confesses Me before men, him the Son of Man also will confess before the angels of God"* (Luke 12:8). Jesus is an advocate of Stephens' defense of the Son of God. "The point must be that Stephen sees Jesus in His role as the Son of man." He sees Him as the One who suffered and was vindicated by God (Luke 9:22) i.e., as a pattern to be followed by Christian martyrs, but also as the One who will vindicate in God's presence those who are not ashamed of Jesus and acknowledge their allegiance to him before men (Luke 12:8)."[25]

The work of the sacrifice for sin is finished. Jesus is at the right hand of God picturing the completeness of redemption. *" ... who being the brightness of His glory and the express image of His person, and upholding all things by the word of His power, when He had by Himself purged our sins, sat down at the right hand of the Majesty on high"* (Hebrews 1:3). He stands picturing his ministering to one of his saints. *"To the angel of the church of Ephesus write, 'These things says He who holds the seven stars in His right hand, who walks in the midst of the seven golden lampstands'"* (Revelation 2:1).

Stephen is stoned to death. Here is the first recorded martyr of the early church. There were witnesses there. These are probably the false witnesses that helped begin this charade in Acts 6:13. Perhaps they had intended a legal counsel to produce legal execution. The scene would be horrific. Yet in the midst of this malady Stephen addressed the Lord " ... Lord, lay not this sin against them". Jesus had been found guilty of blasphemy. Stephen tells the Sanhedrin that Jesus is the Messiah and his crucifixion led Him to the resurrection and he places the verdict for his death squarely on the shoulders of the Sanhedrin.

The Scripture teaches that the dying deacon begs for mercy for his accusers and "fell asleep". This is a term used of the physical death of believers. *These things He said, and after that He said to them, 'Our friend Lazarus sleeps, but I go that I may wake him up.'"* (John 11:11). "But I do not want you to be ignorant, brethren, concerning those who have asleep, lest you sorrow as others who have no hope. For if we believe that Jesus died and rose again, even so God will bring with Him those sleep in Jesus. For this we say to you by the word of the Lord, that we who are alive and remain until the coming of the Lord will by no means precede those who are asleep"* (1 Thessalonians 4:13-15).

From a purely human standpoint, these accusers had no option but to kill Stephen. To do differently would be to admit that the death of Jesus was a mistake.

We are introduced, though briefly here, to a young man named Saul. He is vitriolic in his anger and intent on destroying these hated Christians. In his mind, Stephen was just the first to go!

There are several amazing lessons from this chapter. First in this sermon Stephen details those who persecuted the prophets and God's chosen nation. The opposition came against God's program at times from the people who should have stood up in defense of God's kingdom. Such were the Sanhedrin.

Secondly, God is with His chosen. Such was the case with Joseph. Despite his opposition, "God was with him" (Acts 7:9). On a couple of occasions God calls his own aliens in the world. (Acts 7:6; 7:29).

Thirdly, God welcomes home his people. What a beautiful picture of Stephen being welcomed into the presence of Jesus as He stands in heaven next to His father.

Questions

1. What is the meaning "cut to the heart"?
2. How does Stephen see Jesus as the "Son of Man"?

For Discussion

1. How did Stephen weave the Old Testament prophets into his message?
2. Why did he take this approach? (Your opinion)

11

The Story of Christianity The Main Thing!

(Acts 8:1-18)

And Saul was consenting unto his death. And at that time there was a great persecution against the church which was at Jerusalem; and they were all scattered abroad throughout the regions of Judaea and Samaria, except the apostles. And devout men carried Stephen to his burial, and made great lamentation over him. As for Saul, he made havock of the church, entering into every house, and haling men and women committed them to prison. Therefore they that were scattered abroad went every where preaching the word. Then Philip went down to the city of Samaria, and preached Christ unto them. And the people with one accord gave heed unto those things which Philip spake, hearing and seeing the miracles which he did. For unclean spirits, crying with loud voice, came out of many that were possessed with them: and many taken with palsies, and that were lame, were healed. And there was great joy in that city. But there was a certain man, called Simon, which beforetime in the same city used sorcery, and bewitched the people of Samaria, giving out that himself was some great one: To whom they all gave heed, from the least to the greatest, saying, This man is the great power of God. And to him they had regard, because that of long time he had bewitched them with sorceries. But when they believed Philip preaching the things concerning the kingdom of God, and the name of Jesus Christ, they were baptized, both men and women. Then Simon himself believed also: and when he was baptized, he continued with Philip, and wondered, beholding the miracles and signs which were done. Now when the apostles which were at Jerusalem heard that Samaria had received the word of God, they sent unto them Peter and John: Who, when they were come down, prayed for them, that they might receive the Holy Ghost: (For as yet he was fallen upon none of them: only they were baptized in the name of the Lord Jesus.) Then laid they their hands on them, and they received the Holy Ghost. And when Simon saw that through laying on of the apostles' hands the Holy Ghost was given, he offered them money (Acts 8:1-18 KJV).

Stephen Covey is best remembered for his book "The Seven Habits of Highly Effective People". In the book there are 10 quotes that claim to be life changing. One of these quotes is "to keep the main thing the main thing."[26] What is the main thing of this early group of believers? The main thing that would glorify God is to continue to deliver the life changing message of the resurrection. The growth of this early group is recorded by several major incidents in the next pages of the Acts.

Philip preaching in Samaria (Acts 8:5)

Baptism of the Ethiopian Eunich (Acts 8:38)

Philip in Azotus (Acts 8:40)

Conversion of Simon the Sorcerer (Acts 8:1-31)

Conversion of Saul of Tarsus (Acts 9:1-30) Aeneas healed (Acts 9:34)

Dorcas raised (Acts 9:36) Peter's vision of the Gentiles (Acts 10:9)

Conversion and baptism of Cornelius (Acts 10:34)

James martyred (Acts 12) Peter imprisoned (Acts 12)

Acts continues with some information of the death of Stephen. Saul of Tarsus was introduced in Acts 7 as a man who consented and enthusiastically cheered on the death of Stephen. The Scripture teaches that Saul was consenting to Stephen's death. There are six Greek words that can be rendered consent. This one is *suneudokeo* which means to take pleasure with others in anything, even if it has evil overtones.

Saul was born in the city of Tarsus. He was born to Jewish parents who had citizenship in the Roman Empire. Tarsus is in Cilicia which is modern day Turkey. He was born somewhere around 5 A.D. and historians tend to believe he moved to Jerusalem in 10 A.D. He studied under the famous rabbi, Gamaliel. Saul learned the depth of the law from this teacher. It appears that Jerusalem was his boyhood town. *"I am indeed a Jew, born in Tarsus of Cilicia, but brought up in this city at the feet of Gamaliel taught according to the strictness of our fathers' law, and was zealous toward God as you all are today"* (Acts 22:3). The clothes of Stephen were placed at the feet of Saul. Saul approved with delight the murder of Stephen. Saul hated Christians. He was in every sense a terrorist to the Christian community. Saul is called Paul for the first time in Scripture when he was on the Island of Cyprus. (Acts 1:3). He perhaps was first given the name Paul at birth. He would be a missionary, writer, preacher, teacher, prophet and a tent maker.

As Godly men carried Stephen to his burial, Saul was ravaging the church with a desire to destroy Christianity from off the face of the earth. Acts 8:3 indicates he made havoc of the church. The Greek word havoc is *portheo* referring to wasting or destroying Christianity from off the face of the earth.

Because of the persecution, the apostles stayed put. Others went out preaching the Word of God. The word that is used for preaching here is *evangelizo* which means preaching the good news of the gospel. This is not the usual word for preach but rather a declaration of announcing the good news. It seems that this has to do with the believers. "The great majority of the dispersed Christians held no office in the church, yet they preached wherever they came, and this spread of the gospel without the Holy City, this planting in the churches beyond, was affected not by the apostles but by an entirely voluntary and unofficial agency"[27]

Philip is the deacon. *"I am indeed a Jew, born in Tarsus of Cilicia, but brought up in this city at the feet of Gamaliel, taught according to the strictness of our fathers' law, and was zealous toward God as you all are today"* (Acts 8:5). He comes to Samaria. Jesus had an amazing experience with the woman at Jacob' well (John 4). The city was called Sebaste.

The Greek word in Acts 8:5 is *kerusso*. It means to herald or proclaim. It speaks of preaching as a herald of the truth. The disciples were evangelizing in Acts 8:4. Philip was preaching in Acts 8:5.

Philip's ministry was not just heralding truth. His ministry included miracles. Unclean spirits were delivered. Those that had palsy and those lame were healed. The city had an outbreak of joy (8:8).

As the case is so often, when God is pouring out His blessings, there is opposition. There was a man who performed sorcery. He was a practitioner and probably was one of many in those days who claimed to be a Messiah. His name was Simon. He made grandiose claims of his greatness. His influence was powerful. It is interesting to note that he was called by the greatest to the smallest as the great power of God. A sorcerer was one who pretended to have magic powers. The Greek word *mágos* refers to a wizard, while *pharmakos* speaks of one who used drugs, potions, and spells with the desire to enchant people. Pharmakos is where the English word pharmacy is derived from. This Simon was deceiving many.

As Philip was preaching many came to Christ and were baptized. Simon also believed and was baptized. Simon, however, revealed his true heart when he later tried to buy the gift and work of the Holy Spirit. " ... *saying, 'Give me this power also, that anyone on whom I lay hands may receive the Holy Spirit.'" But Peter said to him, 'Your money perish with you, because you thought that the gift of God could be purchased with money'"* (Acts 8:19-20).

Simon's faith was not a faith unto salvation. There is one requirement to be saved. That requirement is that we are sinners. We don't get saved to a better life, to get healed, to feel better, or any other thing. We are saved because we are sinners in need of a Savior. *"What does it profit, my brethren, if someone says he has faith but does not have works? Can faith save him? If a brother or sister is naked and destitute of daily food, and one of you says to them, 'Depart in peace, be warmed and filled,'" but you do not give them the things which are needed for the body, what does it profit? Thus also faith by itself, if it does not have works, is dead. But someone will say, 'You have faith, and I have works.'" Show me your faith without your works, and I will show you my faith by my works. You believe that there is one God. You do well. Even the demons believe—and tremble! But do you want to know, O foolish man, that faith without works is dead"* (James 2:14-20.

These new followers of Christ were obedient and were baptized. The first step in the Christian life is baptism. Going down in the water reminds us of the death of Christ, being there symbolizes his burial of our sins, and coming out of the water teaches us about the glorious resurrection. However, the gift of the Holy Spirit for these followers was delayed. Peter and John would arrive and lay hands on these new followers of Jesus Christ. Under most circumstances the Holy Spirit is given the moment of faith in Christ. In this situation the Samaritans were to be identified with the apostolic movement and the Jerusalem Church. The goal was not a rivalry with churches, but a blessing of two congregations closely knit and preparing for persecution.

Simon the Sorcerer thought he could buy the gift of God. Peter clearly explains to him that his silver can perish with him. The gift of God is not attained by money. It is a grace gift. Peter urges him to repent. Simon's goal was not to change himself, but to escape punishment. Simon was apostate. Bitterness had crept into his life. He claims faith then denies the claim.

Despite this episode with the gospel, the group heading back to Jerusalem stopping in many Samaritan villages on their way and many believed. Philip's return was interrupted.

The Acts of the Apostles speaks often of the work of the Holy Spirit and the fact of the resurrection of Jesus Christ. In this case the angel of the Lord spoke to Philip. The Great Commission of Acts 1:8 contained our Lord's charge to go into Jerusalem, Judea, Samaria and the uttermost parts of the world. We find Jerusalem is connected with the resurrection in Acts 1:8-8:3 and Judea and Samaria are reached in Acts 8:4-25. Now the ends of the earth will be addressed as we come to Acts 8:26. The Gentile world is included with the unique story of Cornelius, recorded in Acts. 10. There were both Romans and Greeks who viewed Ethiopians as living off the southern end of the earth. An angel of the Lord gives direction. This was not an inner impulse or a dream. This direction is from God. He is told to go to Gaza. This is an old city whose history goes back to the ancient days of Damascus. It is the same city as Azzal in the Old Covenant. *"And the Avim, who dwelt in villages as far as Gaza—the Caphtorim, who came from Caphtor, destroyed them and dwelt in their place"* (Deuteronomy 2:23). It was the southernmost city of the early Canaanites at the border. This area is desert.

Philip goes in obedience to the command and arrives finding an Ethiopian eunuch who is a court official of the queen of the Ethiopians. Her name was Candace. She had a hereditary title of the queen of

Ethiopia – The fact that this man was reading the Scripture reminds us of how far the gospel had traveled. Faithful were these early century believers witnessing of the resurrection.

The Eunuch was reading the book of Isaiah 53. His question is one that has been asked by numerous inquisitors. Who is this about? "Before the coming of Jesus, the Jews understood Isaiah 53 as referring to the Messiah. This interpretation was abandoned as Christians applied the prophecy of Jesus of Nazareth and Isaiah 53 was then considered by the Jews to be referring either to Isaiah himself or to the people of Israel who would be a light to the nations."[28]

The Eunuch sees water and desires to be baptized. Philip responds "If you believe with all your heart, you may" (Acts 8:37). The Eunuch responds and trusts Jesus. Philip then orders the chariot to stop and he take the Eunuch in the water to baptize him.

The Eunuch had been in Jerusalem for worship. Now he meets Jesus through the witness of Philip. This entire chapter is an evidence of how people can come to the Lord and obedient followers of Christ. Despite the hatred of Saul toward Christians and the terrible deception of Simon the Sorcerer and the persecution, the followers of Jesus who were in the midst of the faithful saints, continued to talk of the resurrection of Jesus. Their power came from the Holy Spirit and their message was clear. Jesus Christ of Nazareth rose from the grave. Philip finds himself in Azotus, 20 miles north of Gaza. He settled in Caesarea and spent at least 20 years there. "*On the next day we who were Paul's companions departed and came to Caesarea, and entered the house of Philip the evangelist, who was one of the seven, and stayed with him*" (Acts 21:8).

Questions

1. What is the main thing?
2. What is a sorcerer?

For Discussion

1. What is the purpose of fellowshipping with faithful saints?

CHAPTER

12

The Story of Christianity
An Unbelievable Conversion
by Divine Appointment
(Acts 9)

*And Saul, yet breathing out threatenings and slaughter
against the disciples of the Lord, went unto the high priest,
And desired of him letters to Damascus to the synagogues,
that if he found any of this way, whether they were men or
women, he might bring them bound unto Jerusalem. And as
he journeyed, he came near Damascus: and suddenly there
shined round about him a light from heaven: And he fell to
the earth, and heard a voice saying unto him, Saul, Saul,
why persecutest thou me? And he said, Who art thou, Lord?
And the Lord said, I am Jesus whom thou persecutest: it is
hard for thee to kick against the pricks. And he trembling
and astonished said, Lord, what wilt thou have me to do?
And the Lord said unto him, Arise, and go into the city, and
it shall be told thee what thou must do. And the men which
journeyed with him stood speechless, hearing a voice, but
seeing no man. And Saul arose from the earth; and when
his eyes were opened, he saw no man: but they led him by
the hand, and brought him into Damascus. And he was
three days without sight, and neither did eat nor drink. And*

there was a certain disciple at Damascus, named Ananias;
and to him said the Lord in a vision, Ananias. And he
said, Behold, I am here, Lord. And the Lord said unto him,
Arise, and go into the street which is called Straight, and
enquire in the house of Judas for one called Saul, of Tarsus:
for, behold, he prayeth, And hath seen in a vision a man
named Ananias coming in, and putting his hand on him,
that he might receive his sight. Then Ananias answered,
Lord, I have heard by many of this man, how much evil
he hath done to thy saints at Jerusalem: And here he hath
authority from the chief priests to bind all that call on thy
name. But the Lord said unto him, Go thy way: for he is a
chosen vessel unto me, to bear my name before the Gentiles,
and kings, and the children of Israel: For I will shew him
how great things he must suffer for my name's sake. And
Ananias went his way, and entered into the house; and
putting his hands on him said, Brother Saul, the Lord,
even Jesus, that appeared unto thee in the way as thou
camest, hath sent me, that thou mightest receive thy sight,
and be filled with the Holy Ghost. And immediately there
fell from his eyes as it had been scales: and he received
sight forthwith, and arose, and was baptized. And when
he had received meat, he was strengthened. Then was Saul
certain days with the disciples which were at Damascus.
And straightway he preached Christ in the synagogues, that
he is the Son of God. But all that heard him were amazed,
and said; Is not this he that destroyed them which called
on this name in Jerusalem, and came hither for that intent,
that he might bring them bound unto the chief priests? But
Saul increased the more in strength, and confounded the
Jews which dwelt at Damascus, proving that this is very
Christ. And after that many days were fulfilled, the Jews
took counsel to kill him: But their laying await was known of
Saul. And they watched the gates day and night to kill him.
Then the disciples took him by night, and let him down by
the wall in a basket. And when Saul was come to Jerusalem,
he assayed to join himself to the disciples: but they were all
afraid of him, and believed not that he was a disciple. But

Barnabas took him, and brought him to the apostles, and declared unto them how he had seen the Lord in the way, and that he had spoken to him, and how he had preached boldly at Damascus in the name of Jesus. And he was with them coming in and going out at Jerusalem. And he spake boldly in the name of the Lord Jesus, and disputed against the Grecians: but they went about to slay him. Which when the brethren knew, they brought him down to Caesarea, and sent him forth to Tarsus. Then had the churches rest throughout all Judaea and Galilee and Samaria, and were edified; and walking in the fear of the Lord, and in the comfort of the Holy Ghost, were multiplied. And it came to pass, as Peter passed throughout all quarters, he came down also to the saints which dwelt at Lydda. And there he found a certain man named Aeneas, which had kept his bed eight years, and was sick of the palsy. And Peter said unto him, Aeneas, Jesus Christ maketh thee whole: arise, and make thy bed. And he arose immediately. And all that dwelt at Lydda and Saron saw him, and turned to the Lord. Now there was at Joppa a certain disciple named Tabitha, which by interpretation is called Dorcas: this woman was full of good works and almsdeeds which she did. And it came to pass in those days, that she was sick, and died: whom when they had washed, they laid her in an upper chamber. And forasmuch as Lydda was nigh to Joppa, and the disciples had heard that Peter was there, they sent unto him two men, desiring him that he would not delay to come to them. Then Peter arose and went with them. When he was come, they brought him into the upper chamber: and all the widows stood by him weeping, and shewing the coats and garments which Dorcas made, while she was with them. But Peter put them all forth, and kneeled down, and prayed; and turning him to the body said, Tabitha, arise. And she opened her eyes: and when she saw Peter, she sat up. And he gave her his hand, and lifted her up, and when he had called the saints and widows, presented her alive. And it was known throughout all Joppa; and many believed in the Lord. And it came to pass, that he tarried many days in Joppa with one Simon a tanner (Acts 9 KJV).

A Most Amazing Conversion

The most amazing conversion in the history of the early church is recorded in Acts 9. Other than the Lord Himself, there is no one who has made a greater impact on Christianity than Saul of Tarsus, known as the Apostle Paul. Saul, as the most famous persecutor of the church changed to the most influential and powerful of all the apostles. Paul's writings are some of the earliest of Christian documents. He travels thousands of miles around the Mediterranean Sea as a spokesman for Jesus Christ. His dedication to the cause of Christ is unparalleled and unmatched.

His name means small or humble. He was a Jewish Roman citizen. Paul was a Pharisee. His occupation was that of a tentmaker. Paul was the apostle to the Gentiles. Whereas the other apostles shared the story of the resurrection with the Jews, Paul zeroed in on the Gentiles. 13 New Testament Epistles were written by Paul. Many believe the book of Hebrews could be added to that number. Paul spent much time emphasizing the grace of God and that believers are justified by faith! Faith, not behavior, is the entrance to God. Behavior results in receiving the gift of God.

Divine Appointments

As we approach this chapter, I would like to address this section with the view that God orchestrates in all of our lives, divine appointments.

Divine appointments are seldom in our schedule. As I review a typical day in my life, I initially review my appointment schedule. At the present time I have three people who are my accountability. One is my wife who can change whatever she wants in my schedule but seldom does, my executive assistant who administrates the bookings and my assistant who organizes my speaking schedule. There are many occasions where my schedule is interrupted by God. At times I am not even aware of it. As I reflect back, it is God who has arranged it. Notice in this chapter seven divine appointments.

Saul's Appointment with Christ (Acts 9:1-8) An appointment with destiny

Saul's Appointment with Ananias (Acts 9:9-19) An appointment for direction

Saul's Appointment with his Enemies (Acts 9:20-23) An appointment with deliverance

Saul's Appointment with Protection (Acts 9:24, 25) An appointment with new friends

Saul's Appointment with Barnabus (Acts 9:27-31) An appointment with a deliverer

Peter's Appointment with Aeneas (Acts 9:32-35) An appointment with healing

Peter's Appointment with Dorcas (Acts 9:36-43) An Appointment with the resurrection

Just as those divine appointments occur in Scripture, so you and I will have divine appointments. Take for example the well-known John Newton.

Newton was a sailor who lived a life of debauchery, rebellion and drunkenness. He worked on slave ships. He was frightened by a storm at sea and through the book, Imitation of Christ by Thomas A. Kempis, began thinking about spiritual things. His mother was a Godly and gentle woman who prayed faithfully for her son. One night he was awakened to a violent wave crashing against the boat he was on. He had an exhausting evening of trying to pump the ship of its water and stuffing clothes in the ships holes. Eventually the ship was free of water and that night, March 21, 1747, he asked Jesus to be His Savior. It was Newton who wrote the words of Amazing Grace! It was all by divine appointment.

In each of the sections of Acts 9 we see a divine appointment.

In Saul's Appointment with Christ, he is filled with bitterness and vitriolic anger toward the disciples. He goes to the high priest demanding letters that he could enter the synagogues of Damascus and if necessary, bring Christians bound to Jerusalem. As he approached Damascus his schedule changed abruptly. He had no plan of this happening.

You will notice that the Christians at this point are called people of The Way. The followers were not called Christians until Acts 11:26 in Antioch. The Way was the most often used name. *"But when some were hardened and did not believe, but spoke evil of the Way before the multitude, he departed from them and withdrew the disciples, reasoning daily in the school of Tyrannus"* (Acts 19:9). *"And about that time there arose a great commotion about the Way"* (Acts 19:23). *"But this I confess to you, that according to the Way which they call a sect, so I worship the God of my fathers, believing all things which are written in the Law and in the Prophets"* (Acts 24:14). *"Or else let those who are here themselves say if they found any wrongdoing in me while I stood before the council"* (Acts 24:20).

Jesus said He was the Way in John 14:6 and perhaps this was the reason that the early Christians were simply called "The Way". It was the lifestyle of these early Christians that described them as people of the way.

Damascus is about 150 miles from Jerusalem. Saul has a huge plan that is exhausting. Quickly it all happened. The word suddenly is a word that emphasizes the suddenness of the occasion. I seldom sleep well on an airplane, but on a trip from Mayanmar to Beijing, China recently, I was ill and fell sound asleep. When the plane landed it seemed so sudden and shook my entire being. This is the kind of reaction that Saul has. Another word is hastily. This happened and it shook Saul. Saul falls to the ground and hears the words, *"Saul, Saul, why persecutes thou me?"* (Acts 9:4). Saul perhaps remembers viewing Stephen's death. *"Behold I see the heavens opened, and the Son of man standing on the right hand of God"* (Acts 7:56). Saul viewed Stephen as a blasphemer, yet when he asked God to forgive his accusers He never would forget it. It is interesting how close the unseen world is!

Saul says *"Who are you, Lord?"* The word for Lord is the Greek form of *kurios* which was a form used of Roman or Greek term of civil respect. Jesus responds, *'I am Jesus … "It is hard for you to kick against the pricks."'* This is a proverbial expression referring to an ox goad which is like a piece of painted iron stuck on the end of a stick. It was used to urge the ox to continue plowing. Sometimes an ox would kick against the goad and be wounded. It means it is fruitless and worthless to rebel against authority. The Son of God is about to completely change the life style of Saul. There is a proverb developed that states "Out of bad into worse." In its context here it means 'don't kick against the Holy Spirit'.

Saul had a divine appointment. He is now blind and shook to the core of his being! He asks the Lord for direction. He is told to go into the city and he will find out. Obedient to the One he hated a few moments ago, he is led to the city.

The men who were with him were shocked. They heard someone, but saw no one. They take their leader, who moments before was brazen with pride, and now is led like an elderly blind man into the city. Saul was three days without sight, food, and water.

This was an amazing divine appointment that would change not only Paul's life, but the future of Christianity. This was an appointment with destiny.

The second appointment was Saul with Ananias. He is a disciple of Jesus living at Damascus. The Lord tells Ananias to go to the street called Straight, meet Saul, and minister to him. In humble opposition Ananias tells the Lord that word of Saul's hatred towards Christians is widely known. Yet with assurance from the Lord he obediently goes. Saul receives his sight and Ananias baptized him. Could you imagine being the servant of God who baptizes Saul? This was an appointment for direction.

The third appointment is with enemies. If you live for Jesus there will always be opposition. Saul begins preaching. The people were astonished as they realized that this preacher was the one who had the opposition against Christ and his followers with a desire to bring him bound to the Chief Priests. The unbelieving Jews who were so blessed by Saul are now plotting to kill him. This led to his deliverance.

The next divine appointment is with Paul's new friends who protect him and help him escape by the wall in a basket. When we come to the Lord we have new found friends.

Saul escapes and goes back to Jerusalem where the disciples feared him and did not accept his salvation story. Barnabus becomes a new friend and is a deliverer for Saul. Barnabus defended the apostle. The churches relaxed from this fear and the congregations multiplied.

Peter passes through Lydda. This was a town known for its rich terrain about a day's trip from Jerusalem. It was originally settled by the tribe of Benjamin. It was a place that was the seat of the Rabbinical School. It was here that Peter met with the saints and there was a sick man named Aeneas. He more than likely belonged to the Hellenistic section of the church. He was bedridden for eight years with paralysis. The word bed that is used in verse 34 was a couch and it signified the lower class of people. The disciples had planted churches in this area. Peter tells Aeneas to pick up his bed and walk. What an amazing divine appointment this is. It is interesting to note that no faith on the part of this person was mentioned. He was to be obedient and take up his bed and walk. All the people of the area were astonished of the man's restoration to health.

The final divine appointment is the ministry to Tabitha. Her name in the Greek is Dorcas. She lived in Joppa. The name Tabitha means Gazelle. The woman was full of kindness and love and constantly ministered to people. Dorcas becomes sick and died. With heavy hearts her friends washed her body and put her in an upstairs room. Two men came to Peter begging him to come to the place where the body laid. Peter arrived and went into the upper room and found the widows weeping. They showed the garments Dorcas made. Peter's heart is touched. He requests everyone to leave the room. He then kneels and prays. He says, *"Tabitha, arise"*. Remarkably she opens her eyes and looks at Peter while she is rising. The saints are called in and they are amazed. Word spreads throughout Joppa. Many follow Jesus and believe in Him for their salvation.

Peter decides to stay in Joppa and settles in at a man's house whose name is Simon the tanner; the only reference to a tanner in the Bible. The Jews looked at the occupation with disdain and considered it an undesirable way to make a living because of the unhealthy odors and horrific sights of dealing with dead animals and their skins. There was also the issue of being ceremonially unclean. These tanners had one or two rooms and the front that was near the store helped to eradicate the horrific smell. Tanning was the process of treating skins of animals that produced valuable leather. It is here that Peter resides as a Jewish man with a new friend involved in a work that would be considered unceremonial and unclean. From here Peter would come upon a situation that the next chapter would give information on the amazing grace of God which would go far beyond ceremonial rights.

In Acts 9 we learn of divine appointments. There are four lessons.

1. Lesson One … Their description
   They are made by God. More than likely they are not in your schedule. The appointments are between God and you. They occur at unexpected times. Watch for them. They may occur today!

2. Lesson Two … Their detail
   God has a plan for your life 'For I know the thoughts that I think toward you, says the LORD, thoughts of peace and not of evil, to give you a future and a hope'" (Jeremiah 29:11). God wants a life of fellowship with you. Just as Paul met Jesus in an unexpected way, so God will meet with you and a life of fellowship will develop.

3. Lesson Three … Their drama
   God is always up to something. Look at how Saul's life would be forever changed. God is calling a people to himself. Saul would be exhibit one through history as to what God can do in someone's life. He is the epitome of a divine appointment.

4. Lesson Four … Their design.
   These appointments invoke you! God is working in and through you!

Questions

1. What is a divine appointment?
2. What are 3 characteristics of divine appointments?

For Discussion

1. In your opinion, why did Saul ask the question "Who are you, Lord."?

13

The Story of Christianity
Harmony in the Family

(Acts 10)

*There was a certain man in Caesarea called Cornelius, a
centurion of the band called the Italian band, A devout
man, and one that feared God with all his house, which
gave much alms to the people, and prayed to God alway.
He saw in a vision evidently about the ninth hour of the
day an angel of God coming in to him, and saying unto
him, Cornelius. And when he looked on him, he was afraid,
and said, What is it, Lord? And he said unto him, Thy
prayers and thine alms are come up for a memorial before
God. And now send men to Joppa, and call for one Simon,
whose surname is Peter: He lodgeth with one Simon a
tanner, whose house is by the sea side: he shall tell thee
what thou oughtest to do. And when the angel which spake
unto Cornelius was departed, he called two of his household
servants, and a devout soldier of them that waited on him
continually; And when he had declared all these things unto
them, he sent them to Joppa. On the morrow, as they went
on their journey, and drew nigh unto the city, Peter went
up upon the housetop to pray about the sixth hour: And he
became very hungry, and would have eaten: but while they
made ready, he fell into a trance, And saw heaven opened,*

and a certain vessel descending upon him, as it had been a great sheet knit at the four corners, and let down to the earth: Wherein were all manner of fourfooted beasts of the earth, and wild beasts, and creeping things, and fowls of the air. And there came a voice to him, Rise, Peter; kill, and eat. But Peter said, Not so, Lord; for I have never eaten any thing that is common or unclean. And the voice spake unto him again the second time, What God hath cleansed, that call not thou common. This was done thrice: and the vessel was received up again into heaven. Now while Peter doubted in himself what this vision which he had seen should mean, behold, the men which were sent from Cornelius had made enquiry for Simon's house, and stood before the gate, And called, and asked whether Simon, which was surnamed Peter, were lodged there. While Peter thought on the vision, the Spirit said unto him, Behold, three men seek thee. Arise therefore, and get thee down, and go with them, doubting nothing: for I have sent them. Then Peter went down to the men which were sent unto him from Cornelius; and said, Behold, I am he whom ye seek: what is the cause wherefore ye are come? And they said, Cornelius the centurion, a just man, and one that feareth God, and of good report among all the nation of the Jews, was warned from God by an holy angel to send for thee into his house, and to hear words of thee. Then called he them in, and lodged them. And on the morrow Peter went away with them, and certain brethren from Joppa accompanied him. And the morrow after they entered into Caesarea. And Cornelius waited for them, and he had called together his kinsmen and near friends. And as Peter was coming in, Cornelius met him, and fell down at his feet, and worshipped him. But Peter took him up, saying, Stand up; I myself also am a man. And as he talked with him, he went in, and found many that were come together. And he said unto them, Ye know how that it is an unlawful thing for a man that is a Jew to keep company, or come unto one of another nation; but God hath shewed me that I should not call any man common or unclean. Therefore came I unto you without gainsaying, as soon as

I was sent for: I ask therefore for what intent ye have sent for me? And Cornelius said, Four days ago I was fasting until this hour; and at the ninth hour I prayed in my house, and, behold, a man stood before me in bright clothing, And said, Cornelius, thy prayer is heard, and thine alms are had in remembrance in the sight of God. Send therefore to Joppa, and call hither Simon, whose surname is Peter; he is lodged in the house of one Simon a tanner by the sea side: who, when he cometh, shall speak unto thee. Immediately therefore I sent to thee; and thou hast well done that thou art come. Now therefore are we all here present before God, to hear all things that are commanded thee of God. Then Peter opened his mouth, and said, Of a truth I perceive that God is no respecter of persons: But in every nation he that feareth him, and worketh righteousness, is accepted with him. The word which God sent unto the children of Israel, preaching peace by Jesus Christ: (he is Lord of all:) That word, I say, ye know, which was published throughout all Judaea, and began from Galilee, after the baptism which John preached; How God anointed Jesus of Nazareth with the Holy Ghost and with power: who went about doing good, and healing all that were oppressed of the devil; for God was with him. And we are witnesses of all things which he did both in the land of the Jews, and in Jerusalem; whom they slew and hanged on a tree: Him God raised up the third day, and shewed him openly; Not to all the people, but unto witnesses chosen before God, even to us, who did eat and drink with him after he rose from the dead. And he commanded us to preach unto the people, and to testify that it is he which was ordained of God to be the Judge of quick and dead. To him give all the prophets witness, that through his name whosoever believeth in him shall receive remission of sins. While Peter yet spake these words, the Holy Ghost fell on all them which heard the word. And they of the circumcision which believed were astonished, as many as came with Peter, because that on the Gentiles also was poured out the gift of the Holy Ghost. For they heard them speak with tongues, and magnify God. Then answered

Peter, Can any man forbid water, that these should not be baptized, which have received the Holy Ghost as well as we? And he commanded them to be baptized in the name of the Lord. Then prayed they him to tarry certain days (Acts 10 KJV).

The book of Acts is a document on transition. The gospel is to the Jew first. God chose Abram, a Jew, to establish the Abrahamic Covenant. God chose numerous Jewish writers to pen the Sacred Scriptures. God chose to send His Son to be the world's Savior. The gospel, however, is not distinctively only for the Jew. The gospel is for all. Jew and Gentile (non-Jew) are welcome. This chapter distinctively portrays the worldwide scope of a whosoever will gospel.

There Was a Divine Preparation   The Preparation of Cornelius
(Acts 10:1-20)

The beginning of the chapter introduces us to Cornelius. He was a man who lived in Caesarea. The City was a Roman city along the Mediterranean Sea. The Roman governor of the province of Judea had his headquarters here. I have been there many times. One of its unique characteristics is that there is a stone there with the name Pontius Pilate engraved on it. Cornelius was of the Italian Regiment. He was an officer of the Roman Army. He was a loyalist to Rome and Jewish citizens were concerned of him and had deep commitment to Judaism and prejudice toward Cornelius and his allegiance to Rome. Cornelius had a deep desire to know God. He was a Gentile who feared God but did not want to follow the Jewish rite of circumcision.

God sends an angel to Cornelius. It was 3 p.m. in the middle of the afternoon. Jews prayed during this time. You will remember that Peter and John went to the Temple to pray at 3 p.m. when a crippled man was healed. (Acts 3)

Cornelius has a vision. He is told to send for Peter. Cornelius did not know who Peter was. Peter had a special call. He and Paul are the two key individuals in the book of Acts. The gospel is now going to the world. (Acts 1:8). Peter was given the keys from Jesus when he made his great confession. *"When Jesus came into the region of Caesarea Philippi, He asked His disciples, saying, "Who do men say that I, the Son of Man, am?" So they* said, 'Some say John the Baptist, some Elijah, and others Jeremiah or one of the prophets.'" He said to them, 'But who do you say that I am?'" Simon Peter answered and said, 'You are the Christ, the Son of the living God'" (Matthew 16:13-16). Jesus gave the symbolic keys to Peter to unlock the doors as the church would go into worldwide missions. Peter led the people in the upper room. He gave the famous message on the day of Pentecost. He told the people of the coming of the Holy Spirit. 3,000 were baptized and Peter was there. Peter and John laid hands on the people in Samaria to receive the Holy Spirit. Now he is here as the gospel begins to spread to the Gentile nations. Remember, Peter's life was involved with the Jewish traditions. He is a national Jew steeped in Jewish tradition. He was now living with Simon the tanner. He had a despised trade and yet Peter stayed with him. *"There is neither Jew nor Greek, there is neither slave nor free, there is neither male nor female; for you are all one in Christ Jesus"* (Galatians 3:28). The Jews viewed Gentiles as unclean. God was about to change all that.

Simon is mentioned as a tanner. Often people in Scripture are identified by their trade. Tanners worked with and washed the carcasses of dead animals. Whereas tanning was not forbidden, it was considered an unclean trade based on the teachings of Jewish law. There would be extensive ceremonial washings before tanners would be allowed to hear the Law, worship, or offer any kind of sacrifice in the temple. Yet, it is in this man's house that God prompted Peter to stay. Simon the tanner was evidently a Jew who had turned to Jesus Christ. God was preparing Peter to an unexpected ministry. It would be from this location that the gospel would fulfill the commission to go to the uttermost part of the world. These are four accounts of the Great Commission in the gospel as well as we saw the commission in Acts 1:8.

"And Jesus came and spake unto them, saying, All power is given unto me in heaven and in earth. Go ye therefore, and teach all nations, baptizing them in the name of the Father, and of the Son, and of the Holy Ghost: Teaching them to observe all things whatsoever I have commanded you: and, lo, I am with you always, even unto the end of the earth" (Matthew 28:18-20).

And He said to them, 'Go into all the world and preach the gospel to every creature. He who believes and is baptized will

be saved; but he who does not believe will be condemned'
(Mark 16:15-16).

Then He said to them, 'Thus it is written, and thus it was necessary for the Christ to suffer and to rise from the dead the third day, and that repentance and remission of sins should be preached in His name to all nations, beginning at Jerusalem. And you are witnesses of these things. Behold, I send the Promise of My Father upon you; but tarry in the city of Jerusalem until you are endued with power from on high.' And He led them out as far as Bethany, and He lifted up His hands and blessed them. Now it came to pass, while He blessed them, that He was parted from them and carried up into heaven. And they worshiped Him, and returned to Jerusalem with great joy, and were continually in the temple praising and blessing God. Amen (Luke 24:46-53).

Then, the same day at evening, being the first day of the week, when the doors were shut where the disciples were assembled, for fear of the Jews, Jesus came and stood in the midst, and said to them, ' Peace be with you.' When He had said this, He showed them His hands and His side. Then the disciples were glad when they saw the Lord. So Jesus said to them again, 'Peace to you! As the Father has sent Me, I also send you.' And when He had said this, He breathed on them, and said to them, 'Receive the Holy Spirit. If you forgive the sins of any, they are forgiven them; if you retain the sins of any, they are retained' (John 20:19-23).

And being assembled together with them, He commanded them not to depart from Jerusalem, but to wait for the Promise of the Father, 'which,' He said, 'you have heard from Me; for John truly baptized with water, but you shall be baptized with the Holy Spirit not many days from now.' Therefore, when they had come together, they asked Him, saying, 'Lord, will You at this time restore the kingdom to Israel?' And He said to them, 'It is not for you to know times or seasons which the Father has put in His own authority.

But you shall receive power when the Holy Spirit has come upon you; and you shall be witnesses to Me in Jerusalem, and in all Judea and Samaria, and to the end of the earth' (Acts 1:4-8).

The Preparation of Peter   (Acts 10:9-20)

In Joppa God was preparing his preacher for a monumental task. God not only prepared Cornelius but he also prepared Peter.

Peter falls into a trance. A sheet comes down out of heaven. It was knit at the four corners. The term 'four corners of the earth' refers to all parts of, or the far ends of the earth' Isaiah reminds us ... *"And gathered the dispensed of Judah from the four corners of the earth"* (Isaiah 11:12).

It is interesting to note that the sheet contained both clean and unclean animals. In the Old Testament there were certain Dietary Laws. Furthermore, Israel was not to have social relationships with idolatrous neighbors.

Peter, although the spokesman for the new movement of The Way, kept the Kosher laws. Kosher refers to meals being correct, following the requirements of Jewish law, plus having the divine blessing of the rabbi. If one follows the Kosher system today, it will probably provide a better diet and system of digestion. However, at this event there would be a significant change. There would be the abolishing of the Old Testament restrictions and the Gentiles will be inclusive into God's family as the chosen of God.

Peter is told by the voice three times that what God had cleansed should not be considered common. Often in Scripture God repeats something three times. For example Isaiah went into the temple and saw the seraphim high and lifted up. They cried one to another, "Holy, holy, holy" (Isaiah 6:3) signifying the Trinity and greatness to the Holy One. The number 3 represents divine presence, wholeness, and perfection. To highlight an idea God often used the number 3. "Three is the first number to which the meaning "all" was given. It is the Triad, being the number of the whole as it contains the beginning, a middle and an end. The power of three is universal and is the tripeptide nature of the world as heaven, earth, and its waters. It is human as body, soul and spirit."[29]

The men who are sent by Cornelius find Simon's house. God in His providential sovereignty had led them there.

There was Human Obedience   (Acts 10:21-33)

No self-respecting Jew would give lodging. Cornelius understands this challenge. *"Then he said to them, 'You know how unlawful it is for a Jewish man to keep company with or go to one of another nation. But God has shown me that I should not call any man common or unclean'"* (10:28). The word for lodging in verse 23 mean to "entertain as a guest". On the next day Peter joined the entourage and goes to Caesarea. On arrival at Cornelius' house the host kneels before Peter who quickly reminds him to rise as both are just men.

Peter, somewhat bewildered, remembering his previous vision, asks Cornelius for the purpose of requesting the apostles' visit. It is interesting to note that Cornelius had invited his relatives and close friends to his house. He did not know that the men he sent to get the apostles would be able to bring him from Joppa to Caesarea. Peter brings six brethren with him (Acts 11:12). "Cornelius showed great faith by having the audience already present."[30]

Peter is very clear about the new transition he has experienced. In his vision he learned that God's inclusion into the kingdom was not based on Kosher food or circumcision. It is the reason that he came to see Cornelius. God spoke to him in his quiet time, thus he was doing something he would not normally do. When God speaks in silence, we should not allow anyone to talk us out of what He has spoken.

Cornelius relates his story. He also relates that God commanded him to ask for Simon called Peter to come to see him. The word "commanded" in verse 33 speaks of a commanding, demanding obedience.

When God commands we need to obey.

There is Only One Way to God   (Acts 10:34-43)

The term *"Opening his mouth"* in Acts 10:34 is a colloquial Greek expression that seems to reference someone cutting to the heart of a message. Peter's message is profound yet Peter's message is simple. God does not show partiality.

"For the Lord Your God is God of gods, and Lord of lords, a great God, a mighty and terrible which he does not equal any person" (Deuteronomy 10:17).

There is often discussion on whether or not Cornelius was already saved. It appears that he is a highly religious seeking man who wants desperately to know God. ' … who will tell you words by which you and all your household will be saved'" (Acts 11:14).

When someone comes to Christ, it may take a long time. Sometimes it happens quickly. The book of Acts is full of various time frames when people come to Christ. As we study through this book and seeing the story of Christianity at its beginning, there are various time frames. It is my position that Cornelius accepts Christ as recorded in Acts 10.

In Peter's sermon he addresses the nations and people of the nations who are accepted by God. The word accepted is a term that means marked by a favorable manifestation of divine pleasure. For example, Paul addressed this in 2 Corinthians 6:2. *"For He says: 'In an acceptable time I have heard you, And in the day of salvation I have helped you'" Behold, now is the accepted time; behold, now is the day of salvation"* (2 Corinthians 6:2).

Peter addresses the absolute Lordship of Jesus Christ and gives a brief historical overview of the Lord's death and resurrection.

The word which God sent to the children of Israel, preaching peace through Jesus Christ—He is Lord of all— that word you know, which was proclaimed throughout all Judea, and began from Galilee after the baptism which John preached: how God anointed Jesus of Nazareth with the Holy Spirit and with power, who went about doing good and healing all who were oppressed by the devil, for God was with Him. And we are witnesses of all things which He did both in the land of the Jews and in Jerusalem, whom they killed by hanging on a tree. Him God raised up on the third day, and showed Him openly, not to all the people, but to witnesses chosen before by God, even to us who ate and drank with Him after He arose from the dead. And He commanded us to preach to the people, and to testify that it is He who was ordained by God to be Judge of the living and the dead. To Him all the prophets witness that, through His name, whoever believes in Him will receive remission of sins.' While Peter was still speaking these words, the Holy Spirit fell upon all those who heard the word. And those of the circumcision who believed were astonished, as many as came with Peter, because the gift of the Holy Spirit had been

*poured out on the Gentiles also. For they heard them speak
with tongues and magnify God. Then Peter answered, 'Can
anyone forbid water, that these should not be baptized who
have received the Holy Spirit just as we have?' And he
commanded them to be baptized in the name of the Lord.
Then they asked him to stay a few days* (Acts 10:36-48).

The change is complete. God has accomplished the commission
through the apostles. The world now may hear the story of the resurrection
through the work of the Holy Spirit.

Samuel John Stone captures this thought of the church's place in a
hymn he penned in the 1860's. "The song was written as a direct response
to the schism within the church of South Africa ... [when] the first bishop
of South Africa ... denounced most of the Bible as fictitious."[31] It prompted
Stone to write a set of hymns based on the Apostles' Creed.

"1. The Church's one foundation
Is Jesus Christ her Lord,
She is His new creation
By water and the Word.
From heaven He came and sought her
To be His holy bride;
With His own blood He bought her
And for her life He died.

2. She is from every nation,
Yet one o'er all the earth;
Her charter of salvation,
One Lord, one faith, one birth;
One holy Name she blesses,
Partakes one Holy Food,
And to one Hope she presses,
With every grace endued.

3. The Church shall never perish!
Her dear Lord to defend,
To guide, sustain, and cherish,
Is with her to the end:

Though there be those who hate her,
And false sons in her pale,
Against or foe or traitor
She ever shall prevail.

4. Though with a scornful wonder
Men see her sore oppressed,
By schisms rent asunder,
By heresies distressed:
Yet saints their watch are keeping,
Their cry goes up, "How long?"
And soon the night of weeping
Shall be the morn of song!

5. 'Mid toil and tribulation,
And tumult of her war,
She waits the consummation
Of peace forevermore;
Till, with the vision glorious,
Her longing eyes are blest,
And the great Church victorious
Shall be the Church at rest.

6. Yet she on earth hath union
With God the Three in One,
And mystic sweet communion
With those whose rest is won,
With all her sons and daughters
Who, by the Master's Hand
Led through the deathly waters,
Repose in Eden land.

7. O happy ones and holy!
Lord, give us grace that we
Like them, the meek and lowly,
On high may dwell with Thee:
There, past the border mountains,
Where in sweet vales the Bride

With Thee by living fountains
Forever shall abide! Amen."[32]

This magnificent hymn lays the ground work of the truth found in Scripture of our faith. The emphasis throughout the book of Acts is on the life and ministry of the Lord Jesus Christ.

As we travel through the book of Acts we find the message of the gospel was first given to the Jew and then to the Gentiles.

In Peter's message to Cornelius he made several important declarations, which clearly explains that the early followers of Christ are witnesses of the life, death and resurrection of Jesus Christ. He probably refers to the twelve apostles and the six witnesses he brought with him. The word for witness is the same root used in Acts 1:8 referring to the idea of martyrdom. These early followers were convinced that what they say and heard from their Lord needs to be told. Cornelius was ready to hear the message that Peter delivered. In my own ministry I have been places where the Holy Spirit also prepared people to hear and receive the truth that it almost appears the message needs to be quickly given because the responders are so ready.

There is Power in God's Family
(Acts 10:44-46)

Jews and Gentiles may belong to God's family. The blood of Jesus Christ cleanses all who come to the Savior requesting forgiveness and restoration back to God.

It is important to remember that there were those who were displaced by the Jews. They were the Gentiles who did not keep the laws or practices of Judaism. The Gentiles also looked at the Jews as unclean and not hospitable because of their refusal to enter Gentile homes. Now Simon Peter is staying at a home of a man who is a tanner, an occupation not acceptable to Jews. Peter enters Cornelius home, a place not normally occupied by Jews. The book of Ephesians describes this as a mystery. The word mystery does not mean something scary, but rather something hidden. The Jews and Gentiles are now one in Christ through salvation in the Lord Jesus Christ.

When Jesus gave the Great Commission he said there would be signs that would follow the believers. One of those signs would be " ... they shall speak with new tongues" (Mark 16:17).

The idea of speaking with new tongues is from two Greek words. *glossa* which can be interpreted as language or tongues and *lulia* which means speech.

It means something new to the hearer, or something not understood until that time. If I say that the French language is new to me, it does not mean that I have never heard of the French language, but it means I have never spoken it or understood it. In Acts 2:4 the Scripture teaches *"they began to speak with other tongues"*. The word 'other' refers to the fact that people spoke in languages different from the normal languages being used. In Acts 2:6 the word is *dialekto* meaning dialect.

In the Acts 10 passage the language had a purpose which was to magnify or make much of God. Perhaps it is wise at this point in studying the early days of Christianity to ask the question as to the reason God gave the gift. Let me offer the following.

1. The gift was used to promote the gospel and truthfulness of the resurrection of Jesus Christ. *"Therefore tongues are for a sign, not to those who believe but to unbelievers; but prophesying is not for unbelievers but for those who believe not"* (I Corinthians 14:22). The Scripture uses the word sign which conveys the concept of a message from God to those who are not yet saved. The gifts are not given for self-promotion. The gifts, all of them, are for the purpose of being an instrument for God's glory to give forward the message of the gospel.

2. A second reason was to promote the gospel with a confirmation. *"For as the body is one and has many members, but all the members of that one body, being many, are one body, so also is Christ"* (2 Corinthians 12:12). Unfortunately there are many Christians who disrupt the body of Christ and do not keep the unity of the faith over issues like this. Whereas all may not agree on all issues, the unity of the body is necessary for the lost to be attracted into the body of Christ. The Scripture is clear ' ... *that they all may be one, as You, Father, are in Me, and I in You; that they also may be one in Us, that the world may believe that You sent Me'* (John 17:21).

   Peter then recommended the new believers to be baptized in obedience to the Lord's command (Matthew 28:18-20). After a period of prayer at the request of the people, he stayed for a few days.

The foundation of the Great Commission is now complete. The believers began in Jerusalem and now they have extended to the Gentile world. The world has been changed. It will never be the same again. "According to a 2011 Pew Research Center survey, there are 2.18 billion Christians around the world in 2010, up from 600 million in 1910. A global census study estimates 10,283,700 Muslims converted to Christianity around the world."[33] The Catholic Church claims over 1 billion, Protestants over 800,000,000, Orthodox 260,380,000; other Christian groups 28,430,000."[34] Protestant and other Christianity groups are growing. The Catholic Church and Orthodoxy are declining. "The most fertile countries are Ecuador with a 94% Christian, East Timor with 99% Christian and Armenia with a 98.6% Christian."[35] "Approximately 2.7 million people convert to Christianity ranking first in net gains through religious conversions."[36]

These statistics and others similar to these are easy to find with a little research. How many of these are 'born again' Christians as Jesus defined it in John 3, no one knows but God. The point is from the humble beginning in the early days of Acts, the story of Jesus' resurrection has produced history's greatest movement.

One brief observation before leaving this remarkable chapter. A question. How were people saved in the Old Testament?

In the Old Testament God makes it very clear that people approached Jesus by way of animal sacrifices. The Old Testament saints looked forward to the coming of the Messiah. " ... *knowing that you were not redeemed with corruptible things, like silver or gold, from your aimless conduct received by tradition from your fathers, but with the precious blood of Christ, as of a lamb without blemish and without spot. He indeed was foreordained before the foundation of the world, but was manifest in these last times for you who through Him believe in God, who raised Him from the dead and gave Him glory, so that your faith and hope are in God. Since you have purified your souls in obeying the truth through the Spirit in sincere love of the brethren, love one another fervently with a pure heart, having been born again, not of corruptible seed but incorruptible, through the word of God which lives and abides forever*" (1 Peter 1:18-23). The Old Testament prophets did not grasp the time between the coming of Christ and the glory that was to come. They were, however, sure that the sacrifice would be available for all who believed. " ... *searching what, or what manner of time, the Spirit of Christ who was in them was indicating when He testified beforehand the sufferings of Christ and the glories that would follow. To them it was revealed that, not to themselves, but to us they were ministering the things which now have been reported to you through those who have preached the gospel to you by the Holy Spirit sent from heaven—things which angels desire to look into"* (1 Peter 1:11-12).

"Throughout the history of this world, countless people have discovered that God alone, through Jesus Christ, can meet the deepest longings and needs of the human heart. This is possible because Jesus was fully God and fully man. He died to pay the death penalty for our sin, and He was raised from the dead by the power of God. He is alive today, and He wants to be in your life right now."[37] Salvation has always been through Israel's Messiah, the Lord Jesus Christ.

CHAPTER

14

A New Name

(Acts 11)

And the apostles and brethren that were in Judaea heard
that the Gentiles had also received the word of God. And
when Peter was come up to Jerusalem, they that were of the
circumcision contended with him, Saying, Thou wentest in
to men uncircumcised, and didst eat with them. But Peter
rehearsed the matter from the beginning, and expounded
it by order unto them, saying, I was in the city of Joppa
praying: and in a trance I saw a vision, A certain vessel
descend, as it had been a great sheet, let down from heaven
by four corners; and it came even to me: Upon the which
when I had fastened mine eyes, I considered, and saw
fourfooted beasts of the earth, and wild beasts, and creeping
things, and fowls of the air. And I heard a voice saying unto
me, Arise, Peter; slay and eat. But I said, Not so, Lord: for
nothing common or unclean hath at any time entered into
my mouth. But the voice answered me again from heaven,
What God hath cleansed, that call not thou common. And
this was done three times: and all were drawn up again
into heaven. And, behold, immediately there were three
men already come unto the house where I was, sent from
Caesarea unto me. And the Spirit bade me go with them,
nothing doubting. Moreover these six brethren accompanied
me, and we entered into the man's house: And he shewed us

how he had seen an angel in his house, which stood and said unto him, Send men to Joppa, and call for Simon, whose surname is Peter; Who shall tell thee words, whereby thou and all thy house shall be saved. And as I began to speak, the Holy Ghost fell on them, as on us at the beginning. Then remembered I the word of the Lord, how that he said, John indeed baptized with water; but ye shall be baptized with the Holy Ghost. Forasmuch then as God gave them the like gift as he did unto us, who believed on the Lord Jesus Christ; what was I, that I could withstand God? When they heard these things, they held their peace, and glorified God, saying, Then hath God also to the Gentiles granted repentance unto life. Now they which were scattered abroad upon the persecution that arose about Stephen travelled as far as Phenice, and Cyprus, and Antioch, preaching the word to none but unto the Jews only. And some of them were men of Cyprus and Cyrene, which, when they were come to Antioch, spake unto the Grecians, preaching the Lord Jesus. And the hand of the Lord was with them: and a great number believed, and turned unto the Lord. Then tidings of these things came unto the ears of the church which was in Jerusalem: and they sent forth Barnabas, that he should go as far as Antioch. Who, when he came, and had seen the grace of God, was glad, and exhorted them all, that with purpose of heart they would cleave unto the Lord. For he was a good man, and full of the Holy Ghost and of faith: and much people was added unto the Lord. Then departed Barnabas to Tarsus, for to seek Saul: And when he had found him, he brought him unto Antioch. And it came to pass, that a whole year they assembled themselves with the church, and taught much people. And the disciples were called Christians first in Antioch. And in these days came prophets from Jerusalem unto Antioch. And there stood up one of them named Agabus, and signified by the Spirit that there should be great dearth throughout all the world: which came to pass in the days of Claudius Caesar. Then the disciples, every man according to his ability, determined to send relief unto the brethren which dwelt in Judaea: Which *also they did, and sent it to the elders by the hands of Barnabas and Saul.* (Acts 11:1-30 KJV).

Shock waves were spreading through the Hebrew community. Christianity, considered a sect of Judaism, was now bringing in the Gentile world with full rights and privileges based on the resurrection of the Jewish rabbi who trained twelve followers. The Great Commission would now spread to a Gentile community.

The city mentioned in Acts 11-12 is a good example. The city of Antioch was a major, ancient metropolis. It was the third most powerful city after Rome and Alexandria. It was noted for its culture and commerce. Many Roman trade routes went through the city. There were many learned men and liberal studies. There was an ancient temple named Athena promoting prostitution. The city eventually was called the "cradle of Christianity" because of early Christianity and Hellenistic Judaism and their influence. In the day of the Acts, the city was experiencing some of her glory years. Eventually the city declined because of wear and tear earthquakes, a change in trade routes and the eventual conquest of the Mongols. It was here, in its best of days, that the early believers were first called Christians.

The term Christian was considered to some a term to be used of derision. Christianity has a history of persecution. It was Tertullian, a prolific early Christian author from Carthage in the Roman Empire who demanded legal toleration and that Christians be treated as other sects of the Roman Empire. Tertullian coined the phrase "the blood of the martyrs is the seed of the church."[38] There were so many misunderstandings and misrepresentations of Christianity that persecution broke out in many quarters. The question that seemed to be often debated was to define a Christian.

When the apostles and brethren heard that the Gentiles received the Word of God they took issue with Peter based on his time with Cornelius. In Peter's response he gives some very interesting teaching of the characteristics of the Christian faith. " ... *those who were circumcised* " (Acts 11:2) many were unhappy that Gentiles were entering into the faith without the ritual of circumcision.

Peter's response is brilliant. He begins with a refresher on what occurred in Joppa. (Acts 11:1-10). He rehearses the events that led him to Cornelius. Very carefully he points out to the brethren that he told God he would not eat the four footed animals, wild beasts, and crawling creatures. When God ordered him to understand that what God cleansed cannot be unholy on this occasion, he tells about the three men Cornelius sent who were at the door. Peter, without any reservations, takes six brethren with him and goes to Cornelius' home in Caesarea. He rehearses the story of Cornelius' dream and the revelation that Simon Peter needed to be brought to the Centurion's house. Peter explains that he gave the gospel teaching and carefully states, *"Therefore if God gave them the same gift as He gave to us also after believing in the Lord Jesus Christ who was I that I could stand in God's way"* (Acts 10:17). The conclusion is that repentance has been granted to the Gentiles. It is here that we can understand the marvelous truth of grace. We do nothing to receive it that can be accounted as works. There are three distinct thoughts in this passage of Scripture.

Grace

Grace is seen in our salvation. *"For by grace you have been saved through faith, and that not of yourselves; it is the gift of God, not of works, lest anyone should boast"* (Ephesians 2:8, 9).

Grace is realized in our security *"For the grace of God that brings salvation has appeared to all men"* (Titus 2:11). *" ... to the praise of the glory of His grace, by which He made us accepted in the Beloved"* (Ephesians 1:6).

Grace is seen in a desire to serve *"And of His fullness we have all received, and grace for grace"* (John 1:16).

Grace keeps on through suffering *"Let us therefore come boldly to the throne of grace, that we may obtain mercy and find grace to help in time of need"* (Hebrews 4:16).

Grace to look for the Second Coming *" ... teaching us that, denying ungodliness and worldly lusts, we should live soberly, righteously, and godly in the present age, looking for*

*the blessed hope and glorious appearing of our great God
and Savior Jesus Christ* (Titus 2:12-13).

Grace provides inner satisfaction *"You therefore, my son, be
strong in the grace that is in Christ Jesus"* (2 Timothy 2:1).

Growth

A second indication of the early Christians and who they were was
the growth. There was growth within. *"When they heard these things they
became silent; and they glorified God, saying, 'Then God has also granted
to the Gentiles repentance to life'"* (Acts 11:18). Jerusalem was the starting
point. Antioch would now replace Jerusalem as the key Christian city. The
early days of missionary activities and enterprises started here. In Acts 6,
we previously studied that the early deacons were Greeks. Nicholas was a
proselyte from Antioch. *"From there they sailed to Antioch, where they had
been commended to the grace of God for the work which they had completed*
(Acts 14:26). *" ... it seemed good to us, being assembled with one accord,
to send chosen men to you with our beloved Barnabas and Paul"* (Acts
15:35). *"And when he had landed at Caesarea, and gone up and greeted
the church, he went down to Antioch"* (Acts 18:22). These verses indicate
the importance of the city of Antioch. Bible believing Christianity desires
growth through the process of the Great Commission that we describe in
Acts 1:8.

Men from Cyprus and Cyrene came to Antioch to preach.

The growth of the ministry was based on the hand of the Lord being
with them (Acts 10:21). The hand of God in the Bible describes blessings.
It speaks of the power and strength of God. The men who came from
Cyrene came from an area in northern Africa. It was actually a Greek city
in the province of Cyrenaica. It was an early center of Christianity. This
area is north-eastern Libya today. Cyprus was one of the largest islands of
the Mediterranean Sea. It was the original home of Barnabus. Paul's first
missionary journeys were here. *"When we had sighted Cyprus, we passed
it on the left, sailed to Syria, and landed at Tyre; for there the ship was to
unload her cargo"* (Acts 21:3). *"When we had put to sea from there, we sailed
under the shelter of Cyprus, because the winds were contrary"* (Acts 27:4).

The work that God was doing in Antioch reached the Jerusalem church.
They sent Barnabus to see them. What did he find? The outpouring of

God's grace. Barnabus did what he did best. He encouraged the people. He is described as a good man who was filled with the Holy Spirit. His ministry was always welcomed. It was Barnabus who convinced the apostle and early Christians of the reality and genuineness of the conversion of Saul. *"But Barnabas took him and brought him to the apostles. And he declared to them how he had seen the Lord on the road, and that He had spoken to him, and how he had preached boldly at Damascus in the name of Jesus"* (Acts 9:27). He emphasizes that the work in Antioch is of God. *"Then news of these things came to the ears of the church in Jerusalem, and they sent out Barnabas to go as far as Antioch. When he came and had seen the grace of God, he was glad, and encouraged them all that with purpose of heart they should continue with the Lord. For he was a good man, full of the Holy Spirit and of faith. And a great many people were added to the Lord"* (11:22-24). He encouraged Paul on their first missionary journey. *"Then the proconsul believed, when he saw what had been done, being astonished at the teaching of the Lord"* (Acts 13:12). He was very helpful in defending the message of grace when the debates, discussions, and decisions were made in Jerusalem.

> *Then all the multitude kept silent and listened to Barnabas and Paul declaring how many miracles and wonders God had worked through them among the Gentiles. And after they had become silent, James answered, saying, "Men and brethren, listen to me: Simon has declared how God at the first visited the Gentiles to take out of them a people for His name. And with this the words of the prophets agree, just as it is written: 'After this I will return And will rebuild the tabernacle of David, which has fallen down; I will rebuild its ruins, And I will set it up; So that the rest of mankind may seek the LORD, Even all the Gentiles who are called by My name, Says the LORD who does all these things.' Known to God from eternity are all His works. Therefore I judge that we should not trouble those from among the Gentiles who are turning to God, but that we write to them to abstain from things polluted by idols, from sexual immorality, from things strangled, and from blood. For Moses has had throughout many generations those who preach him in every city, being read in the synagogues every Sabbath.' Then it*

pleased the apostles and elders, with the whole church, to send chosen men of their own company to Antioch with Paul and Barnabas, namely, Judas who was also named Barsabas and Silas, leading men among the brethren. They wrote this letter by them: The apostles, the elders, and the brethren, To the brethren who are of the Gentiles in Antioch, Syria, and Cilicia: Greetings. Since we have heard that some who went out from us have troubled you with words, unsettling your souls, saying, 'You must be circumcised and keep the law'—to whom we gave no such commandment—it seemed good to us, being assembled with one accord, to send chosen men to you with our beloved Barnabas and Paul (Acts 15:12-25).

From Antioch Barnabus goes to Tarsus to get Saul. He found him, brought him to Antioch, and for a year they faithfully taught the believers who are now called Christians.

Saul had returned to Tarsus and also spent time in Syria and Cilicia. *"Afterward I went into the regions of Syria and Cilicia"* (Galatians 1:21). Paul was there about five years. *"Then Barnabas departed for Tarsus to seek Saul. And when he had found him, he brought him to Antioch. So it was that for a whole year they assembled with the church and taught a great many people. And the disciples were first called Christians in Antioch"* (Acts 11:25, 26).

The early church had growth both internally and externally. There was a huge move of God.

Giving

Some prophets came to Antioch from Jerusalem. As large numbers were following the faith (Acts 11), one of these prophets is mentioned. His name is Agabus. He predicts a severe famine. The famine came during the reign of Claudius. "The fourth century historian, Orasius, mentions this famine in Syria which occurred in 46 and 47 A.D."[39] "Herod, the brother of Agrippa who had perished, was allowed to govern Claudius. He asked Claudius Caesar for control over the temple along with the sacred treasury and the ability to choose the high priests ... Around this time lived queen Helena ... Her arrival was of great help to the masses in Jerusalem for there was a great famine in the land that overtook them, and many died in starvation."[40]

The disciple, knowing the needs, sent funds through trusted men, Barnabus and Saul, to the elders to the needy in Judea. These funds were sent to the elders. The elders have a two-fold meaning in Scripture. An elder may be an older or wiser man. In the Old Testament elders were usually older men responsible for making decisions. They were community leaders (Genesis 50:7). Moses had seventy elders who were selected as the governing group under Moses. *"So the LORD said to Moses: 'Gather to Me seventy men of the elders of Israel, whom you know to be the elders of the people and officers over them; bring them to the tabernacle of meeting, that they may stand there with you'"* (Numbers 11:16).

In the New Testament there are three words used interchangeably that appear to be the same office. One is bishop. *"This is a faithful saying: If a man desires the position of a bishop, he desires a good work"* (1 Timothy 3:1). Note the word bishop and elder is used interchangeably. *"For this reason I left you in Crete, that you should set in order the things that are lacking, and appoint elders in every city as I commanded you-For a bishop must be blameless, as a steward of God, not self-willed, not quick-tempered, not given to wine, not violent, not greedy for money"* (Titus 1:5,7). The term pastor is also used. He is the under shepherd. *"And He Himself gave some to be apostles, some prophets, some evangelists, and some pastors and teachers, for the equipping of the saints for the work of ministry, for the edifying of the body of Christ"* (Ephesians 4:11-12). *"The elders who are among you I exhort, I who am a fellow elder and a witness of the sufferings of Christ, and also a partaker of the glory that will be revealed: Shepherd the flock of God which is among you, serving as overseers, not by compulsion but willingly, not for dishonest gain but eagerly; nor as being lords over those entrusted to you, but being examples to the flock; and when the Chief Shepherd appears, you will receive the crown of glory that does not fade away"* (1 Peter 5:1-4). "Elders are recognized by other elders."[41] *"Do not neglect the gift that is in you, which was given to you by prophecy with the laying on of the hands of the eldership"* (1 Timothy 4:14). "His duties are ruling (5:17), pastoring or shepherding the flock (Acts 20:28, 1 Peter 5:2), guarding the truth (Titus 1:9), and general oversight of the work."[42] According to Acts 11:31 the elders were in charge of receiving the gift.

In the early church, these new groups of Christians are characterized in this chapter as people who received grace, they grew internally and externally and they were givers.

Questions and Discussion

Questions

1. What were some of the early reactions to the name Christian?
2. What 3 terms describe the leadership of the church? How is each term described?

For Discussion

1. What do you sense that the early church of Antioch was like?

CHAPTER

15

The Story of Christianity
A Miracle of Prayer
(Acts 12)

Now about that time Herod the king stretched forth his hands to vex certain of the church. And he killed James the brother of John with the sword. And because he saw it pleased the Jews, he proceeded further to take Peter also. (Then were the days of unleavened bread.) And when he had apprehended him, he put him in prison, and delivered him to four quaternions of soldiers to keep him; intending after Easter to bring him forth to the people. Peter therefore was kept in prison: but prayer was made without ceasing of the church unto God for him. And when Herod would have brought him forth, the same night Peter was sleeping between two soldiers, bound with two chains: and the keepers before the door kept the prison. And, behold, the angel of the Lord came upon him, and a light shined in the prison: and he smote Peter on the side, and raised him up, saying, Arise up quickly. And his chains fell off from his hands. And the angel said unto him, Gird thyself, and bind on thy sandals. And so he did. And he saith unto him, Cast thy garment about thee, and follow me. And he went out, and followed him; and wist not that it was true which was done by the angel; but thought he saw a vision. When they were past the first and the second ward, they came unto the iron gate that leadeth unto the city; which opened to them of his own accord: and they went out, and passed on through one street; and forthwith the angel departed from him. And when Peter was come to himself, he said, Now I know of a surety, that the Lord hath sent his angel, and hath delivered me out of the hand of Herod, and from all the expectation of the people of the Jews. And when he had considered the thing, he came to the house of Mary the mother of John, whose surname was Mark; where many were gathered together praying. And as Peter knocked at the door of the gate, a damsel came to hearken, named Rhoda. And when she knew Peter's voice, she opened not the gate for gladness, but ran in, and told how Peter stood before the gate. And they said unto her, Thou art mad. But she constantly affirmed that it was even so. Then said they, It is his angel. But Peter continued knocking: and when they had opened the door, and saw him, they were astonished. But he, beckoning unto them with the hand to hold their peace, declared unto them how the Lord had brought him out of the prison. And he said, Go shew these things unto James, and to the brethren. And he departed, and went into another place. Now as soon as it was day, there was no small stir among the soldiers, what was become of Peter. And when Herod had sought for him, and found him not, he examined the keepers, and commanded that they should be put to death. And he went down from Judaea to Caesarea, and there abode. And Herod was highly displeased with them of Tyre and Sidon: but they came with one accord to him, and, having made Blastus the king's chamberlain their friend, desired peace; because their country was nourished by the king's country. And upon a set day Herod, arrayed in royal apparel, sat upon his throne, and made an oration unto them. And the people gave a shout, saying, It is the voice of a god, and not of a man. And immediately the angel of the Lord smote him, because he gave not God the glory: and he was eaten of worms, and gave up the ghost. But the word of God grew and multiplied. And Barnabas

*and Saul returned from Jerusalem, when they had fulfilled
their ministry, and took with them John, whose surname was
Mark.* (Acts 12:1-25 KJV).

There is a war that rages all around us. The war is between God
and Satan. The outcome is not in doubt. Jesus wins! Despite
this outcome, it does not lesson the challenge of struggle that
Christians will face. This chapter relates the truth of the struggle and the
need for prayer in all of our lives.

As we enter Acts 12, we have found a very powerful move of God
evidenced by the amazing things that have happened. Each chapter in
Acts describes great preaching, multiple conversions and numerous other
miraculous experiences. There have been some challenges, like the death
of Stephen, but even in that episode there is a mighty scene of the deacon's
entrances into heaven. Great conversions include the man who hated
Christianity enough to attempt to destroy it, Saul and the Gentile Roman
centurion, Cornelius, whose story opens up the gospel to the world.

Herod's Outcome

In Acts 12 we see Herod deciding to harass and harm the church.
This is Herod Agrippa. He is the grandson of Herod the Great. Herod
the Great ruled during the days of the birth of our Lord Jesus Christ.
Herod Agrippa was the nephew of Herod Antipas. Herod Antipas is
the individual who was involved in the trial of Jesus. Luke records that
narrative in Luke 23:7-12. *"And as soon as he knew that He belonged
to Herod's jurisdiction, he sent Him to Herod, who was also in Jerusalem
at that time. Now when Herod saw Jesus, he was exceedingly glad; for he
had desired for a long time to see Him, because he had heard many things
about Him, and he hoped to see some miracle done by Him. Then he
questioned Him with many words, but He answered him nothing. And the
chief priests and scribes stood and vehemently accused Him. Then Herod,
with his men of war, treated Him with contempt and mocked Him, arrayed
Him in a gorgeous robe, and sent Him back to Pilate. That very day Pilate
and Herod became friends with each other, for previously they had been at
enmity with each other"* (Luke 23:7-12).

There are many leaders who dislike Christians. Herod, for political
reasons, sets out to cause great harm to the early Christians. It would appear

that this Herod was at least outwardly in favor of Jewish ceremonies and a patriot of Judaism.

James, the apostle of our Lord, is the first apostle to die and the first to be martyred. James had a unique relationship with Jesus. He is often mentioned as being part of the inner three associates with our Lord. *"And He took with Him Peter and the two sons of Zebedee, and He began to be sorrowful and deeply distressed"* (Matthew 26:37); *"And He permitted no one to follow Him except Peter, James, and John the brother of James"* (Mark 5:37).

It is interesting to note that James and his brother, John, came to Jesus requesting to be seated on each side of Him in the kingdom. They wanted to go up the ladder to success! When they made the request, Jesus responded in the following manner. *"Then James and John, the sons of Zebedee, came to Him, saying, 'Teacher, we want You to do for us whatever we ask.'" And He said to them, 'What do you want Me to do for you?'" "They said to Him, 'Grant us that we may sit, one on Your right hand and the other on Your left, in Your glory.'" But Jesus said to them, 'You do not know what you ask. Are you able to drink the cup that I drink, and be baptized with the baptism that I am baptized with?'" They said to Him, 'We are able'" So Jesus said to them, 'You will indeed drink the cup that I drink, and with the baptism I am baptized with you will be baptized; but to sit on My right hand and on My left is not Mine to give, but it is for those for whom it is prepared'"* (Mark 10:35-40). Little did they know at this time what was ahead for them. On other occasions Jesus warned his followers of persecution. Now it was very real! None of us know what the future looks like but we do know that one day we will be with our Lord!

James is put to death by the sword. This indicates that this man was beheaded. It is interesting to note that James is not replaced as an apostle. The Apostles of our Lord were given specific tasks. It appears there would come a day when the office would not be needed in the specific role of telling the resurrection story from a first-hand account.

Herod's persecutions were politically motivated. Saul of Tarsus had sincere religious convictions. Misguided as they were, he believed strongly in his religious views until the day he met Jesus on the Damascus Road.

The Jews were very happy with Herod's decision to execute James. He now decides to go after the 'main guy'. He goes after Peter!

Herod arrests Peter at the feast of Unleavened Bread. "Unleavened bread is any of a wide variety of breads which are not prepared with raising agents such as yeast. Unleavened breads are usually flat breads."[43]

"On the fourteenth day of the first month at twilight is Yahweh's Passover. And on the fifteenth day of the same month is the Feast of Unleavened Bread to Yahweh. On the first day you shall have a holy convocation, you shall have no customary work on it."[44]

The Scripture indicates that this was during the days of Unleavened Bread. During the Passover no leavened bread is eaten. Passover was called the Feast of Unleavened Bread. Matzo is traditionally eaten during Passover.

It seems that Herod decides to hold Peter until after the Passover. He doesn't need an outbreak of a mob mentality that would result from killing this high profile figure. It would not be expedient for this politically motivated leader.

Passover is one of Israel's important yearly festivals. The others are Booths and Pentecost. Passover commemorates the Jewish deliverance under Moses. It is celebrated on the fourteenth of Nisan. This is the March-April time frame. It was followed by the Feast of Unleavened Bread which would continue from the fifteenth to twenty-sixth.

From the first four verses of Acts 12 we leap ahead to see the results of Herod's life. Through the power of prayer Peter is delivered from prison. An outraged Herod proceeds to kill the guards who were trying to find the apostle. (12:19)

Herod leaves Judea and goes to Caesarea. He was angry with the people of Tyre and Sidon. These areas needed to import grains from the agricultural bason of the fields of Galilee. The people of Tyre and Sidon have been working with Blastus, the king's chamberlain. He was the mediator between the people and the king. It seems he is bribed to come on the side of the people! People in the position of Blastus normally had great influence with their masters! Herod is eaten with worms and dies. Why? Because he did not give God the glory! Herod's goal in life was self-exaltation and a desire to please people! God will share His glory with no one! *"How can you believe, who receive honor from one another, and do not seek the honor that comes from the only God"* (John 5:44).

According to the historian, Josephus, Agrippa came to Caesarea and a great multitude of families gathered to listen to him. His garment was made of silver and with it being illuminated by the sun. It shone out and was resplendent to spread a horror over those who looked intently on him. As they spoke about him being a god it was not for his good. "On the second day of which shows he put on a garment made wholly of silver, and of a contexture truly wonderful, and came into the theatre early in the morning; at which the silver of his garment being illuminated by the fresh reflection of the sun's rays upon it, shone out after a surprising manner, and was so resplendent as to spread horror over those who looked intently upon him; and presently his flatterers cried out, one from one place, and another from another (though not for good) that he was a god …"[45] "A terrible pain entered his belly and an intestinal struggle was violent. According to Josephus he said that he would have to accept what God would give him. What a tragic way to end one's life.

The Angel of the Lord strikes Herod. This is the Greek word *patasso*. It is the same word that occurs in verse seven of this chapter when Peter woke up from his sleep. When the angel struck Herod, it was not fatal, but it began a terrible intestinal struggle Herod would face.

Peter's Outcome

Peter is off to prison. Four squads mean there were four soldiers for each six hour shifts. It appears two soldiers were chained to Peter, while two others were available to watch for any intruders.

Despite the prospects of death, Peter is calmly accepting his fate. What a difference in Peter at this event in comparison to his denial of Jesus at the cross. The difference? Peter is now filled with the Holy Spirit. Four interesting things occur in verse five. First "prayer was made". The people who loved their leader were praying and believe their prayer was specifically about his deliverance. Secondly, the prayer was not general. It was specific. Thirdly, it was made fervently. The word fervently is the Greek *ektenes*, which means strained, stretched. It means both instantly and earnestly. Finally the whole church was praying. They spoke specifically to God about Peter.

Amazingly, Peter is sleeping between the two soldiers. There are times when we pray and there is such comfort in God's promises. Jesus promised Peter that he would live to an old age. *"Most assuredly, I say to you, when you were younger, you girded yourself and walked where you wished; but when you are old, you will stretch out your hands, and another will gird you and carry you where you do not wish"* (John 21:18). Perhaps the apostle remembered this.

The angel of the Lord strikes Peter's side and orders the apostle to get up. He adds 'quickly'. The Word means with swiftness or with speed.

Miraculously the chains fall off the apostle. He is told to put on his cloak and sandals and leave the prison following the angel.

It is possible he had been wakened so suddenly or for some other reason, he does not recognize this is really happening, but senses that he is dreaming (vv 9). The angel leads him by the guards and into the street and Peter finds himself now all alone. He then comes to his senses and recognizes he is delivered.

When he considered what had taken place, he fully realized what had happened. He decides to go to the house of Mary. "Traditionally it was here that the Last Supper was held and here now was the nerve center of the church in Jerusalem."[46] This was the mother of John Mark. "Among the Mary's mentioned in the New Testament, Mary the mother of Mark who wrote the second gospel, is spoken of but once, yet this brief description of her is suggestive of her life and labors ... Scottish archeologist and New Testament scholar, Sir William Ramsey, holds that the narrative of Mary in the Acts was by Mark, which would account for the details of his mother's large house becoming a well-known center of Christian life and worship. There is a legend to the affect that this same house was the scene of a still more sacred gathering when, in its upper room, Jesus observed the Lord's Supper on the night of his betrayal."[47]

Peter knocked at the door. The servant, Rhoda, comes and recognizes Peter's voice. She does not answer the door, but rushes in to tell the people who are praying that Peter is at the door! Their prayers have specifically been answered! I take great delight in this fact. Those prayer warriors, the heart of the early church, struggled believing that God would do what they prayed for. I have found this to be true in my own prayer life. There are times God wants to answer our prayers and we doubt. Thank God for His faithfulness and grace. These early saints go so far as to basically tell Rhoda she is out of her mind and they say it is his angel. This reference probably speaks to his guardian angel.

Peter kept knocking. Finally the door is opened. They see Peter and are absolutely amazed!

Peter tells the disciples to be quiet. He relates the story, tells the people to report this to Pastor James and then leaves. We are not told here where he went. The next day there is chaos. Whatever has happened to Peter? Soldiers will now lose their lives. The word 'stir' is the Greek word *torachos* which means trouble! Trouble is brewing. Peter escaped! The soldiers, under law must die for losing the prisoner.

Such are the stories of how Christianity began. Despite constant struggles to stop these followers of Jesus, there was a greater power that would not be stopped. The Acts tells us that power is the Holy Spirit. There is the message that this Jewish rabbi named Jesus of Nazareth rose again. The persecution is just starting but the growth of these followers will become a world record!

Questions

1. What were the 4 principles in verse 12 describing prayer?
2. Why did Herod kill the guards who were in charge of Peter?
3. What are the 3 major feasts of Israel?

For Discussion

1. What do you think the emotional state of the people praying for Peter's deliverance was? How do you think you would react?

16

The Story of Christianity
The Gospel Travels

(Acts 13)

Now there were in the church that was at Antioch certain prophets and teachers; as Barnabas, and Simeon that was called Niger, and Lucius of Cyrene, and Manaen, which had been brought up with Herod the tetrarch, and Saul. As they ministered to the Lord, and fasted, the Holy Ghost said, Separate me Barnabas and Saul for the work whereunto I have called them. And when they had fasted and prayed, and laid their hands on them, they sent them away. So they, being sent forth by the Holy Ghost, departed unto Seleucia; and from thence they sailed to Cyprus. And when they were at Salamis, they preached the word of God in the synagogues of the Jews: and they had also John to their minister. And when they had gone through the isle unto Paphos, they found a certain sorcerer, a false prophet, a Jew, whose name was Barjesus: Which was with the deputy of the country, Sergius Paulus, a prudent man; who called for Barnabas and Saul, and desired to hear the word of God. But Elymas the sorcerer (for so is his name by interpretation) withstood them, seeking to turn away the deputy from the faith. Then Saul, (who also is called Paul,) filled with the Holy Ghost, set his eyes on him. And said, O full of all

*subtilty and all mischief, thou child of the devil, thou enemy
of all righteousness, wilt thou not cease to pervert the right
ways of the Lord? And now, behold, the hand of the Lord
is upon thee, and thou shalt be blind, not seeing the sun
for a season. And immediately there fell on him a mist
and a darkness; and he went about seeking some to lead
him by the hand. Then the deputy, when he saw what
was done, believed, being astonished at the doctrine of the
Lord. Now when Paul and his company loosed from Paphos,
they came to Perga in Pamphylia: and John departing from
them returned to Jerusalem. But when they departed from
Perga, they came to Antioch in Pisidia, and went into the
synagogue on the sabbath day, and sat down. And after
the reading of the law and the prophets the rulers of the
synagogue sent unto them, saying, Ye men and brethren, if
ye have any word of exhortation for the people, say on. Then
Paul stood up, and beckoning with his hand said, Men of
Israel, and ye that fear God, give audience. The God of this
people of Israel chose our fathers, and exalted the people
when they dwelt as strangers in the land of Egypt, and
with an high arm brought he them out of it. And about
the time of forty years suffered he their manners in the
wilderness. And when he had destroyed seven nations in
the land of Chanaan, he divided their land to them by lot.
And after that he gave unto them judges about the space
of four hundred and fifty years, until Samuel the prophet.
And afterward they desired a king: and God gave unto
them Saul the son of Cis, a man of the tribe of Benjamin,
by the space of forty years. And when he had removed him,
he raised up unto them David to be their king; to whom
also he gave their testimony, and said, I have found David
the son of Jesse, a man after mine own heart, which shall
fulfil all my will. Of this man's seed hath God according
to his promise raised unto Israel a Saviour, Jesus: When
John had first preached before his coming the baptism of
repentance to all the people of Israel. And as John fulfilled
his course, he said, Whom think ye that I am? I am not he.
But, behold, there cometh one after me, whose shoes of his*

feet I am not worthy to loose. Men and brethren, children of the stock of Abraham, and whosoever among you feareth God, to you is the word of this salvation sent. For they that dwell at Jerusalem, and their rulers, because they knew him not, nor yet the voices of the prophets which are read every sabbath day, they have fulfilled them in condemning him. And though they found no cause of death in him, yet desired they Pilate that he should be slain. And when they had fulfilled all that was written of him, they took him down from the tree, and laid him in a sepulchre. But God raised him from the dead: And he was seen many days of them which came up with him from Galilee to Jerusalem, who are his witnesses unto the people. And we declare unto you glad tidings, how that the promise which was made unto the fathers, God hath fulfilled the same unto us their children, in that he hath raised up Jesus again; as it is also written in the second psalm, Thou art my Son, this day have I begotten thee. And as concerning that he raised him up from the dead, now no more to return to corruption, he said on this wise, I will give you the sure mercies of David. Wherefore he saith also in another psalm, Thou shalt not suffer thine Holy One to see corruption. For David, after he had served his own generation by the will of God, fell on sleep, and was laid unto his fathers, and saw corruption: But he, whom God raised again, saw no corruption. Be it known unto you therefore, men and brethren, that through this man is preached unto you the forgiveness of sins: And by him all that believe are justified from all things, from which ye could not be justified by the law of Moses. Beware therefore, lest that come upon you, which is spoken of in the prophets; Behold, ye despisers, and wonder, and perish: for I work a work in your days, a work which ye shall in no wise believe, though a man declare it unto you. And when the Jews were gone out of the synagogue, the Gentiles besought that these words might be preached to them the next sabbath. Now when the congregation was broken up, many of the Jews and religious proselytes followed Paul and Barnabas: who, speaking to them, persuaded them to continue in the grace of God. And the next sabbath day came almost the whole city together to hear the word of God. But when the Jews saw the multitudes, they were filled with envy, and spake against those things which were spoken by Paul, contradicting and blaspheming. Then Paul and Barnabas waxed bold, and said, It was necessary that the word of God should first have been spoken to you: but seeing ye put it from you, and judge yourselves unworthy of everlasting life, lo, we turn to the Gentiles. For so hath the Lord commanded us, saying, I have set thee to be a light of the Gentiles, that thou shouldest be for salvation unto the ends of the earth. And when the Gentiles heard this, they were glad, and glorified the word of the Lord: and as many as were ordained to eternal life believed. And the word of the Lord was published throughout all the region. But the Jews stirred up the devout and honourable women, and the chief men of the city, and raised persecution against Paul and Barnabas, and expelled them out of their coasts. But they shook off the dust of their feet against them, and came unto Iconium. And the disciples were filled with joy, and with the Holy Ghost (Acts 13 KJV).

The close of Acts 12 describes the story of Barnabus and Saul's trip to Jerusalem with the relief fund. This fund was described in Acts 11:30. *"This they also did, and sent it to the elders by the hands of Barnabas and Saul"* (Acts 11:30).

Herod dies. The trip for Saul is easier. It is now time for another transition. There is a shift from Jerusalem and Judea. The shift is into the bubbling community of Antioch. There are prophets and teachers expounding the Word of God to the Christian community. Several leaders emerged. Barnabus was first mentioned by Luke. He has been a leading figure in the Jerusalem church. This encouraging, good man would have been a delight to listen to.

The Teachers of Antioch

Simeon, who is called Niger is different from Simon the tanner and the apostle Peter. Lucius may have been a Gentile.

He is from North Africa. He may have been among the Cyrenian group that preached in Antioch. (Acts 11:20).

Manaen is an interesting person. His name means comforter. He was raised with Herod the Tetrarch. This is the Herod that Jesus once called a fox. *"And He said to them, 'Go, tell that fox, 'Behold, I cast out demons and perform cures today and tomorrow, and the third day I shall be perfected.'"* (Luke 13:32). This Herod was the one who imprisoned and had John the Baptist killed. It is interesting to notice that Manaen was raised with Herod. He turned to God. Herod turned away from God! One is a Christian leader while the other is best known for his killing of John the Baptist.

Saul is the fifth member of this team. He is listed last yet he will shortly be the main character of God's work in the early days of Christianity.

Those early leaders are fasting and praying. Fasting is for more than health purposes. Fasting is a spiritual discipline that is found in both covenants. Jesus strongly emphasized fasting. *'And Jesus said to them, 'Can the friends of the bridegroom mourn as long as the bridegroom is with them? But the days will come when the bridegroom will be taken away from them, and then they will fast'"* (Matthew 9:15). Jesus taught that after his departure there would be change and transition.

Biblical fasting should done in humility. *"But you, when you fast, anoint your head and wash your face, so that you do not appear to men to be fasting, but to your Father who is in the secret place; and your Father who sees in secret will reward you openly"* (Matthew 6:17-18).Fasting results in our motives directed to glorify God and help others. *"Is this not the fast that I have chosen: To loose the bonds of wickedness, To undo the heavy burdens, To let the oppressed go free, And that you break every yoke? Is it not to share your bread with the hungry, And that you bring to your house the poor who are cast out; When you see the naked, that you cover him, And not hide yourself from your own flesh"* (Isaiah 58:6-7). As we fast the exercise can bring us in a closer relationship with God.

In Acts 13 it seems to indicate that the fasting and prayer is for the purpose of finding direction with the transition that is taking place: "The importance of the present narrative is that it describes the first piece of planned 'overseas mission' carried out by representatives of a particular church decision, inspired by the Spirit, rather than somewhat more as a result of persecution."[48]

The gospel is preparing to go to the Roman Empire. Saul is about to have his life changed as dramatically as when he was walking the Damascus Road and the Great light shown from heaven.

The process of laying on of hands takes place and Saul and Barnabus are set apart for this endeavor.

The Trip

The final missionary trip is embarked on. Saul and Barnabus leave from Seleucia. The trip will last about 3 years. Seleucia is 16 miles from Antioch. They are heading toward the island of Cypress, a trip of 200 miles, the homeland of Barnabus.

Accompanying Saul and Barnabus is John Mark. It appears he is to be a helper and servant to Saul and Barnabus.

They will also go to Paphos which is about 90 miles southwest of Salamis. The proconsul is Sergius Paulus. He requests a meeting with the travelers. It is interesting to note that there were leaders in the Roman Empire who desired to know more about these Christians. Sergius Paulus desired to hear the Word of God. It is here that Saul's name is referred to Paul. The name and its transition is mentioned in verse nine in a manner of fact way which assumes this fact was not unfamiliar to others. Saul was a Jewish name. Paul is now more acceptable to the new Gentile world he is heading into. "Saul was his Jewish name and Paul his Roman name or Gentile name. Both were given at the time of his birth, but now he begins to use his Gentile name in this Gentile environment."[49]

There is a friend and counsellor to Sergius Paulus named Bar Jesus, also called Elymas the sorcerer. A sorcerer is a magus. The sorcerer asks Sergio Paulus to pay no attention to the message of Paul. He is concerned about losing his position or influence with the proconsul. His power and influence was from Satan.

The apostle Paul, filled with the Holy Spirit, begins to bring a scorching message to Bar Jesus. Two issues found over and over again in the book of Acts are the filling of the Holy Spirit and the message of the resurrection of Jesus Christ. The name Bar Jesus means 'son of Jesus'. It is interesting to note that Paul calls him the opposite. "O full of deceit and fraud, you son of the devil ..." (Acts 13:10). Paul pronounces a curse upon this man! He loses his sight. Sergius Paulus was overwhelmed. He believes in the message of Paul, but Bar Jesus must be an imposter. This is the last we hear of Sergius Paulus. The text says the leader was astonished. This means he was amazed or beside himself with wonderment.

Here was the sorcerer who was the advisor to the proconsul. Now he is seeking someone to lead him around.

The group sail to Perga, a river port about 12 miles from Atlalia. John Mark returns to Jerusalem. This action will eventually lead to a major disagreement and discord among these leaders.

They leave Perga and go to Antioch in Pisidia. There were actually 16 or 17 cities named Antioch in the ancient world. Pisidia Antioch was located in Southwest Asia Minor and is between the districts of Pisidia and Phrygia. This is not to be confused with the Antioch of Syria.

Paul's sermon is very typical of many of the sermons in Acts. There is a series of historical facts and propositions leading to Jesus and the resurrection. The key theme of his sermons would be the resurrection.

The Sermon   (Acts 13:15-47)

An outline of the sermon could be as follows.

1. The Situation (13:13-15)
2. The Shepherding Hand of God on Israel (13:16-25)
3. The Sovereign Truth of the Gospel (13:26-31)
4. The Source of the Resurrection (13:32-39)
5. The Spoken Warning (13:40-43)

Note now the exposition of the sermon.

The Situation   (Acts 13:13-15)

After the traditional readings, the new arrivals, Peter and Barnabus, are asked to bring a word of exhortation. John Mark has left the group. We do not know why. Paul is now in charge. Perhaps John Mark's relationship to Paul changed things. John Mark was closely aligned to Barnabus.

The Shepherding of God in Israel   (Acts 13:16-25)

Paul beckons with his hand. This was a gesture that commanded silence and attention. He opens the address with the very respectful,

"Men of Israel, and you that fear God". "Give audience" speaks about the importance of the speech he is about to deliver.

God is a shepherding God. He regularly is overseeing the people that are His to lead them in their journey of life. Here the emphasis is the time spent in the journey from Egypt of over 400 years. The nations that were destroyed are the Hittites, the Girgashites, the Amorites, the Canaanites, the Perizzites, the Hivitites, and the Jebusites. "*When the Lord your God brings you into the land which you go to possess, and has cast out many nations before you, the Hittites and the Girgashites and the Amorites and the Canaanites and the Perizzites and the Hivites and the Jebusites, seven nations greater and mightier than you*" (Dueteronomy 7:1). The command of God was destruction. " *... and when the* LORD *your God delivers them over to you, you shall conquer them and utterly destroy them. You shall make no covenant with them nor show mercy to them*" (Dueteronomy 7:2). "From the Hebrew root word for 'devote' meaning here to devote to destruction to exterminate the Canaanites, the most morally, corrupt people of that time and haters of God (7:10) deserved to die for their sins."[50] " *... and He repays those who hate Him to their face, to destroy them. He will not be slack with him who hates Him; He will repay him to his face*" (Deuteronomy 7:10). "*It is not because of your righteousness or the uprightness of your heart that you go in to possess their land, but because of the wickedness of these nations that the* LORD *your God drives them out from before you, and that He may fulfill the word which the* LORD *swore to your fathers, to Abraham, Isaac, and Jacob*" (Deuteronomy 9:5).

Paul continues to rehearse Israel's history. He reminds the listeners of the 450 year reign of various judges followed by the prophet Samuel. When the people desired a king, God gave them Saul. Eventually, God placed David in the royal position (13:22). David was a man who will always be remembered as a man after God's heart. From this seed came a Savior. Paul identifies Him as Jesus. When the forerunner, John the Baptist, came on the scene the message was that he was not worthy to loose the sandals of the Lord.

The Sovereign Truth of the Gospel   (Acts 13:26-31)

Paul now calls to all the followers of Abraham and broadens his message to any who fear God that the word of salvation has been sent. He begins to remind the listeners of the message of the gospel. Although there was no cause to kill Jesus, kill Him they did. He was put in a sepulcher. Then Paul states the majestic truth *"But God raised him from the dead."* (Acts 13:20).

There were numerous witnesses of the resurrection. Many came with Him from Galilee to Jerusalem.

In God's appointed time His sovereign rule was enforced. God exercises permanent authority over His world. In His time table the gospel was fulfilled. *"But when the fullness of the time had come, God sent forth His Son, born of a woman, born under the law"* (Galatians 4:4).

The Source of the Resurrection   (Acts 13:32-39)

The gospel is a beautiful word. "The word gospel literally means 'good news' and occurs 93 times in the Bible, exclusively in the New Testament. In Greek, it is the word *evaggelion*, from which we get our English words evangelist, evangel, and evangelical."[51] The good news is that Jesus died to pay for our sins, He was buried to bury our sins and He rose from the dead giving evidence that He is the Son of God.

Verse 32 can be rendered glad tiding or good news. It seems that the whole of the incarnation, gospel events, and His ascension and exaltation are at least hinted of in verse 33. Psalm 2:7 is quoted. *"I will declare the decree: The LORD has said to Me 'You are My Son, Today I have begotten You"* (Psalm 2:7).

Paul speaks of the beloved David. David died. His body decayed. David had a purpose. He fulfilled it. Now he mentions that the decay or corruption in David's body is typical to all bodies who die waiting for the resurrection. Jesus, however, did not undergo decay and He rose from the grave. Jesus death, burial, and resurrection provide forgiveness of sin and this is the message that Paul is proclaiming. The heart of these early Christians foundational beliefs was the surety of the resurrection of Jesus. Paul concludes this section with an amazing, startling, and life changing statement. The law of Moses is revered and honored as a document. It could never declare someone righteous. Only Christ can do that. *"Therefore by the deeds of the law no flesh will be justified in His sight, for by the law is the knowledge of sin. But now the righteousness of God apart from the law is revealed, being witnessed by the Law and the Prophets, even the righteousness of God, through faith in Jesus Christ, to all and on all who believe. For there is no difference; for all have sinned and fall short of the glory of God, being justified freely by His grace through the redemption that is in Christ Jesus"* (Romans 3:20-24). The purpose of the law is to reveal the truth of the knowledge of our sin.

The Spoken Warning   (Acts 13:40-42)

Perhaps Paul remembered in Stephen's earlier sermon the stern words he spoke. *"Then God turned and gave them up to worship the host of heaven, as it is written in the book of the Prophets: 'Did you offer Me slaughtered animals and sacrifices during forty years in the wilderness, O house of Israel'"* (Acts 7:42). He now uses a passage from the Old Testament to describe those who are wandering aimlessly away from God and not giving attention to the gospel. He uses these words to also explain to those who insist on the law to provide righteousness. In the Old Testament, the prophet Habakkuk wrote, *"Look among the nations and watch—Be utterly astounded! For I will work a work in your days Which you would not believe, though it were told you"* (Habakkuk 1:5).

This is a very unique message. On this occurrence this sermon promotes the apostle to a position that previously had been held by Peter. Paul will now be the primary leader of the Christians who declare, Jesus is Risen!

His warning is clear. For salvation there is only one way. It is through Jesus Christ.

Paul's sermon has ended. The interest level in what he is teaching is off the charts. He has emphasized the grace of God and Jew and Gentiles want to hear more. The proselytes speak of converts to Judaism, foreign converts to the Jewish faith. These people probably lived abroad. The message they now wanted was the message of grace. The Greek word for grace is *charis*, which literally means favor. Its literal meaning has the idea of bending or stooping in kindness. God stooped to give God the Son to die for the sins of the world and we do not deserve it nor can we earn it. It is all of grace. Grace is the unmerited gift of God. Mercy is compassion shown toward someone when it is in the power to discipline, punish, or harm someone. The listeners to Paul want to hear more!

Paul and Barnabus accept the invitation and continue to preach. When the Jewish leaders saw the crowds they were jealous. They began contradicting what was being taught. Paul's direct message to them was simple. In essence he said the message was given to the Jews first, and they rejected it. The message would be delivered to the Gentiles. The

Great Commission that Jesus left with his followers was not to be fulfilled. Paul used the prophet Isaiah as his basis. "I, the LORD, *have called You in righteousness, And will hold Your hand; I will keep You and give You as a covenant to the people, As a light to the Gentiles*" (Isaiah 42:6). "*Indeed He says, 'It is too small a thing that You should be My Servant To raise up the tribes of Jacob, And to restore the preserved ones of Israel; I will also give You as a light to the Gentiles, That You should be My salvation to the ends of the earth'*" (Isaiah 49:6). The light of the gospel is now for the nations.

The Gentiles were thrilled. They gloried that God's Word was available directly to them. The Word of God spread like wildfire in a forest. Many believed. The Jews incited distinguished men and women to turn on the preachers. Paul and Barnabus were driven out of the area. The term "shake off the dust" was a break of fellowship. It was stating that the responsibility for the community was not something they would shoulder.

The Gentiles openness to the gospel and the rejection by the Jews is now an ongoing theme in the Acts. God loves both Jew and Gentile. However, there is a coldness and jealousy that begins to develop.

So the preachers are off to Iconium. The disciples are filled with the Holy Spirit and joy radiates their hearts!

Questions:

1. What approach did Paul use to explain to his listeners what was happening?
2. Why did the Jewish leaders turn on Paul for his preaching?
3. What does 'shake off the dust' mean?

For Discussion:

What do you think your emotions would be in the situation Paul and Barnabus were in?

17

The Story of Christianity Unity and Disunity on the Missionary Journey

Acts 14

And it came to pass in Iconium, that they went both together into the synagogue of the Jews, and so spake, that a great multitude both of the Jews and also of the Greeks believed. But the unbelieving Jews stirred up the Gentiles, and made their minds evil affected against the brethren. Long time therefore abode they speaking boldly in the Lord, which gave testimony unto the word of his grace, and granted signs and wonders to be done by their hands. But the multitude of the city was divided: and part held with the Jews, and part with the apostles. And when there was an assault made both of the Gentiles, and also of the Jews with their rulers, to use them despitefully, and to stone them, They were ware of it, and fled unto Lystra and Derbe, cities of Lycaonia, and unto the region that lieth round about: And there they preached the gospel. And there sat a certain man at Lystra, impotent in his feet, being a cripple from his mother's womb, who never had walked: The same heard Paul speak: who stedfastly beholding him, and perceiving that he had faith to be healed, Said with a loud voice, Stand upright on thy feet. *And he leaped and walked. And when the people saw what Paul had done, they lifted up their voices, saying in the speech of Lycaonia, The gods are come down to us in the likeness of men. And they called Barnabas, Jupiter; and Paul, Mercurius, because he was the chief speaker. Then the priest of Jupiter, which was before their city, brought oxen and garlands unto the gates, and would have done sacrifice with the people. Which when the apostles, Barnabas and Paul, heard of, they rent their clothes, and ran in among the people, crying out, And saying, Sirs, why do ye these things? We also are men of like passions with you, and preach unto you that ye should turn from these vanities unto the living God, which made heaven, and earth, and the sea, and all things that are therein: Who in times past suffered all nations to walk in their own ways. Nevertheless he left not himself without witness, in that he did good, and gave us rain from heaven, and fruitful seasons, filling our hearts with food and gladness. And with these sayings scarce restrained they the people, that they had not done sacrifice unto them. And there came thither certain Jews from Antioch and Iconium, who persuaded the people, and having stoned Paul, drew him out of the city, supposing he had been dead. Howbeit, as the disciples stood round about him, he rose up, and came into the city: and the next day he departed with Barnabas to Derbe. And when they had preached the gospel to that city, and had taught many, they returned again to Lystra, and to Iconium, and Antioch, Confirming the souls of the disciples, and exhorting them to continue in the faith, and that we must through much tribulation enter into the kingdom of God. And when they had ordained them elders in every church, and had prayed with fasting, they commended them to the Lord, on whom they believed. And after they had passed throughout Pisidia, they came to Pamphylia. And when they had preached the word in Perga, they went down into Attalia: And thence sailed to Antioch, from whence they had been recommended to the grace of God for the work which they fulfilled. And when they were come, and had gathered the church together,*

they rehearsed all that God had done with them, and how
he had opened the door of faith unto the Gentiles. And there
they abode long time with the disciples (Acts 14:1-28 KJV).

Division

P aul and Barnabus chose to begin their ministry in synagogues
of the cities they visited. As they travel Paul is the speaker
and Barnabus goes with him. As the encourager I am sure he
spends much time with Paul in hiding him, especially through much
tribulation. Large numbers of both Jews and Greeks are coming to the
faith. Opposition abounds. It begins with some Jews who could not accept
the apostolic message of the resurrection. The Jews were influencing the
Gentiles. The term evil affected (KJV) is a verb. In the Greek is means
ill-treat or affected by evil. It speaks to harm, vexation, or hurt. It is the
same word that is used in Acts 7:6, 9. *"But God spoke in this way: that his*
descendants would dwell in a foreign land, and that they would bring them
into bondage and oppress them four hundred years" (Acts 7:6). *"This man*
dealt treacherously with our people, and oppressed our forefathers, making
them expose their babies, so that they might not live" (Acts 7:19). The
opposition did not hinder these early leaders. They continued to speak
boldly, depending on the Lord to help them. The key to their message
was the gift of God's grace through Jesus Christ. "The miraculous signs
and wonders confirmed the truthfulness of the message."[52] *"Truly the signs*
of an apostle were accomplished among you with all perseverance, in signs
and wonders and mighty deeds" (2 Corinthians 12:12).

Disunity developed. Some sided with the Jews. Others with the Apostles.
The tension grew. The signs and wonders were continuing the support of
the veracity and visibleness of the resurrection of Jesus Christ. A plan is put
in place by the opposition. The goal is to stone these missionaries.

Paul and Barnabus leave the area and went to Lystra and Derbe,
cities of Lyconia. They continued their preaching ministry presenting the
gospel to those who would listen. "Paul and Barnabus flee some eighteen
and then sixty miles to the southeast, finding refuge in Lyconian Roman
outposts of Lystra and Derbe. They act from prudence, not cowardice, for
they continued to preach the good news."[53]

In an evening service a man sits and listens to Paul preach. Paul gazed
at the man and sees that he has faith to be made whole. Faith is a gift

from God. *"For by grace you have been saved through faith, and that not of yourselves; it is the gift of God, not of works, lest anyone should boast"* (Ephesians 2:8-9). Paul commands the man to stand. He leaps up and begins to walk. The man healed in Acts 3 shows no faith. This man has faith. Healing, is in my estimation, a gift God gives. Perfect healing is when we are in the presence of the Lord.

When the crowds saw what had happened they said, 'The gods have become like men and have come down to us.' A well-known poet, Ovid, lived from 43 BC to 17 AD. He was considered one of three great poets (Virgil and Horace). He often wrote of the last of the gods. His most famous work was Metamorphoses. The gods become like humans. His writings are very intriguing and perhaps the Lyconians had this in mind when addressing this issue with Paul and Barnabus. In a passage we read, "Ovid, a Roman poet has Zeus known, in the Roman contact as Jupiter, describes the punishment of an impious king named Lycaon for failing to recognize the god and worship him."[54] Zeus was the chief god of the Greek patron and Ibermes was considered the performance god for those who were public speakers and oratorical messages were their claim to fame. There were two legends from Greek mythology where Zeus and Hermos had come down and were like men.

The message of the resurrection of Jesus was such a powerful force in the lives of these early missionaries that the teachings that gave worship to other gods was not tolerated. Paul's explosive message reminds the people of the goodness of God. Even when the nations turned from God He did not forsake them and took care of their crops. (Acts 14:16-17).

For this Paul is stoned. He is left outside of the city to die. He is dragged out and left to beasts, predators, and dogs. Paul had many close calls. His body bore the bruises. He often spoke of them.

> *From now on let no one trouble me, for I bear in my body the marks of the Lord Jesus"* (Galatians 6:17). Paul's testimonial continues. *'I say again, let no one think me a fool. If otherwise, at least receive me as a fool, that I also may boast a little. What I speak, I speak not according to the Lord, but as it were, foolishly, in this confidence of boasting. Seeing that many boast according to the flesh, I also will boast. For you put up with fools gladly, since you yourselves are wise! For you put up with it if one brings*

you into bondage, if one devours you, if one takes from you, if one exalts himself, if one strikes you on the face. To our shame I say that we were too weak for that! But in whatever anyone is bold—I speak foolishly—I am bold also. Are they Hebrews? So am I. Are they Israelites? So am I. Are they the seed of Abraham? So am I. Are they ministers of Christ?—I speak as a fool—I am more: in labors more abundant, in stripes above measure, in prisons more frequently, in deaths often. From the Jews five times I received forty stripes minus one. Three times I was beaten with rods; once I was stoned; three times I was shipwrecked; a night and a day I have been in the deep; in journeys often, in perils of waters, in perils of robbers, in perils of my own countrymen, in perils of the Gentiles, in perils in the city, in perils in the wilderness, in perils in the sea, in perils among false brethren; in weariness and toil, in sleeplessness often, in hunger and thirst, in fastings often, in cold and nakedness— besides the other things, what comes upon me daily: my deep concern for all the churches. Who is weak, and I am not weak? Who is made to stumble, and I do not burn with indignation? If I must boast, I will boast in the things which concern my infirmity. The God and Father of our Lord Jesus Christ, who is blessed forever, knows that I am not lying. In Damascus the governor, under Aretas the king, was guarding the city of the Damascenes with a garrison, desiring to arrest me; but I was let down in a basket through a window in the wall, and escaped from his hands (2 Corinthians 11:16-33).

It is here that we can speculate. Paul was left for dead. Perhaps he did die. The people supposed he was dead. *"I know a man in Christ who fourteen years ago—whether in the body I do not know, or whether out of the body I do not know, God knows—such a one was caught up to the third heaven. And I know such a man—whether in the body or out of the body I do not know, God knows— how he was caught up into Paradise and heard inexpressible words, which it is not lawful for a man to utter"* (2 Corinthians 12:2-4). Paul describes here an experience of being caught up into heaven. He was given visions he could not find in himself to speak about. Paul was in the dwelling place of God. The experience was unbelievably magnificent for the apostle. The stoning at Lystra was about 14 years prior to his writing 2 Corinthians 12. It is considered to be around 45-46 A.D. Some historians put it around 43-44 A.D. The fact is, it was this kind of stoning that left Stephen dead and the mob thought Paul was dead. Paul, like Stephen, was being stoned for blasphemy. Paul amazingly gets up and heads to Lystra. It is this experience that teaches Paul about the tribulations that are to come. " ... *strengthening the souls of the disciples, exhorting them to continue in the faith, and saying, 'We must through many tribulations enter the kingdom of God'"* (Acts 14:22).

There is speculation concerning the timing of Paul's death bed scene. It is not speculation when we realize the struggles this man went through to bring the gospel to the Gentile world.

Appointments

Paul and Barnabus "appoint Pastors (Elders)". The term appoint speaks to ordination. It means chosen. These elders are chosen of God. Paul and Barnabus have been given the authority to appoint these elders. *"Then, having fasted and prayed, and laid hands on them, they sent them away"* (Acts 13:3). This appointment actually came from the church at Antioch. Paul and Barnabus go through Pisidia, Pamphylia, and Purga proclaiming the Word, then arrive back in Antioch and give a report of their trip. They are commended for their trip. The word commended is a confidence given to someone whereby they are trusted to protect and proclaim a very important message. Paul and Barnabus have proved they are trustworthy.

Can you imagine listening to this report? What a story and what marvelous results. The door is now wide opened to the Gentiles. Now for a long period Paul and Barnabus will relax with the disciples, getting their minds and bodies ready for their next event!

Questions

1. What is the background to cause people to think of the gods coming speaking through Paul?
2. What was the reason Paul was stranded and left for dead?

For Discussion

1. Do you think Paul's heavenly vision is the result of being stoned and left for dead at Lystra?
2. What kinds of persecution are you personally aware of in your life?

CHAPTER

18

The Story of Christianity
Solving Doctrinal Dissension
(Acts 15)

And certain men which came down from Judaea taught the brethren, and said, Except ye be circumcised after the manner of Moses, ye cannot be saved. When therefore Paul and Barnabas had no small dissension and disputation with them, they determined that Paul and Barnabas, and certain other of them, should go up to Jerusalem unto the apostles and elders about this question. And being brought on their way by the church, they passed through Phenice and Samaria, declaring the conversion of the Gentiles: and they caused great joy unto all the brethren. And when they were come to Jerusalem, they were received of the church, and of the apostles and elders, and they declared all things that God had done with them. But there rose up certain of the sect of the Pharisees which believed, saying, That it was needful to circumcise them, and to command them to keep the law of Moses. And the apostles and elders came together for to consider of this matter. And when there had been much disputing, Peter rose up, and said unto them, Men and brethren, ye know how that a good while ago God made choice among us, that the Gentiles by my mouth should hear the word of the gospel, and believe. And

God, which knoweth the hearts, bare them witness, giving them the Holy Ghost, even as he did unto us; And put no difference between us and them, purifying their hearts by faith. Now therefore why tempt ye God, to put a yoke upon the neck of the disciples, which neither our fathers nor we were able to bear? But we believe that through the grace of the Lord Jesus Christ we shall be saved, even as they. Then all the multitude kept silence, and gave audience to Barnabas and Paul, declaring what miracles and wonders God had wrought among the Gentiles by them. And after they had held their peace, James answered, saying, Men and brethren, hearken unto me: Simeon hath declared how God at the first did visit the Gentiles, to take out of them a people for his name. And to this agree the words of the prophets; as it is written, After this I will return, and will build again the tabernacle of David, which is fallen down; and I will build again the ruins thereof, and I will set it up: That the residue of men might seek after the Lord, and all the Gentiles, upon whom my name is called, saith the Lord, who doeth all these things. Known unto God are all his works from the beginning of the world. Wherefore my sentence is, that we trouble not them, which from among the Gentiles are turned to God: But that we write unto them, that they abstain from pollutions of idols, and from fornication, and from things strangled, and from blood. For Moses of old time hath in every city them that preach him, being read in the synagogues every sabbath day. Then pleased it the apostles and elders with the whole church, to send chosen men of their own company to Antioch with Paul and Barnabas; namely, Judas surnamed Barsabas and Silas, chief men among the brethren: And they wrote letters by them after this manner; The apostles and elders and brethren send greeting unto the brethren which are of the Gentiles in Antioch and Syria and Cilicia. Forasmuch as we have heard, that certain which went out from us have troubled you with words, subverting your souls, saying, Ye must be circumcised, and keep the law: to whom we gave no such commandment: It seemed good unto us, being assembled with one accord, to send chosen men unto you with our beloved Barnabas and Paul, Men that have hazarded their lives for the name of our Lord Jesus Christ. We have sent therefore Judas and Silas, who shall also tell you the same things by mouth. For it seemed good to the Holy Ghost, and to us, to lay upon you no greater burden than these necessary things; That ye abstain from meats offered to idols, and from blood, and from things strangled, and from fornication: from which if ye keep yourselves, ye shall do well. Fare ye well. So when they were dismissed, they came to Antioch: and when they had gathered the multitude together, they delivered the epistle: Which when they had read, they rejoiced for the consolation. And Judas and Silas, being prophets also themselves, exhorted the brethren with many words, and confirmed them. And after they had tarried there a space, they were let go in peace from the brethren unto the apostles. Notwithstanding it pleased Silas to abide there still. Paul also and Barnabas continued in Antioch, teaching and preaching the word of the Lord, with many others also. And some days after Paul said unto Barnabas, Let us go again and visit our brethren in every city where we have preached the word of the Lord, and see how they do. And Barnabas determined to take with them John, whose surname was Mark. But Paul thought not good to take him with them, who departed from them from Pamphylia, and went not with them to the work. And the contention was so sharp between them, that they departed asunder one from the other: and so Barnabas took Mark, and sailed unto Cyprus; And Paul chose Silas, and departed, being recommended by the brethren unto the grace of God. And he went through Syria and Cilicia, confirming the churches.(Acts 15: 1-40 KJV).

What Christians believe is important. Standing true to orthodoxy and determining what is essential to the Christian faith is foundation to a belief system. In the history of Christianity of the first centuries there are seven ecumenical councils that helped frame various Christian positions. The Eastern Orthodox Church and Catholic

Church accepted these councils and pronounced them legitimate. A brief overview of these councils is as follows:

The First Council was of Nicaea held May 20-June 19 in 325 A.D. It was ordered by Emperor Constantine 1st. There were over 300 in attendance and the topic was the nature of Christ. The theological term was Arianism. Other issues included how to celebrate Easter, ordinations, the validity of baptism by heretics and numerous other matters.

The First Council of Constantinople was held May-July 38 A.D. and was ordered by Emperor Theodosius. Approximately 150 attended and the issues were Arianism, Apollinarism, and the Holy Spirit, plus other issues.

The Council of Ephesus was held June 22-July 31 and was ordered by Theodosius 2nd. Over 200 attended and the issues were Pelegianism, Nestorianism, and several other issues.

The Council of Chalcedon occurred October 8 – November 1 under emperor Marcion. Over 500 were in attendance and numerous topics were discussed and debated including issues involving the divinity and humanity of Jesus.

The Second Council of Constantinople occurred May 5 –June 2, 553 A.D., under Justinian 1st. Over 150 attended and Nestorianism was a major point of discussion.

The Third Council of Constantinople was held November 7-September 16, 680-681 A.D. under Constantine IV with around 300 in attendance, and the humanity and divine will of Jesus were major issues.

The seventh of these councils was the Second Council of Nicaea. September 24-October 23, 787 A. D. under Constantine VI and Empress Irene. About 350 attending and the topic was Iconoclasm.

There are many resources on the specifics of these councils. The point here is that the Christian faith was taken very seriously and Christian leaders were impressed with getting truth rightfully disseminated.

In Acts 15 we have the first of these type of situations. The question to be discussed makes this council the most significant. What should a person do in order to be saved? That is the discussion.

"The wholesale entrance of Gentiles into the church was very disturbing and threatening to some of the Jewish believers. Many believed that Gentiles who wanted to become Christians had to become Jewish proselytes. They saw Christianity as the culmination of Judaism. That Gentiles were short-circuiting the process and becoming Christians without first becoming Jewish proselytes shocked and overwhelmed them.

They could not conceive that pagans could simply enter the church and immediately be on an equal basis with Jewish believers. That seemed unfair to those who had devoted their lives to keeping God's Law. They feared, too, that in an increasingly Gentile church, Jewish culture, traditions, and influence would be lost."[55]

The question was not one of rights. Gentiles could be saved. The question was how were they too be saved? Could they come directly and did they need to come through the process of Judaism?

The Commencement of the Discussion   (Acts 15:1-5)

As Paul and Barnabus arrived 'back home' in Jerusalem they testified of some of the amazing things God had done in their journeys. A teaching began to permeate the followers of Christ that unless the custom of circumcision be practiced, that some could not be saved. Remember Paul and Barnabus in Antioch? The teaching of these Judaizers sparked a discussion that turned into debate. Since Jerusalem was the sending church, the brethren decided to go to the headquarters and hear the matter out.

These early Christians went through Phoenicia and Samaria and described the conversion of the Gentiles. This one was populated by Samaritans and the Hellenistic Jews who were more open to what God was doing in the Gentile world than the Palestinian Jews were.

Upon arrival, the testimony of God's great work as it was in Antioch is all given back to God. "*Now when they had come and gathered the church together, they reported all that God had done with them, and that He had opened the door of faith to the Gentiles*" (Acts 14:27).

Members of the sect of Pharisees insisted circumcision and observance of the moral law is necessary for Gentile salvation.

"The problems raised by the presence of Gentiles in the church now come to a head. Peter had learned that no man be called unclean – not even a Gentile – (10:34) and the Jerusalem church had accepted the first Gentile converts on an equal basis with Jewish converts, without the necessity of being circumcised."[56]

"To add anything to Christ as being necessary to salvation, say circumcision or any human work of any kind, is to deny that Christ is the complete Savior, is to put something human on a par with him, yet to make it the crowning point. That is fatal. A bridge to make it the crowning point.

A bridge to heaven that is built of 99/100 of Christ and even only 1/100 of anything human, breaks down at the joint and ceases to be a bridge."[57]

"A parallel question was also being raised: Should there be unrestricted social contact between Jewish and Gentile Christians? The Judaistic party separated themselves from those who did not follow the dietary laws and would not partake of the meals."[58] These are two issues that were up for grabs in this very important Jerusalem Council.

The Content of the Discussion   (Acts 15:6-18)

The discussion became a debate. Peter presents a very clear message on the gospel. His thesis is clear. *"But we believe that through the grace of the Lord Jesus Christ we shall be saved in the same manner as they"* (15:11). Paul and Barnabus began to tell the story of the remarkable work of the gospel in the areas they just ministered to.

It is interesting to note that it is James who speaks up to decide the matter. There seems to be perhaps six people who are named James in the New Testament. The brother of John, James, and James the son of Alphaeus are apostles. There is James, the brother of Jesus. The son of Mary is James. The pastor of Jerusalem is James and the father of the apostle, Jude, is James. It is interesting that many scholars are cautious in identifying this James in chapter 15. I sense this is our Lord's brother and writer of the epistle with his name, based upon the fact that he is accepted as the one to bring this matter to a conclusion. Remember Jesus' brothers were present at the Jerusalem council. He appears later in Acts as the leader of the church in Jerusalem. I believe he is the pastor Paul mentions seeing James. *"But I saw none of the other apostles except James, the Lord's brother"* (Galatians 1:19).

James was originally opposed to Jesus' ministry. *"Is this not the carpenter's son? Is not His mother called Mary? And His brothers James, Joses, Simon, and Judas? And His sisters, are they not all with us? Where then did this Man get all these things"* (Matthew 13:55-56). *"But when His own people heard about this, they went out to lay hold of Him, for they said, 'He is out of His mind'"* (Mark 3:21). *"For even His brothers did not believe in Him"* (John 7:5). Several historical writers including Clement of Alexandria, Eusebius, and Hegesippus teach that James is the leader of Jerusalem. When he speaks in this passage there is broad acceptance of his presentation. As strong as Peter and Paul are presented in the Acts, it is James who leads here.

His opening statement is basically, "Listen to me!" He endorses Peter's message that God had saved by grace many before the Cornelius episode. He quotes from Amos 9:11-12. '*On that day I will raise up The tabernacle of David, which has fallen down, And repair its damages; I will raise up its ruins, And rebuild it as in the days of old; That they may possess the remnant of Edom, And all the Gentiles who are called by My name,*'" "*Says the LORD who does this thing*" (Amos 9:11-12). "After these things" speaks to the world wide witness. After the return of the Lord, the tabernacle will be established. Both Jew and Gentile can know the Lord. God's plan for Israel has not been rescinded nor abandoned because Gentiles came into the church. James very clearly explains that the Gentiles should not be circumcised in order to enter God's family. The Gentiles should not "be troubled" over this issue.

James solves the deeply imbedded theological issue. He now addresses the practical matter of social relationships between the Jew and Gentile. The danger here is a danger in any age. With salvation that is totally of grace, there is a tendency to promote freedom over obedience. James plan appears brilliant. He proposes a letter be written to the Gentiles to abstain from four practices that would be very offensive to the Jews. To violate these Mosaic sanctions would give the church less credibility. To do it would be to abuse the freedom we have in Christ.

The four issues were as follows:

> Things contaminated by idols. This refers to various foods that would be offered to false gods that would eventually be on the market place. Eating foods that were offered to idols is not to be practiced.

> Fornication – This term signifies sexual sin. It refers to illicit sexual intercourse. It includes all sexual activity outside of marriage and anything associated in this area that would lead to pagan idolatry. The Greek word is *porneia*. It is the foundation word that we get the word pornography from.

> What is strangled refers to the dietary laws. '*This shall be a perpetual statute throughout your generations in all your dwellings: you shall eat neither fat nor blood.*'"

(Leviticus 3:17); *"Therefore I said to the children of Israel, 'No one among you shall eat blood, nor shall any stranger who dwells among you eat blood. Whatever man of the children of Israel, or of the strangers who dwell among you, who hunts and catches any animal or bird that may be eaten, he shall pour out its blood and cover it with dust; for it is the life of all flesh. Its blood sustains its life.'" "Therefore I said to the children of Israel, 'You shall not eat the blood of any flesh, for the life of all flesh is its blood. Whoever eats it shall be cut off'"* (17:12-14).

The issue with blood ... What is from blood? The blood would need to be drained from animals. It is not James' desire to withhold these laws from the Gentiles. Yet these attitudes toward Jewish believers seem to be some requirements for fellowship.

Jewish Christians could have social gatherings with the Gentile Christians. *"Therefore, if food makes my brother stumble, I will never again eat meat, lest I make my brother stumble"* (1 Corinthians 8:13).

Paul and Barnabus head back to Antioch. The conclusion as specified in the letter pleased the congregation at Antioch.

In the letter it is pointed out that Paul and Barnabus have risked their lives (vv 26). Judas and Silas will be sent to verify the ministry and walk of Paul and Barnabus.

The Conclusion to the First Church Council

The reading of the letter was well received. The people rejoiced. Salvation by grace alone will always have the respondence who are thankful. The people were thankful. Legalism has a way of producing false guilt and arrogance. Grace was very obviously a big part of the letter. Two prophets, Paul and Silas, encouraged the people with positive and uplifting sermons. Paul and Barnabus continued with their ministry.

Here are two observations. The early church had just survived a major challenge. Salvation is by grace alone. The resurrection of Jesus Christ is based on the sacrificial death of Jesus and his burial of our sins. He did it all! The greater days of the church are just ahead and the blessing of the foundational truth of salvation is settled.

A second observation is the wisdom and calm that is exercised by James. He is the leader. He is the pastor. Not Peter, Paul, or Barnabus. God placed him in a position of leadership and God directs him to the answer. Wise, godly leadership needs to be exercised by pastors. God gives to leaders what they need for their situations. I like to think of it as an anointing from God. A special touch by God for the task at hand. To all Christian leaders reading this you will find that God gives you a special endowment of wisdom just when you need it. There are times, I believe, when God removes that. It is then that God may lead you into the next harvest field waiting for you.

Questions

1. What were the four things that James told the Gentiles in Antioch to do in order to respect the Jewish customs?
2. What is meant by salvation by grace?
3. What characteristics are seen in the life of James when he led the people through the theological challenge?

For Discussion

1. What are some theological challenges facing the church today and how should they be dealt with based on principles found in Acts 15?

19

The Story of Christianity
The Second Missionary Journey
(Acts 15:36 and 16:1-40)

And some days after Paul said unto Barnabas, Let us go again and visit our brethren in every city where we have preached the word of the Lord, and see how they do (Acts 15:36). Then came he to Derbe and Lystra: and, behold, a certain disciple was there, named Timotheus, the son of a certain woman, which was a Jewess, and believed; but his father was a Greek: Which was well reported of by the brethren that were at Lystra and Iconium. Him would Paul have to go forth with him; and took and circumcised him because of the Jews which were in those quarters: for they knew all that his father was a Greek. And as they went through the cities, they delivered them the decrees for to keep, that were ordained of the apostles and elders which were at Jerusalem. And so were the churches established in the faith, and increased in number daily. Now when they had gone throughout Phrygia and the region of Galatia, and were forbidden of the Holy Ghost to preach the word in Asia, After they were come to Mysia, they assayed to go into Bithynia: but the Spirit suffered them not. And they passing by Mysia came down to Troas. And a vision appeared to Paul in the night; There stood a man of Macedonia, and prayed him, saying, Come over into Macedonia, and help us. And after he had seen the vision, immediately we endeavoured to go into Macedonia, assuredly gathering that the Lord had called us for to preach the gospel unto them. Therefore loosing from Troas, we came with a straight course to Samothracia, and the next day to Neapolis; And from thence to Philippi, which is the chief city of that part of Macedonia, and a colony: and we were in that city abiding certain days. And on the sabbath we went out of the city by a river side, where prayer was wont to be made; and we sat down, and spake unto the women which resorted thither. And a certain woman named Lydia, a seller of purple, of the city of Thyatira, which worshipped God, heard us: whose heart the Lord opened, that she attended unto the things which were spoken of Paul. And when she was baptized, and her household, she besought us, saying, If ye have judged me to be faithful to the Lord, come into my house, and abide there. And she constrained us. And it came to pass, as we went to prayer, a certain damsel possessed with a spirit of divination met us, which brought her masters much gain by soothsaying: The same followed Paul and us, and cried, saying, These men are the servants of the most high God, which shew unto us the way of salvation. And this did she many days. But Paul, being grieved, turned and said to the spirit, I command thee in the name of Jesus Christ to come out of her. And he came out the same hour. And when her masters saw that the hope of their gains was gone, they caught Paul and Silas, and drew them into the marketplace unto the rulers, And brought them to the magistrates, saying, These men, being Jews, do exceedingly trouble our city, And teach customs, which are not lawful for us to receive, neither to observe, being Romans. And the multitude rose up together against them: and the magistrates rent off their clothes, and commanded to beat them. And when they had laid many stripes upon them, they cast them into prison, charging the jailor to keep them safely: Who, having received such a charge, thrust them into the inner prison, and made their feet fast in the stocks. And at midnight Paul and Silas prayed, and sang praises unto God: and the prisoners heard them. And suddenly there was a great earthquake, so that the foundations of the prison were shaken: and immediately all the doors were opened, and every one's bands were loosed. And the keeper of the prison awaking out of his sleep, and seeing the prison doors open, he drew out his sword, and would have killed himself, supposing that the prisoners had been fled. But Paul cried with a loud voice, saying, Do thyself no harm: for we are all here. Then he called for a light, and sprang in, and came trembling, and fell down before Paul and Silas, And brought them out, and said, Sirs, what must I do to be saved? And they said, Believe on the Lord Jesus Christ, and thou shalt be saved, and thy house. And they spake unto him the word of the Lord, and to all that were in his house. And he took them the same hour of the night, and washed their stripes; and was baptized, he and all his, straightway. And when he had brought them into his house, he set meat before them, and rejoiced, believing in God with all his house. And when it was day, the magistrates sent the serjeants, saying, Let those men go. And the keeper of the prison told this saying to Paul, The magistrates have sent to let you go: now therefore depart, and go in peace. But Paul said unto them, They have beaten us openly uncondemned, being Romans, and have cast us into prison; and now do they thrust us out privily? nay verily; but let them come themselves and fetch us out. And the serjeants told these words unto the magistrates: and they feared, when they heard that they were Romans. And they came and besought them, and brought them out, and desired them to depart out of the city. And they went out of the prison, and entered into the house of Lydia: and when they had seen the brethren, they comforted them, and departed. (Acts 16:1-40 KJV)

The second missionary journey of Paul is initiated and recorded beginning in Acts 15:36. The goal was to revisit those that were ministered to on the first visit. The well documented division between Paul and John Mark appears because of differences of personality.

Barnabus chooses to take John Mark and they went to Cyprus. Paul selects Silas. Silas was known as a faithful brother. *"By Silvanus, our faithful brother as I consider him, I have written to you briefly, exhorting and testifying that this is the true grace of God in which you stand"* (1 Peter 5:12). He was a Helenistic Jew but also a Roman citizen. *"But Paul said to them, 'They have beaten us openly, uncondemned and have thrown us into prison. And now do they put us out secretly? No indeed! Let them come themselves and get us out'"* (Acts 16:37). He is also mentioned in Scripture with the name Silvanus. Remember he is the man chosen to give the Jerusalem's council to the believers in Antioch. He will become a very important person in this missionary journey.

In the first verse of Acts 16:1 we are brought into acquaintance with a young man who has a Greek father and Jewish mother. His name is Timothy. His mother's name was Eunice and his grandmother was Lois (2 Timothy 1:5). Paul had Timothy circumcised because of his Jewish heritage with his mother. This would allow him to have a greater impact into the Jewish community with the gospel. They traveled with the decrees that were the decisions made at the Jerusalem council. The churches continued growing and they grew in their faith. (Acts 16:5).

Since Barnabus took John Mark with him to Cypress, Paul, Silas, and Timothy travel through Syria and Cilicia. To go there it meant traveling through the Toareas Mountains. These mountains are a complex group in Southern Turkey. There are actually tours today that will follow the footsteps of Paul going through this area. Here they go … Paul the leader … His new right hand man … Silas, his companion.

They passed through the cities of Galatia. As they went, the churches were strengthened. This was a customary statement that seems to permeate the writings of The Acts. The churches continued to grow. *"Then those who gladly received his word were baptized; and that day about three thousand souls were added to them"* (Acts 2:41); *" … praising God and having favor with all the people. And the Lord added to the church daily those who were being saved"* (2:47); *"However, many of those who heard the word believed; and the number of the men came to be about five thousand"* (4:4); *"And believers were increasingly added to the Lord, multitudes of both men and women"* (5:14); *"Then the word of God spread, and the number of the disciples multiplied greatly in Jerusalem, and a great many of the priests were obedient to the faith"* (6:7); *"Then the churches throughout all Judea, Galilee, and Samaria had peace and were edified. And walking in the* fear of the Lord and in the comfort of the Holy Spirit, they were multiplied" (9:31). As they passed through Phrygia and the areas of Galatia they moved west to Asia. However, the Holy Spirit did not permit them to continue. *"Now when they had gone through Phrygia and the region of Galatia, they were forbidden by the Holy Spirit to preach the word in Asia. After they had come to Mysia, they tried to go into Bithynia, but Spirit did not permit them"* (Acts 16:6, 7).

The Macedonian Call   (Acts 16:9-10)

A vision appears to Paul. A man of Macedonia requests that the missionaries come and help them. It is here that Paul received what is commonly referred to as the Macedonian call. Luke writes in verse 10, " ... when he had seen the vision, immediately we sought to go into Macedonia..." Luke now joins the team.

Here in Macedonia, across from the Aegean Sea in Greece, were the cities of Philippi and Thessalonica. The gospel was now making its entrance into Europe. It is interesting to see God open and close doors. One of the great challenges of life is this issue. Watch where God is leading and get in the middle!

Ministry to Women   (Acts 16:13-18)

From Samothrace to Neopolis, the team eventually stayed at Philippi! This was a leading city. It was named after Phillip 2. He was the father of Alexander the Great. The city was named a Roman Colony by Octavian. It also was a part of the Roman highway that was named Egnatian Way.

On the Sabbath they go to a place to pray. Paul customarily preached in the synagogues and his messages were on the gospel with special emphasis on the truth of the resurrection. Paul was mentored under Gamaliel who was considered the greatest Rabbi. "In the Christian tradition, Gamaliel is recognized as a Pharisee doctor of Jewish law. The Acts of the Apostles, chapter 5, speaks of Gamaliel as a man held in great esteem by all Jews, who spoke to not condemn the apostle of Jesus in Acts 5:34 to death, and as Jewish law teaches of the Apostle in Acts 22:3."[59] His name in Hebrew means reward of God. Because of Paul's relationship to the rabbi, it appears he was welcomed initially in the synagogue.

~ 190 ~

It is interesting to note that there is no synagogue mentioned here. Ten Jewish men were required to begin a synagogue. These are women here.

One woman was a business woman named Lydia. She sold purple fabric and had a heart for worshipping God. She listened to the apostle and opened her heart to his message. Perhaps near this place of prayer was a body of water. She and whoever the individuals that made up her household are baptized.

She then proceeds to invite the missionaries into her home. She tells them if they sense her faithfulness to accept her offering of hospitality.

Just before I came into my study to write the words to this chapter, I had the privilege of having a couple take my wife and I out and they paid for our meal. What a wonderful time we spent together with their hospitality. Back in the days of the early Christians many inns were unsafe, dirty and dangerous. Making provisions for traveling Christians was important. *"Do not let a widow under sixty years old be taken into the number, and not unless she has been the wife of one man, well reported for good works: if she has brought up children, if she has lodged strangers, if she has washed the saints' feet, if she has relieved the afflicted, if she has diligently followed every good work"* (1 Timothy 5:9-10).

Just as there is a woman who is Christ-like, there was another woman. She was a slave who had the spirit of divination. This woman was possessed and her master exploited her. *"But when her masters saw that their hope of profit was gone, they seized Paul and Silas and dragged them into the marketplace to the authorities"* (Acts 16:19). "Luke notes that the demon-possessed girl was bringing her masters much profit by fortunetelling. Such people were believed to be able to predict the future, a valuable commodity in the Greco-Roman culture."[60] "Greeks and Romans put great stock on augury and divination. No commander would set out on a major military campaign nor would an emperor make an important decree without first consulting an oracle to see how things might turn out. A slave girl with a clairvoyant gift was thus a veritable gold mine for her owners."[61] This pitiful woman kept following Paul and his comrades. Her statement seemed to endorse the work of the missionaries. *"This girl followed Paul and us, and cried out, saying, 'These men are the servants of the Most High God, who proclaim to us the way of salvation'"* (Acts 16:17).

The form Most High God spoke of Israel's God and his authority over the people. *"Then they remembered that God was their rock, And the Most High God their Redeemer"* (Psalm 78:35). Realizing the demonic activity, Paul finally commands the demon to come out of her. The demon comes out!

Chaos in the City   (Acts 16:19-24)

The woman was delivered but in accomplishing this, the men who owned her (masters) lost their ability to financially profit because of her divining the future. Judaism was accepted but the publishing publically of it was considered a difficult challenge, especially when it affected business enterprises. At this point Paul and Silas are considered Jews. Remember Christianity was considered a sect of Judaism.

Persecution is challenging. Facing persecution is difficult. Taking a beating for what one believes is unthinkable. Here Paul and Silas are falsely accused. They are then given a terrible beating. In this case, as it is so true in other similar circumstances, God will turn what appears to be chaos and calamity into spiritual victory. You see, Satan does not like God's work proceeding forward. God's plan is bigger that what we think. We are simply a part of the greater plan of God. There are numerous examples of Satanic opposition in Scripture. There is Joseph who ends up in Egypt. A demoniac delivered from possession and the people who are more concerned about the swine who died. (Mark 5)

The world is run by money. The fact is the love of money clouds our spiritual growth. Money in itself is not evil and quite frankly, is very necessary. Yet it takes many into a world they wish they never entered. *"And having food and clothing, with these we shall be content. For the love of money is a root of all kinds of evil, for which some have strayed from the faith in their greediness, and pierced themselves through with many sorrows"* (1 Timothy 6:8, 10).

There was a place in communities called the marketplace. It was the public square somewhere in the center of a city. It was the social center. Court cases were judged here. According to Roman law, a person could be brought there to try the grievance. Every Roman colony had two chief magistrates. The charge against Paul and Silas appears ludicrous, yet it sticks. They are charged with proclaiming customs not lawful to accept. This was true. There were laws forbidding any foreign religion to be practiced. However, the charge rumored that these missionaries were causing chaos in the city appears untrue. A crowd rises up against Paul and Silas. There is no investigation and a proper hearing is not arranged.

The police who were called lictors beat the missionaries. Paul endured this kind of punishment three times in his life. *"Three times I was beaten with rods; once I was stoned; three times I was shipwrecked; a night and a day I have been in the deep"* (2 Corinthians 11:25). So it appears Paul and Silas are beaten illegally and imprisoned unjustly.

Amazingly, this did not stop the missionaries from witnessing. *"But even after we had suffered before and were spitefully treated at Philippi, as you know, we were bold in our God to speak to you the gospel of God in much conflict"*(1 Thessalonians 2:2). This event did not hinder the work of God. *"All the saints greet you, but especially those who are of Caesar's household"* (Philippians 4:22). *"Yes, and if I am being poured out as a drink offering on the sacrifice and service of your faith, I am glad and rejoice with you all"* (Philippians 2:17).

Calm in the Prison   (Acts 16:26-29)

This is one of the most helpful passages on worship in Scripture. Real worship is not based on our situation. Worship is based on the greatness of Christ. *"Rejoice in the Lord always. Again I will say, rejoice"* (Philippians 4:4). *"And we know that all things work together for good to those who love God, to those who are the called according to His purpose"* (Romans 8:28). *"Therefore we do not lose heart. Even though our outward man is perishing, yet the inward man is being renewed day by day. For our light affliction, which is but for a moment, is working for us a far more exceeding and eternal weight of glory"* (2 Corinthians 4:16-17). *"And He said to me, 'My grace is sufficient for you, for My strength is made perfect in weakness. Therefore most gladly I will rather boast in my infirmities, that the power of Christ may rest upon me. Therefore I take pleasure in infirmities, in reproaches, in needs, in persecutions, in distresses, for Christ's sake. For when I am weak, then I am strong'"* (2 Corinthians 12:9-10 KJV).

The book of Acts has two major themes. One is the resurrection. The other is the work of the Holy Spirit. Ephesians 5:18 declares *"And do not be drunk with wine, in which is dissipation; but be filled with the Spirit"*. Colossians 3:16 teaches *"Let the word of Christ dwell in you richly in all wisdom, teaching and admonishing one another in psalms and hymns and spiritual songs, singing with grace in your hearts to the Lord"*. The filling of the Spirit is in close relationship to the filling of lives with God's Word. The result in both passages is the filling of God's Word anonymous with

His Spirit filling us. In the Ephesians passage the result is melody in your heart (5:19), a thankful spirit (5:20), subjection to Christ (5:21), a growing relationship at home (5:22-6:4); a giving relationship in our work (6:5-9). The same characteristics are found in Colossians 3:17-4:2.

Paul and Silas are put into the most secure area of the prison and with their feet in stocks. Only God could miraculously deliver them. There they are in the filth of the prison.

Paul and Silas are singing praises to God and are interrupted with an earthquake. The quake was so powerful that the doors were opened and the chains that held their feet in stocks were unfastened. Roman soldiers would lose their lives if they lost prisoners. It would be the height of embarrassment and peak of humiliation to lose a prisoner and it was a normal decision to kill himself if this happened. The words of Paul had to be most refreshing. "Do thyself no harm, for we are all here!"

The event shook the jailer to the core of his being.

Comfort for the Jailer

The jailer and his entire household are saved. There are four facts that reveal the genuiness of his salvation.

He takes Paul and Silas into his keeping and cares for them by washing their wounds. True Christianity shows our concern for one another.

Secondly, he and his family follow through with baptism. The book of Acts has numerous passages describing the initial step of our faith which is baptism.

He continues to express his new found faith by feeding Paul and Silas. *"What does it profit, my brethren, if someone says he has faith but does not have works? Can faith save him? If a brother or sister is naked and destitute of daily food, and one of you says to them, "Depart in peace, be warmed and filled. Thus also faith by itself, if it does not have works, is dead"* (James 2:14-17).

He had a heart change. After the earthquake he considered suicide. Now he is thankful and rejoices with what God has provided.

The Conviction of the Missionaries

The apostle Paul, as we have previously mentioned, is a Jewish man with Roman citizenship. When the Christian leaders are released by the magistrate, it would seem that there would be great relief. However, Paul had a point to make. He did not make it for selfish reasons. He did not want this episode to become a precedent. It would be possible others would experience this dangerous ill-treatment. Paul, with full legal rights demands that the magistrates come and release them because of his full legal rights as a citizen of Rome. The fact is, a very ill advised error has occurred. Corporal punishment was a violation of Roman law and to do it without a trial was illegal. This could now mean the removal of office with loss of benefits for the magistrates. Paul demands the leaders come to him and show proper respect to the Roman citizens they have unjustly beaten and imprisoned. The magistrates come to Paul and Silas and release them, begging them to leave the city. Here they are ... Humbled and humiliated before God's servants!

Paul and Silas leave and go to the house of Lydia and they encouraged each other in the faith.

Questions:

1. Where did the missionaries customarily go when they initially enter a city?
2. Why was it illegal to imprison Paul and Silas?
3. What four things occurred in the jailer's life that gave evidence of his salvation?

For Discussion:

1. What are some areas of persecution you face in your life?
2. How do you deal with them?

20

The Story of Christianity Turning the World Upside Down

Acts 17

Now when they had passed through Amphipolis and Apollonia, they came to Thessalonica, where was a synagogue of the Jews: And Paul, as his manner was, went in unto them, and three sabbath days reasoned with them out of the scriptures, Opening and alleging, that Christ must needs have suffered, and risen again from the dead; and that this Jesus, whom I preach unto you, is Christ.And some of them believed, and consorted with Paul and Silas; and of the devout Greeks a great multitude, and of the chief women not a few. But the Jews which believed not, moved with envy, took unto them certain lewd fellows of the baser sort, and gathered a company, and set all the city on an uproar, and assaulted the house of Jason, and sought to bring them out to the people. And when they found them not, they drew Jason and certain brethren unto the rulers of the city, crying, These that have turned the world upside down are come hither also; Whom Jason hath received: and these all do contrary to the decrees of Caesar, saying that there is another king, one Jesus. And they troubled the people and the rulers of the city, when they heard these things. And when they had taken security of Jason, and of the other, they let them go. And the brethren immediately sent away Paul and Silas by night unto Berea: who coming thither went into the synagogue of the Jews. These were more noble than those in Thessalonica, in that they received the word with all readiness of mind, and searched the scriptures daily, whether those things were so. Therefore many of them believed; also of honourable women which were Greeks, and of men, not a few. But when the Jews of Thessalonica had knowledge that the word of God was preached of Paul at Berea, they came thither also, and stirred up the people. And then immediately the brethren sent away Paul to go as it were to the sea: but Silas and Timotheus abode there still. And they that conducted Paul brought him unto Athens: and receiving a commandment unto Silas and Timotheus for to come to him with all speed, they departed. Now while Paul waited for them at Athens, his spirit was stirred in him, when he saw the city wholly given to idolatry. Therefore disputed he in the synagogue with the Jews, and with the devout persons, and in the market daily with them that met with him. Then certain philosophers of the Epicureans, and of the Stoicks, encountered him. And some said, What will this babbler say? other some, He seemeth to be a setter forth of strange gods: because he preached unto them Jesus, and the resurrection. And they took him, and brought him unto Areopagus, saying, May we know what this new doctrine, whereof thou speakest, is? For thou bringest certain strange things to our ears: we would know therefore what these things mean. (For all the Athenians and strangers which were there spent their time in nothing else, but either to tell, or to hear some new thing.) Then Paul stood in the midst of Mars' hill, and said, Ye men of Athens, I perceive that in all things ye are too superstitious. For as I passed by, and beheld your devotions, I found an altar with this inscription, To The Unknown God. Whom therefore ye ignorantly worship, him declare I unto you. God that made the world and all things therein, seeing that he is Lord of heaven and earth, dwelleth not in temples made with hands; Neither is worshipped with men's hands, as though he needed any thing, seeing he giveth to all life, and breath, and all things; And hath made of one blood all nations of men for to dwell on all the face of the earth, and hath determined the times before appointed, and the bounds of their habitation; That they should seek the Lord, if haply they might feel after him, and find him, though he be not far from every one of us: For in him we live, and move, and have our being; as certain also of your own poets have said, For we are also his offspring. Forasmuch then as we are the offspring of God, we ought not to think that the Godhead is like unto gold, or silver, or stone, graven by art and man's device. And the times of this ignorance God winked at; but now commandeth all men every where to repent: Because he hath appointed a day, in the which he will judge the world in righteousness by that man whom he hath ordained; whereof he hath given assurance unto all men, in that he hath raised him from the dead. And when they heard of the resurrection of the dead, some mocked: and others said, We will hear thee again of this matter. So Paul departed from among them. Howbeit certain men clave unto him, and believed: among the which was Dionysius the Areopagite, and a woman named Damaris, and others with them. (Acts 17 KJV).

The World Turned Upside Down is an English ballad. It was first published as a protest against the policies of Parliament in England. It had to do with limiting the celebration of Christmas. There may be evidence that the tune was placed where Lord Cornwallis surrendered at Yorktown. However, many centuries prior to this episode there were others who were accused of turning the world upside down. They were the Christian leaders in the early days of Christianity.

As Paul and Silas picked up from Phillipi, they went through Amphipolis and Apollonia arriving in Thessalonica. Today, Thessalonica is a Greek port along the Aegean Sea. The name in Bible days meant "Victory against the Thessalians".[62] There was a large Jewish population there as well as Greek converts to Christianity. It was about 100 miles from Philippi.

In Paul's day the city was the capital of Macedonia. It is unclear who founded it. The city was a major port.

When Christ is proclaimed, the devil with all of his power would like to stifle the work. G. Campbell Morgan wrote:

"No propagative work is done save at cost: and every genuine triumph of the Cross brings after it the travail of some new affliction, and come new sorrow. So we share the travail that makes the Kingdom come."[63]

This chapter is a continuation of a message that is so powerful, yet so truthful. A man has risen from the grave and he is Jesus of Nazareth who is truly the God/Man!

The Occasion   (Acts 17:1-3)

Paul regularly went to the synagogue as his first stop in a new city. This is what he did in Thessalonica. Paul declared in 1 Corinthians 1 the response to the gospel. *"For since, in the wisdom of God, the world through wisdom did not know God, it pleased God through the foolishness of the message preached to save those who believe. For Jews request a sign, and Greeks seek after wisdom; but we preach Christ crucified, to the Jews a stumbling block and to the Greeks foolishness, but to those who are called, both Jews and Greeks, Christ the power of God and the wisdom of God. Because the foolishness of God is wiser than men, and the weakness of God is stronger than me"* (1 Corinthians 1:21-25).

Christ crucified was a stumbling block to Jews. The Jews wanted a social political savior. The Greeks looked at the message as foolishness since someone who would be crucified would have no authority. The passion in Paul's life was to clearly proclaim the resurrection!

For three weeks the apostle reasoned from the Scriptures in the synagogue. His style here was discussion. The word reasoned is the Greek *dialegomai* from which we get our English word dialogue. Paul would use the resource the Jewish leaders clung to, the Old Testament Scriptures. Many believed.

The Growth   (Acts 17:4-12)

When Paul was on the Damascus road I mentioned his vitriolic behavior towards people of The Way and now that same intolerance was manifested by Jewish religionists. They grab a man named Jason looking for the missionaries. When they did not find them, they took Jason, shouting the men who had turned the world upside down were now in Thessalonica.

Demanding a pledge from Jason and the others they released them. It is interesting to note the loyalty towards Caesar because of the fear of the popularity of Jesus which was based on the resurrection.

Individuals sent Paul and Silas on to Berea. They left at night and upon arrival went immediately to the synagogue and found a group of believers who were turning to Christ. Many of these were Greek women.

The Scripture says they were examining the Scriptures. The word is one that is used of Judicial investigation. They had carefully sought out the truth and found the Word of God Paul preached and taught was on target. Jesus is the Christ. The resurrection proves it. The Thessalonians came and joined the study.

The Conflict   (Acts 17: 13-19)

Again there is conflict. Paul is escorted away to Athens. It doesn't matter where he goes, everywhere there is conversion and conflict. When Paul arrives in Athens his spirit is provoked within him because of the idolatry that abounds.

As Paul is moved on it appears people are orchestrating it. The fact is he is being moved on by God's direction and the eternal plan is that he will stand before powerful individuals who have no idea of God, Jesus, and certainly not the resurrection message. Paul goes to the synagogue and is reasoning with God-fearing Gentiles and Jews. They were a group of pantheistic worshipers, known as the Epicureans. Epicureans lived from 314-270 B.C. Their creed was that happiness was the chief end of life. This philosophy leads to such sadness. People leave families, have sex changes, build huge greed, steal, kill or whatever it takes to find some kind of elusive happiness. This group believed that. Happiness is the chief end of life. The founder was considered to be Zeno. He lived 75 years and he taught for years in Athens. His teaching included emphasizing the rational over the emotional. They were naturalists. Nature mattered. They were very disciplined in their pursuit.

Paul continued his discussion into the market place. Paul preached Jesus and the resurrection. These philosophies tried to belittle him and decided they would put him into the Areopagus. This was a very respectable and venerable group who had charge of the important matters including education, humanitarian, and religious issues. The common belief is this was located on the hill known as the Areopagus.

The Message   (Acts 17: 20-29)

At the point of writing this book I preach almost every Sunday in a different church. Many churches call my office requesting my sermon title and a Scripture passage. What would you and I title this message? There is no time to think ahead about it. The time is now. The request is " ... so we want to know what these things mean?" Many of the Athenians simply want to hear something new.

Perhaps Paul has a flashback to the sermon he heard from Stephen. Perhaps he remembers the amazing anointing. In my opinion, Paul could not have said it better or been more prepared. He tells them about God!

In the world we live in we need to hear about God. We do not only need just pragmatism, psychology, or other ideologues. We need to know God!

The city of Athens had passed Corinth as the city of political and commercial influence in Greece. It was the philosophical center of the ancient world. Numerous gods were worshipped in Athens.

Idolatry is the worship of an idol. It is cultish. Anything that is worshipped apart from God is idolatry. I have been to over 30 countries preaching and spoke in most of the states of the union and everywhere there is idolatry. False gods, fetishes, immoralities, and imposters. Only God is to be worshipped! The triune God will not share His glory with another. *"But the hour is coming, and now is, when the true worshipers will worship the Father in spirit and truth; for the Father is seeking such to worship Him. God is Spirit, and those who worship Him must worship in spirit and truth"* (John 4: 23-24).

Paul's message? You got it – the resurrection! Note the message.

The Reality of God

Paul mentions that there is a statue altar to the Unknown God. He congratulates them in their recognition that there is a God. The Bible's approach is that God simply is. Although there are numerous arguments for God, the Scripture declares Him. *"In the beginning God ..."* (Genesis 1:1). There are four familiar arguments about God. First there is Teleological argument which states there is an order to the universe. The Cosmological argument states there is a cause behind the universe. The moral argument is the Anthropological issue that claims humans are different than the animal world. The Ontological argument states that there must be a perfect being somewhere behind everything. Yet preceding any of this is the fact of God.

The Person of God

Paul proceeds to explain God! He begins by stating that God made all things. This runs into the basic teaching of the Epicureans who believed there is no creator and matter was eternal. The Stoics were Pantheists and believed everything was part of God. Paul affirms that God made the world. *"For by Him all things were created that are in heaven and that are on earth, visible and invisible, whether thrones or dominions or principalities or powers. All things were created through Him and for Him"* (Colossians 1:16). " *... and to make all see what is the fellowship of the mystery, which from the beginning of the ages has been hidden in God who created all things through Jesus Christ"* (Ephesians 3:9). *"You are worthy, O Lord, To receive glory and honor and power; For You created all things, And by Your will they exist and were created"* (Revelation 4:11)

Paul further emphasizes that the God of heaven and earth does not dwell in temples made with hands. *"Give unto the* LORD, *O you mighty ones, Give unto the* LORD *glory and strength"* (Psalm 29:1). *"But will God indeed dwell on the earth? Behold, heaven and the heaven of heavens cannot contain You. How much less this temple which I have built"* (1 Kings 8:27).

God is also the one who controls all things. All people are welcome into God's family. Some Greeks who sensed they were far better than others are now told all people have their place on the face of the earth.

Because of these opposite propositions of God the people of the world should seek Him. There is the natural revelation of God in the conscience of a human being. " *... for when Gentiles, who do not have the law, by nature do the things in the law, these, although not having the law, are a law to themselves, who show the work of the law written in their hearts, their conscience also bearing witness, and between themselves their thoughts accusing or else excusing them"* (Romans 2:14-15). The nature of the world itself speaks of God. *"For the wrath of God is revealed from heaven against all ungodliness and unrighteousness of men, who suppress the truth in unrighteousness, because what may be known of God is manifest in them, for God has shown it to them. For since the creation of the world His invisible attributes are clearly seen, being understood by the things that are made even His eternal power and Godhead, so that they are without* excuse, because, although they knew God, they did not glorify Him as God, nor were thankful, but became futile in their thoughts, and their foolish hearts were darkened. Professing to be wise, they became fools, and changed the glory of the incorruptible God into an image made like corruptible man— and birds and four-footed animals and creeping things. Therefore God also gave them up to uncleanness, in the lusts of their hearts, to dishonor their bodies among themselves, who exchanged the truth of God for the lie, and worshiped and served the creature rather than the Creator, who is blessed forever. Amen. For this reason God gave them up to vile passions. For even their women exchanged the natural use for what is against nature" (Romans 1:18-26). All are accountable.

In loving, firm and through direct proposition the apostle has laid the case for God.

The Words of God   (Acts 17:30-31)

God is very gracious. His longsuffering is depicted by the fact that "God overlooked the times of ignorance." God doesn't always send swift judgment. The time has come when repentance must be declared. The overriding truth is clear. The book of Acts declares it over and over again. Here the apostle brings it home to these brilliant, yet lost people. Jesus has risen from the grave. When the resurrection was mentioned, some sneered. "We will hear you again ..." was their excuse to leave. Some men believed. A member of the court, Dionysius, a woman named Damaris, and others knew not just an unknown God, but now the God of the universe.

An amazing brief message through a spirit-filled messenger exalting the risen Christ brings strength to this community. Paul is just beginning a ministry to the Gentile community which includes some very powerful people.

Questions

1. What does the Scriptures mean that the new faith had turned the world upside down?
2. What was the starting point of the apostle on his message to the philosophers?
3. List several evidences of the God Paul spoke of.

For Discussion

1. What are some of the ways to bring people to Jesus who have a philosophical approach to Jesus? Have you done some of these approaches? What are the results?

21

The Story of Christianity
Encouragement in a
Discouraging World
(Acts 18:1-28)

*After these things Paul departed from Athens, and came
to Corinth; And found a certain Jew named Aquila, born
in Pontus, lately come from Italy, with his wife Priscilla;
(because that Claudius had commanded all Jews to depart
from Rome:) and came unto them. And because he was of
the same craft, he abode with them, and wrought: for by
their occupation they were tentmakers. And he reasoned in
the synagogue every sabbath, and persuaded the Jews and
the Greeks. And when Silas and Timotheus were come from
Macedonia, Paul was pressed in the spirit, and testified to
the Jews that Jesus was Christ. And when they opposed
themselves, and blasphemed, he shook his raiment, and
said unto them, Your blood be upon your own heads; I am
clean; from henceforth I will go unto the Gentiles. And he
departed thence, and entered into a certain man's house,
named Justus, one that worshipped God, whose house
joined hard to the synagogue. And Crispus, the chief ruler
of the synagogue, believed on the Lord with all his house;
and many of the Corinthians hearing believed, and were*

baptized. Then spake the Lord to Paul in the night by a vision, Be not afraid, but speak, and hold not thy peace: For I am with thee, and no man shall set on thee to hurt thee: for I have much people in this city. And he continued there a year and six months, teaching the word of God among them. And when Gallio was the deputy of Achaia, the Jews made insurrection with one accord against Paul, and brought him to the judgment seat, Saying, This fellow persuadeth men to worship God contrary to the law. And when Paul was now about to open his mouth, Gallio said unto the Jews, If it were a matter of wrong or wicked lewdness, O ye Jews, reason would that I should bear with you: But if it be a question of words and names, and of your law, look ye to it; for I will be no judge of such matters. And he drave them from the judgment seat. Then all the Greeks took Sosthenes, the chief ruler of the synagogue, and beat him before the judgment seat. And Gallio cared for none of those things. And Paul after this tarried there yet a good while, and then took his leave of the brethren, and sailed thence into Syria, and with him Priscilla and Aquila; having shorn his head in Cenchrea: for he had a vow. And he came to Ephesus, and left them there: but he himself entered into the synagogue, and reasoned with the Jews. When they desired him to tarry longer time with them, he consented not; But bade them farewell, saying, I must by all means keep this feast that cometh in Jerusalem: but I will return again unto you, if God will. And he sailed from Ephesus. And when he had landed at Caesarea, and gone up, and saluted the church, he went down to Antioch. And after he had spent some time there, he departed, and went over all the country of Galatia and Phrygia in order, strengthening all the disciples. And a certain Jew named Apollos, born at Alexandria, an eloquent man, and mighty in the scriptures, came to Ephesus. This man was instructed in the way of the Lord; and being fervent in the spirit, he spake and taught diligently the things of the Lord, knowing only the baptism of John. And he began to speak boldly in the synagogue: whom when Aquila and Priscilla had heard, they took him

unto them, and expounded unto him the way of God more
perfectly. And when he was disposed to pass into Achaia, the
brethren wrote, exhorting the disciples to receive him: who,
when he was come, helped them much which had believed
through grace: For he mightily convinced the Jews, and that
publicly, shewing by the scriptures that Jesus was Christ
(Acts 18:1-28 KJV).

❝❞ **T**he combination of early limited success at Athens, loneliness
and prospect of facing the city, with its commerce and vice,
accounts for the weakness and fear that gripped the apostle
as he arrived to begin his work."[64] Paul the apostle would now enter Corinth.
Corinth was an influential city that was located on a narrow isthmus
between two seas, the Aegean and the Adriatic. Corinth was a wealthy port
and commercial hub. It was dangerous to travel around the southern tip
of Greece. Therefore, many ships came across the isthmus. Corinth was a
most impressive city. There was an outdoor theater that would hold 70,000.
The temple of Aphrodite was there. The city was very immoral. Corinth
was well known for its lewdness, debauchery, and drunkenness.

Paul arrives and begins to preach in the synagogue. He is forced out
of the synagogue by religious opposition and goes next door to the house
of Titus Justus ... Paul stays in the city initially for 18 months. This was a
wild city. Only the tough could survive such circumstances. A discouraged
apostle enters into this city.

Companionship of Friends   (Acts 18:1-4)

An important edict by Claudius, the Roman emperor, drove the Jews
out of Rome. Claudius was a member of the Julio Claudian dynasty. The
dynasty consisted of the first five Roman imperial emperors – Augustus,
Tiberius, Caligalo, Nero, and this Claudius. He was the first Roman
emperor outside of Italy.

Paul connects with Aquila and Priscilla. Aquila, like Paul, was a
tentmaker. Aquila and Paul earned their income with this trade and Paul
was dialoguing in the synagogue trying to persuade Jews and Greeks. Silas
and Timothy came down from Macedonia and joined the apostle who had
devoted himself to the Word of God. Paul received huge opposition from
the Jews who were blaspheming the truth and Paul clearly told them, "Your

blood be on your hands. I am clean. I will go the Gentiles" (Paraphrase of Acts 18:6). He found a new friend in Titus Justus. Crispus, who was the leader of the synagogue, also believed along with many of the Corinthians and they followed the Lord in baptism.

It is interesting to notice how God brought people into the life of Paul. This is true with all followers of Jesus. Keep your mind open to people you meet. They are people God brings to you by way of divine appointments.

Fellowship with God   (Acts 18:9-11)

In a night vision, a dream, the Lord speaks to Paul and says, *"Do not be afraid any longer, but go on speaking and do not be silent; for I am with you, and no man will attack you in order to harm you, for I have many people in this city"* (Acts 18:9-10).

For 18 months he preached. What a privilege this must have been for the people to hear the apostle expound the Scriptures.

Persecution of the Enemies   (Acts 18:12-17)

"Gallio was proconsul of Achaia. He was characterized by contemporaries as an amiable, witty, and loveable person."[65] Under Roman law Judaism was licensed. Christianity was considered a sect of Judaism. I assume that Jewish religionists probably complained that these people of the city should not be considered a sect of Judaism. The religionists bring Paul to Gallio and he tells them to work out their own squabbles amongst themselves. Gallio drives them away from the town square where there was a judgment seat. Another leader of the synagogue is Sosthenes. He was head of the anti-Paul group in the synagogue. He was a Jew. He is mentioned in 1 Corinthians 1:1. *"Paul, called to be an apostle of Jesus Christ through the will of God, and Sosthenes our brother"* (1 Corinthians 1:1). It appears this beating, that Paul did not deserve, caused him to become a Christian.

The Completed Journey   (Acts 18:18-22)

Paul has his hair cut. It was the sign of the Nazarite vow. *"Then the Nazirite shall shave his consecrated head at the door of the tabernacle of meeting, and shall take the hair from his consecrated head and put it on the fire which is under the sacrifice of the peace offering*" (Numbers 6:18). There is no evidence given concerning the reason for him to take the vow. Cenchrea was the eastern part of Corinth. While Paul was in Corinth he wrote the two epistles to the Thessalonians.

Paul went to Ephesus, ministered there, then despite the request by the people to stay, he went to Caesarea and from there, back down to Antioch.

Commencement of the Third Missionary Journey   (Acts 18:23-28)

The commencement of the third missionary journey begins here. Paul meets up with a very eloquent and powerful preacher named Apollos. He was considered a polished preacher. His message, however, had a deficiency. He was an Alexandrian and mighty in the Scriptures, but did not understand believers' baptism. He was very aware of John's baptism.

Aquila and Priscilla lovingly take him aside and shared with him the truth of baptism. Being an obedient servant of God he accepts the encouragement. He desired to go to Achaia and the brethren wrote to the disciples to welcome him. This powerful preacher refuted the Jews and through the Scriptures proclaimed that Jesus Christ is the resurrected Lord.

Questions and Discussion

Questions

1. What was Paul's reaction to those who opposed him in Corinth?
2. How long did Paul preach in Corinth?
3. What was Gallio's response to the Jews who wanted to persecute the Christian leaders?

Discussion

1. Apollos was a powerful and eloquent preacher of the Word of God. Who are some preachers you know who preach today like this and what is their effectiveness?

22

The Story of Christianity
The Work of the Holy Spirit
(Acts 19)

And it came to pass, that, while Apollos was at Corinth, Paul having passed through the upper coasts came to Ephesus: and finding certain disciples, He said unto them, Have ye received the Holy Ghost since ye believed? And they said unto him, We have not so much as heard whether there be any Holy Ghost. And he said unto them, Unto what then were ye baptized? And they said, Unto John's baptism. Then said Paul, John verily baptized with the baptism of repentance, saying unto the people, that they should believe on him which should come after him, that is, on Christ Jesus. When they heard this, they were baptized in the name of the Lord Jesus. And when Paul had laid his hands upon them, the Holy Ghost came on them; and they spake with tongues, and prophesied. And all the men were about twelve. And he went into the synagogue, and spake boldly for the space of three months, disputing and persuading the things concerning the kingdom of God. But when divers were hardened, and believed not, but spake evil of that way before the multitude, he departed from them, and separated the disciples, disputing daily in the school of one Tyrannus. And this continued by the space of two years; so that all they which dwelt in Asia heard the word of the Lord Jesus, both Jews and Greeks. And God wrought special miracles by the hands of Paul: So that from his body were brought unto the sick handkerchiefs or aprons, and the diseases departed from them, and the evil spirits went out of them. Then certain of the vagabond Jews, exorcists, took upon them to call over them which had evil spirits the name of the Lord Jesus, saying, We adjure you by Jesus whom Paul preacheth. And there were seven sons of one Sceva, a Jew, and chief of the priests, which did so. And the evil spirit answered and said, Jesus I know, and Paul I know; but who are ye? And the man in whom the evil spirit was leaped on them, and overcame them, and prevailed against them, so that they fled out of that house naked and wounded. And this was known to all the Jews and Greeks also dwelling at Ephesus; and fear fell on them all, and the name of the Lord Jesus was magnified. And many that believed came, and confessed, and shewed their deeds. Many of them also which used curious arts brought their books together, and burned them before all men: and they counted the price of them, and found it fifty thousand pieces of silver. So mightily grew the word of God and prevailed. After these things were ended, Paul purposed in the spirit, when he had passed through Macedonia and Achaia, to go to Jerusalem, saying, After I have been there, I must also see Rome. So he sent into Macedonia two of them that ministered unto him, Timotheus and Erastus; but he himself stayed in Asia for a season. And the same time there arose no small stir about that way. For a certain man named Demetrius, a silversmith, which made silver shrines for Diana, brought no small gain unto the craftsmen; Whom he called together with the workmen of like occupation, and said, Sirs, ye know that by this craft we have our wealth. Moreover ye see and hear, that not alone at Ephesus, but almost throughout all Asia, this Paul hath persuaded and turned away much people, saying that they be no gods, which are made with hands: So that not only this our craft is in danger to be set *at nought; but also that the temple of the great goddess Diana should be despised, and her magnificence should be destroyed, whom all Asia and the world worshippeth. And when they heard these sayings, they were full of wrath, and cried out, saying, Great is Diana of the Ephesians. And the whole city was filled with confusion: and having caught Gaius and Aristarchus, men of Macedonia, Paul's companions in travel, they rushed with one accord into the theatre. And when Paul would have entered in unto the people, the disciples suffered him not. And certain of the chief of Asia, which were his friends, sent unto him, desiring him that he would not adventure himself into the theatre. Some therefore cried one thing, and some another: for the assembly was confused: and the more part knew not wherefore they were come together. And they drew Alexander out of the multitude, the Jews putting him forward. And Alexander beckoned with the hand, and would have made his defence unto the people. But when they knew that he was a Jew, all with one voice about the space of two hours cried out, Great is Diana of the Ephesians. And when the townclerk had appeased the people, he said, Ye men of Ephesus, what man is there that knoweth not how that the city of the Ephesians is a worshipper of the great goddess Diana, and of the image which fell down from Jupiter? Seeing then that these things cannot be spoken against, ye ought to be quiet, and to do nothing rashly. For ye have brought hither these men, which are neither robbers of churches, nor yet blasphemers of your goddess. Wherefore if Demetrius, and the craftsmen which are with him, have a matter against any man, the law is open, and there are deputies: let them implead one another. But if ye enquire any thing concerning other matters, it shall be determined in a lawful assembly. For we are in danger to be called in question for this day's uproar, there being no cause whereby we may give an account of this concourse. And when he had thus spoken, he dismissed the assembly.* (Acts 19 KJV).

T he work of the Holy Spirit drives people to the message of the cross. At the outset of this volume I mentioned that work of God was done in redemption. The work of God in evangelism is not done. It continues until the coming of our Lord.

Contemporary evangelism often reflects shallowness. I use the word contemporary as belonging to the present period of time. Because something is contemporary doesn't make it right or wrong. It simply states its time period as being modern. The fact is that contemporary when used in the past is not always clear. In this case we are viewing evangelism in the twenty-first century.

Sometimes evangelism is too ecclesiastical. We simply invite people to church. Sometimes emotionalism appeals to decisions without an adequate basis of understanding. Other times it is superficial which involves brief encounters with the expectation of unusual results. There are also occasions when the gospel is too empty and we try to live the gospel and never get to the message. There are occasions when the gospel is mechanical. We only try to win someone with a special system. Perhaps the biggest is that we do not depend on God's Holy Spirit to empower us.

A weak gospel never offends, loses contact, strives to be entertaining and is not life changing. As we enter Acts 19 the issue involves God the Holy Spirit working through the Word of God in the time of transition.

The chapter begins with a question. "Did you receive the Holy Spirit when you believed?" Paul is on his third missionary journey. The response was clear. "No, we have not even heard whether this is a Holy Spirit." Their baptism was John's baptism. It appears there were Old Testament saints who were in transition. As Paul explains to them the significance of John's baptism, they are then baptized and the apostle lays his hand on them as an affirmation of their faith. Author David Williams explains this conversation. "His criterion for what distinguished the Christian is significant. So, too, is the way in which his question is framed. It implies that the Holy Spirit is received at a definite point in time and that that moment is the moment of initial belief (the aorist participle, piseusontes, being construed here as coincidental with the verb, elabete)."[66]

These men began to speak with tongues and prophesy. "That was a further indication that they were now part of one true church (cf 11:15, 57). And since they had not even heard that the Spirit had come, they needed tangible proof that He had indeed come into their lives."[67]

From here on the Holy Spirit would come to people of salvation. The theological term is the indwelling of the Holy Spirit (1 Corinthians 6:19-20). The filling of the Spirit is the consuming, controlling, and completing work that works in believer's lives after salvation.

The Spoken Word Proclaimed   (Acts 19:8-12)

Paul returns to Ephesus and goes to a familiar spot, the synagogue. For three months he proclaims the Word of God. As previously mentioned, there are four aspects of the kingdom. First, there is the spiritual aspect of the kingdom. To enter the kingdom one needs to be born again. *"There was a man of the Pharisees named Nicodemus, a ruler of the Jews. This man came to Jesus by night and said to Him, 'Rabbi, we know that You are a teacher come from God; for no one can do these signs that You do unless God is with him.'" Jesus answered and said to him, 'Most assuredly, I say to you, unless one is born again, he cannot see the kingdom of God.'" Nicodemus said to Him, 'How can a man be born when he is old? Can he enter a second time into his mother's womb and be born?'" Jesus answered, 'Most assuredly, I say to you, unless one is born of water and the Spirit, he cannot enter the kingdom of God'"* (John 3:1-5).

The second aspect is the kingdom is moral. Jesus in the Sermon on the Mount emphasized the beatitudes. *"Blessed are the poor in spirit, For theirs is the kingdom of heaven. Blessed are those who mourn, For they shall be comforted. Blessed are the meek, For they shall inherit the earth. Blessed are those who hunger and thirst for righteousness, For they shall be filled. Blessed are the merciful, For they shall obtain mercy. Blessed are the pure in heart, For they shall see God. Blessed are the peacemakers, For they shall be called sons of God. Blessed are those who are persecuted for righteousness' sake, For theirs is the kingdom of heaven. Blessed are you when they revile and persecute you, and say all kinds of evil against you falsely for My sake. Rejoice and be exceedingly glad, for great is your reward in heaven, for so they persecuted the prophets who were before you"* (Matthew 5: 3-12).

Thirdly, the kingdom is literal. (Revelation 20:1-6.) The eschatological thousand-year reign of Jesus Christ on the earth is literal.

Finally, the kingdom is eternal. *"And the king gave the command, and they brought those men who had accused Daniel, and they cast them into the den of lions—them, their children, and their wives; and the lions overpowered them, and broke all their bones in pieces before they ever came to the bottom of the den. Then King Darius wrote: To all peoples, nations, and languages that dwell in all the earth: Peace be multiplied to you. I make a decree that in every dominion of my kingdom men must tremble and fear before the God of Daniel. For He is the living God, And steadfast forever; His kingdom is the one which shall not be destroyed, And His dominion shall endure to the end"* (Daniel 6: 24-26).

The preaching of God's Word can be life changing to the hearers. The preaching of God's Word can also be rejected. There were some who spoke evil of the Way. They were hardened. *"But when some were hardened and did not believe, but spoke evil of the Way before the multitude, he departed from them and withdrew the disciples, reasoning daily in the school of Tyrannus"* (19:9). The word hardened is in imperfect tense referring to a process that takes time. When a heart is hardened it will speak evil. Those listeners spoke evil of those who were members of the Way. The goal became one of destroying the influence of the apostle.

Sensing that there was no reason to stay, Paul changed locations to the school of Tyrannus. Tyrannus was a Greek rhetorician. A rhetorician is considered to be an excellent writer or an eloquent speaker. "Tyrannus no doubt held his classes in the early morning hours. Public activity ceased in the cities of Ionia for several hours at 11 a.m. and … more people would be asleep at 1 a.m. of the day. But Paul, after spending the early hours of the day at his tentmaking (cf. Ch. 20:34) devoted the hours of the day and heat to his more important and more exhausting business, and must have infected his hearers with his own energy and zeal, so that they were willing to sacrifice their siesta for the sake of listening to Paul."[68]

In the early days of Christianity God provided miracles as evidence of the resurrection of Jesus Christ. It is important to remember that the New Testament was not yet in the Canon of Scripture. A term used in describing what books belong in Holy Scripture is Canon. It comes from the Greek word *kanon* meaning measurement. A canonical is one that will measure up the Holy Scriptures standard. Briefly speaking, criteria included authorship, witness of the spirit, and acceptance of the nature of God and Jesus. The authentication of the apostolic message was signs and wonders. Evidently, there was common belief in the days of the apostle that healing could be magically transmitted. *"For she said to herself, 'If only I may touch His garment, I shall be made well'"* (Matthew 9:21). These miracles were important for the Ephesian people to know that the apostle and more importantly, the message was from God.

The Exorcists   (19:13-20)

A group of exorcists were observing the Holy Spirit's ministry through the apostle Paul. It appears they assumed they could reproduce similar miracles. These are called exorcists. Their goal was to bind demons and expel them by utilizing another powerful evil spirit. The presence of exorcists was very common. They immediately began by utilizing the Jesus whom Paul preached urging demons to leave. There was a priest by the name of Sceva. He had seven sons. In a conversation they mentioned they knew Jesus and Paul but did not know the man who had an evil spirit. With an enormous amount of strength the evil spirit overpowered them and they left the house naked, bruised, and wounded. The exorcists' fate spread throughout the people of Ephesus. Recognition spread about the power of the very name of Jesus Christ.

The people began to tell their stories and brought books and burned them. 50,000 pieces of silver was the value of the literature. "The staggering value of it, noted as fifty pieces of silver (equivalent to 50,000 days wages for an average laborer) was given to indicate Ephesus's widespread involvement in the magic acts."[69]

The Word of God has enormous power! Magical acts, evil influence, and Satanic influence cannot stand against it!

More Persecution   (Acts 19:21-41)

Persecution grew the Christian faith. Religious groups were involved in trying to halt Christianity (Acts 4 -5; 6; 8) in Jerusalem. At Antioch the issue was envy (Acts 13). Paganism reared its head of opposition in Lystra (Acts 14). It was demonism in Philippi (Acts 16:16-40). Jealous religious leaders provoked an unruly mob (Acts 17). The gospel was opposed in Athens by worldly philosophers (Acts 17). In Acts 18 the opposition is in a Roman Court with Jewish religionists leading the opposition.

Despite the opposition Paul has a plan. Paul will head to Jerusalem to help with an offering for the poor, go to Macedonia and Achaia to collect offerings and eventually head to Rome.

He decides to send to Macedonia two who ministered to him, Timothy and Erastus. He would stay in Asia for a period of time.

The Christians, called the Way (19:23), have a huge opposition against them. A man named Demetrius is a silversmith. His name was a common name and he was well known. He made silver shrines of the goddess Artemis and evidently had a lucrative business. Ancient Roman temples were important. Roman culture emphasized these structures. The structure of Artemis was rebuilt three times and became known as one of the Seven Wonders of the Ancient World in the final form. This temple had local and international influence and prestige. Demetrius is the head of the silversmiths' guild.

Ephesus was a center of magic, a university town, but it was best known for this seventh Wonder of the World. Artemis (Diana) was a temple full of shrines. Often older shrines were removed by the priests to make room for more.

The influence of Paul was mighty. As Demetrius emphasized the influence of Paul, he mentions the danger of losing the magnificent power of the world worship of Diana. The people become indignant and begin to cry out saying, "Great is Diana of the Ephesians" (19:28). The city becomes a riot. The whole city rushed into the theater with one accord and seize Gaius and Aristarchus, Paul's traveling companions.

It is also interesting how Demetrius delivered his speech. The temple had received gifts from many rulers. To lose any profit would lower the stature of the prominence of Ephesus.

It is interesting to notice the anger that was exhibited. The anger was similar to when Stephen was martyred and when the mob went after Paul and Silas at Philippi. From anger there was unmitigated confusion. So often when a demonstration breaks out there are many who do foolish things. They seized Aristarchus, a beloved friend of the apostle who would be imprisoned with Paul in Rome. "*Aristarchus my fellow prisoner greets you, with Mark the cousin of Barnabas (about whom you received instructions: if he comes to you, welcome him*" (Colossians 4:10).

The theater, the center of town meetings, could hold around 25,000 people. The disciples would not let Paul go in for safety reasons. Paul had friends in places of position who would not let him go in. The people who gathered were not sure why they had gathered. (19:32).

The riot continued and finally the town clerk, Alexander, motioned to the people to listen to him. He calmly tells the people the temple of Artemis is safe. He mentions an image which fell down from heaven (19:35). It was commonly believed the meteorites were associated with the worship of Artemis. He mentioned the star falling from Zeus and it is possible this is what he is referring to.

The town clerk defends the leaders of the Way and states they are neither thieves nor blasphemers. If Demetrius and any of his craftsmen has an issue, it can be brought before the courts. The law with lawful assembly will decide the cause. He states the people here met with a disorderly gathering and the people leave as he dismisses them.

Questions

1. What does a weak gospel produce?
2. How did the town clerk appeal to the mob? What was the result?
3. How influential was the Temple of Diana?

For Discussion

1. The big issue for the people in Ephesus was the loss of income from false worship. Where does money fit into your priority list?

23

The Story of Christianity
The Importance of the Local Church
(Acts 20)

And after the uproar was ceased, Paul called unto him the disciples, and embraced them, and departed for to go into Macedonia. And when he had gone over those parts, and had given them much exhortation, he came into Greece, And there abode three months. And when the Jews laid wait for him, as he was about to sail into Syria, he purposed to return through Macedonia. And there accompanied him into Asia Sopater of Berea; and of the Thessalonians, Aristarchus and Secundus; and Gaius of Derbe, and Timotheus; and of Asia, Tychicus and Trophimus. These going before tarried for us at Troas. And we sailed away from Philippi after the days of unleavened bread, and came unto them to Troas in five days; where we abode seven days. And upon the first day of the week, when the disciples came together to break bread, Paul preached unto them, ready to depart on the morrow; and continued his speech until midnight. And there were many lights in the upper chamber, where they were gathered together. And there sat in a window a certain young man named Eutychus, being fallen into a deep sleep: and as Paul was long preaching, he sunk down with sleep, and fell down from the third loft, and was taken up dead.

And Paul went down, and fell on him, and embracing him said, Trouble not yourselves; for his life is in him. When he therefore was come up again, and had broken bread, and eaten, and talked a long while, even till break of day, so he departed. And they brought the young man alive, and were not a little comforted. And we went before to ship, and sailed unto Assos, there intending to take in Paul: for so had he appointed, minding himself to go afoot. And when he met with us at Assos, we took him in, and came to Mitylene. And we sailed thence, and came the next day over against Chios; and the next day we arrived at Samos, and tarried at Trogyllium; and the next day we came to Miletus. For Paul had determined to sail by Ephesus, because he would not spend the time in Asia: for he hasted, if it were possible for him, to be at Jerusalem the day of Pentecost. And from Miletus he sent to Ephesus, and called the elders of the church. And when they were come to him, he said unto them, Ye know, from the first day that I came into Asia, after what manner I have been with you at all seasons, Serving the Lord with all humility of mind, and with many tears, and temptations, which befell me by the lying in wait of the Jews: And how I kept back nothing that was profitable unto you, but have shewed you, and have taught you publicly, and from house to house, Testifying both to the Jews, and also to the Greeks, repentance toward God, and faith toward our Lord Jesus Christ. And now, behold, I go bound in the spirit unto Jerusalem, not knowing the things that shall befall me there: Save that the Holy Ghost witnesseth in every city, saying that bonds and afflictions abide me. But none of these things move me, neither count I my life dear unto myself, so that I might finish my course with joy, and the ministry, which I have received of the Lord Jesus, to testify the gospel of the grace of God. And now, behold, I know that ye all, among whom I have gone preaching the kingdom of God, shall see my face no more. Wherefore I take you to record this day, that I am pure from the blood of all men. For I have not shunned to declare unto you all the counsel of God. Take heed therefore unto yourselves, and to all the flock, over the which the Holy Ghost hath made you overseers, to feed the church of God, which he hath purchased with his own blood. For I know this, that after my departing shall grievous wolves enter in among you, not sparing the flock. Also of your own selves shall men arise, speaking perverse things, to draw away disciples after them. Therefore watch, and remember, that by the space of three years I ceased not to warn every one night and day with tears. And now, brethren, I commend you to God, and to the word of his grace, which is able to build you up, and to give you an inheritance among all them which are sanctified. I have coveted no man's silver, or gold, or apparel. Yea, ye yourselves know, that these hands have ministered unto my necessities, and to them that were with me. I have shewed you all things, how that so labouring ye ought to support the weak, and to remember the words of the Lord Jesus, how he said, It is more blessed to give than to receive. And when he had thus spoken, he kneeled down, and prayed with them all. And they all wept sore, and fell on Paul's neck, and kissed him, Sorrowing most of all for the words which he spake, that they should see his face no more. And they accompanied him unto the ship (Acts 20:1-38 KJV).

The history of Christianity includes the story of the importance of the local church. History is replete with stories of people who loved the church. The early Puritans in America had many pastors who continued to preach the Word of God when they were forbidden to do so. John Bunyan, an English writer and Puritan preacher, best remembered with a Christian allegory, Pilgrim's Progress, loved the church and was imprisoned. Robert Murray McChayne, an outstanding minister in the church of Scotland from 1835 to 1943 died having giving his life fully to the church. Charles Haddon Spurgeon, perhaps the best known preacher from Britain, lost his health and died rather young. Spurgeon deeply loved his church. Paul writes about his love for the church in Philippians 1:3-7. *"I thank my God upon every remembrance of you, always in every prayer of mine making request for you all with joy, for your fellowship in the gospel from the first day until now, being confident of this very thing, that He who has begun a good work in you will complete it until the day of Jesus Christ;*

just as it is right for me to think this of you all, because I have you in my heart, inasmuch as both in my chains and in the defense and confirmation of the gospel, you all are partakers with me of grace" (Philippians 1:3-7).

In the America I live in, the church is well down on the list of priorities for many Christians. Church hopping caused by a search for the church with the best music, teaching, or children's program is common.

In Acts 20 Paul goes to Greece, ministers at Troas, arrives at Miletus, but spends most of the chapter speaking of his love for the church at Ephesus.

In this chapter there are four things the church is a place for.

A Place of Exhortation   (Acts 20: 1-2)

Paul returned after the chaotic uproar. He embraces the people and heads to Macedonia. He encourages the people with many words and then heads to Greece. Paul was constantly teaching and preaching.

> *"And He commanded us to preach to the people, and to testify that it is He who was ordained by God to be Judge of the living and the dead"* (Acts 10: 42).

> *"And when they arrived in Salamis, they preached the word of God in the synagogues of the Jews. They also had John as their assistant"* (Acts 13:5).

> *"And we declare to you glad tidings—that promise which was made to the fathers"* (Acts 13:32).

> *"And they were preaching the gospel there"* (Acts 14:7).

> *"... and saying, "Men, why are you doing these things? We also are men with the same nature as you, and preach to you that you should turn from these useless things to the living God, who made the heaven, the earth, the sea, and all things that are in them"* (Acts 14:15).

> *"But the unbelieving Jews stirred up the Gentiles and poisoned their minds against the brethren"* (Acts 14:2).

"Paul and Barnabas also remained in Antioch, teaching and preaching the word of the Lord, with many others also" (Acts 15:35).

"Now after he had seen the vision, immediately we sought to go to Macedonia, concluding that the Lord had called us to preach the gospel to them" (Acts 16:10).

"... explaining and demonstrating that the Christ had to suffer and rise again from the dead, and saying, "This Jesus whom I preach to you is the Christ" (Acts 17:3).

"But when the Jews from Thessalonica learned that the word of God was preached by Paul at Berea, they came there also and stirred up the crowds" (Acts 17:13).

"And indeed, now I know that you all, among whom I have gone preaching the kingdom of God, will see my face no more" (Acts 20:25).

"... preaching the kingdom of God and teaching the things which concern the Lord Jesus Christ with all confidence, no one forbidding him" (Acts 28:31).

Since I was a teenager God has allowed me to preach. I love proclaiming the Word of God. I pastored 2 churches over a 40 years span and most recently spent over 10 years in itinerate ministry. The joy of preaching in a local church, Bible conference, or other setting is very special and if one is called to it, I encouraged them to be faithful to the calling. I remember one month when I delivered thirteen commencement addresses along with speaking a minimum of 4 times a week at my church. It was exhausting, yet deeply fulfilling. God is so good to provide the strength and wisdom.

Everyone needs community. The essential place for community that is ordained by God is the home and local church. In Acts 20 there are a number of qualities that a church provides for the family of God. It is at the church we are fed with the preaching of God's Word.

History is full of examples of people who loved the church.

The Church is a Place of Giving

Paul went through the Greek districts of Macedonia; Israel had suffered a severe famine. Queen Helena had organized relief efforts. This period appears to be longer than at first glance because of the many communities visited.

The term "much encouragement" (v, 2) spoke to the apostle giving the Scripture as the source of their life and strength. The church needs sound preaching, for by it the people can be fed and, therefore, serve the Lord. A part of understanding God's Word is the emphasis of giving. In 2 Corinthians Paul devotes two chapters about the collection for the saints. (2 Corinthians 8, 9). He addresses the offering needed in his writing to the church at Rome. *"But now I am going to Jerusalem to minister to the saints. For it pleased those from Macedonia and Achaia to make a certain contribution for the poor among the saints who are in Jerusalem. It pleased them indeed, and they are their debtors. For if the Gentiles have been partakers of their spiritual things, their duty is also to minister to them in material things. Therefore, when I have performed this and have sealed to them this fruit, I shall go by way of you to Spain"* (Romans 15:25-28). Paul had a love for the people of the first church in Jerusalem. Persecution came on the residents there as well as those who came to the city to stay on the Day of Pentecost.

The book of Acts regularly addresses the issue of giving from the heart. The example is our Lord Himself who gave His life for us. *"By this we know love, because He laid down His life for us. And we also ought to lay down our lives for the brethren. But whoever has this world's goods, and sees his brother in need, and shuts up his heart from him, how does the love of God abide in him? My little children, let us not love in word or in tongue, but in deed and in truth"* (1 John 3:16-18).

The Church is a Place of Faithfulness   (Acts 20: 3-6)

The Jews formed a plot against Paul. Although details are missing here it is obvious that the apostle would be an easy target on a small ship. His countrymen were intent on harming him. *" … in journeys often, in perils of waters, in perils of robbers, in perils of my own countrymen, in perils of the Gentiles, in perils in the city, in perils in the wilderness, in perils in the sea, in perils among false brethren"* (2 Corinthians 11:26). Paul decides to go to Palestine by traveling through Macedonia. "He would retrace his steps through Achaia north of Macedonia. From there he would cross the Aegean Sea to board another ship in Asia Minor headed toward Israel. That delay and detour cost Paul his opportunity to be in Jerusalem for Passover; all he could hope for now was to arrive in time for Pentecost, fifty days after Passover. (20:16)"[70]

Community is important. Paul had a group of companions that had been with him where he ministered in Roman provinces. This group probably had taken up collections in various churches for the poor in Jerusalem.

Sopater from Berea was the son of Pyrrhas, Aristarcho, and Secundus from Thessalonia. There was Gaius and the young Timothy. Tychicus and Trophimus were from Ephesus. *"For they had previously seen Trophimus the Ephesian with him in the city, whom they supposed that Paul had brought into the temple"* (Acts 21:29).

A group had gone ahead to Troas (vv.4). Luke used the pronoun "is' and "we" as a reminder that he is with the group.

Paul and Luke sailed from Philippi to Troas. It was a five day journey. The group stayed in Troas for five days.

The Church is a Place of Christian Worship   (Acts 20:7-38)

Acts 2:41-47 describes an early church's worship context. There is worship, praise, prayer, teaching of doctrine, fellowship, the Lord's Table, and baptism. This section of Scripture gives a description of a Christian worship service. My wife and I are normally in a different church most Sundays. We have chosen and decided that we will worship and enjoy whatever worship style is there. We have found a great delight in enjoying churches.

A major question that arises is the day of meeting. The day of rest is a Biblical concept. God rested on the seventh day as an example to people that our bodies need a day of rest. The Sabbath was given to the nation of Israel. It was actually a sign of the covenant God gave to Moses. *"Therefore the children of Israel shall keep the Sabbath, to observe the Sabbath throughout their generations as a perpetual covenant. It is a sign between Me and the children of Israel forever; for in six days the LORD made the heavens and the earth, and on the seventh day He rested and was refreshed"* (Exodus 31:16-17). *"You made known to them Your holy Sabbath,*

And commanded them precepts, statutes and laws, By the hand of Moses Your servant" (Nehemiah 9:14). In the New Testament the Sabbath day principle is given (Hebrews 4). There is no command in the New Covenant to keep the Sabbath prior to Moses. In the council at Jerusalem there was no imposition of the Sabbath laid on Gentile believers. *"You observe days and months and seasons and years. I am afraid for you, lest I have labored for you in vain"* (Galatians 4:10-11). The observance of the Sabbath as the seventh day is to be a matter of preference among completed Jews. Many Jewish friends practice the Shabbat (Sabbath) faithfully. The principle is important, both spiritually and physically.

The early church fathers observed the Lord's Day. "Let every friend of Christ keep the Lord's Day as a festival, the resurrection-day, the queen and chief of all days."[71]

"On the first day of the week … this became the regular day of worship for Christians in remembrance of Christ's resurrection Sunday. The meeting was held Sunday night because many had to work during the day time."[72]

The early church often met in homes. *"Greet Philologus and Julia, Nereus and his sister, and Olympas, and all the saints who are with them"* (Romans 16:15). *"to the beloved Apphia, Archippus our fellow soldier, and to the church in your house"* (Philemon 2). Paul preached but he also had discussions. Questions and answers were a part of the early church. It is my opinion that if there is a question and answer time, it is mandatory for the person who is answering the questions to be a strong student of Scripture who can rightly divide the Word of God.

Paul began preaching and his sermon went into the late hours of the night. An individual names Eutychus was sitting in the window sill and fell asleep and he fell off and down three floors. The term 'young man' refers to the idea that he was very young, perhaps pre-teen or in his early teens. The believers were shocked and gathered around his body. Paul realizes that Eutychus has died. *"And in a window sat a certain young man named Eutychus, who was sinking into a deep sleep. He was overcome by sleep; and as Paul continued speaking, he fell down from the third story and was taken up dead"* (vv. 9) When he mentions that his 'life is in him', it seems to refer to the fact that his life has been restored. The boy is brought back to life. Paul continues the service until daybreak.

There is a love feast and observance of the Lord's Table. This service would be one that those who attended would never forget.

Paul's selfless love for his Savior and the church is obvious. He ministers all night then takes a 20 mile journey. After the lengthy walk the apostle meets his fellow workers at Assos. The ship then went to Mitylene, Chios, and Somos and eventually arrived at Miletus. Paul's goal was to be in Jerusalem on the day of Pentecost. You will remember that there was a plot against his life in Corinth that delayed him from arriving in Jerusalem on Passover. Pentecost, 50 days after Passover, was now his goal. The elders at Ephesus were requested to come to Miletus to meet the apostle there.

Paul is now ready to deliver his farewell speech to the leaders of the Ephesian church. Paul was an example. He was an example of "do what I do". No one could question his loyalty to Christ and the church except those who constantly tried to stop his message and practice.

Paul was first and foremost a servant of God, not man. " ... *knowing that from the Lord you will receive the reward of the inheritance; for you serve the Lord Christ"*(Colossians 3:24). The word serving is from the verb bond servant or slave. "Paul uses the verb form seventeen times in his epistles, primarily to refer to obedience to the Lord. He considered it a great honor and privilege to serve the King of Kings and Lord of Lords"[73]

Paul emphasized that he did his ministry with humility. He once called himself *"the least of the saints"* (1 Timothy 1:15). Great leaders in kingdom work are humble people. Paul was moved emotionally as a leader. He writes about the tears he often experienced. Paul was moved to tears over those individuals who were lost without a Savior. " ... *that I have great sorrow and continual grief in my heart. For I could wish that I myself were accursed from Christ for my brethren, my countrymen according to the flesh"* (Romans 9:2-3). He had a burden over Christians who continued struggling with their sins instead of enjoying the victory they had in Christ. Another huge burden the apostle had were those, especially religionists, who were not following Christ. *"For I know this, that after my departure savage wolves will come in among you, not sparing the flock. Also from among yourselves men will rise up, speaking perverse things, to draw away the disciples after themselves"* (Acts 20:29-30). *"For many walk, of whom I have told you often, and now tell you even weeping, that they are the enemies of the cross of Christ"* (Philippians 3:18). Paul is a great example of the many pastors who love God and their congregations for the passion and compassion they experience. *"For do I now persuade men, or God? Or do I seek to please men? For if I still pleased men, I would not be a bondservant of Christ"* (Galatians 1:10).

Of the many responsibilities the apostle had at the top would be teaching. Teachers are to 'equip the saints'. Paul clearly emphasizes that he taught with doctrine, clarity of admonitions, practicality in wisdom, and helpful advice. *"All Scripture is given by inspiration of God, and is profitable for doctrine, for reproof, for correction, for instruction in righteousness"* (2 Timothy 3:16) Paul's ministry of teaching included going house to house.

When I am asked about what are the needs of the church today I immediately respond with teaching. Churches that have one service in a week need to emphasize the importance in teaching. The old fashioned Sunday School, life groups, or some form of program needs to be in instituted for the congregation to learn theological and practically how to live out their faith.

The apostle emphasizes repentance. The word means to change one's mind or purpose. A person turns from his sins to God because they have changed their mind on the subject. *"Therefore bear fruits worthy of repentance, and do not begin to say to yourselves, 'We have Abraham as our father.'" For I say to you that God is able to raise up children to Abraham from these stones"* (Luke 3:8). *"I have not come to call the righteous, but sinners, to repentance"* (Luke 5:32). *" ... but declared first to those in Damascus and in Jerusalem, and throughout all the region of Judea, and then to the Gentiles, that they should repent, turn to God, and do works befitting repentance"* (Acts 26:20). The gospel also is a belief in the finished work of Jesus Christ on the cross.

Paul was very content on his calling in life. He had a single-mindedness about himself. He had a message. It was the message of the cross. *"But God forbid that I should boast except in the cross of our Lord Jesus Christ, by whom the world has been crucified to me, and I to the world"* (Galatians 6:14). It was the truth of the gospel, the good news! *"Moreover, brethren, I declare to you the gospel which I preached to you, which also you received and in which you stand, by which also you are saved, if you hold fast that word which I preached to you—unless you believed in vain. For I delivered to you first of all that which I also received: that Christ died for our sins according to the Scriptures, and that He was buried, and that He rose again the third day according to the Scriptures, and that He was seen by Cephas, then by the twelve"* (1 Corinthians 15:1-5). It was the message of God's grace - The gift we do not deserve - punishment for our sins. This is the message that needs to be preached and taught over and over again.

The end of Acts 20:25-38 is a charge to leaders. There are numerous passages on leadership. *"By me kings reign, And rulers decree justice"* (Proverbs 8:15); *"Divination is on the lips of the king; His mouth must not transgress in judgment"* (16:10); *"A king who sits on the throne of judgment scatters all evil with his eyes"* (20:8). These are examples of poor leadership throughout Scripture. *"The prophets prophesy falsely, And the priests rule by their own power; And My people love to have it so. But what will you do in the end"* (Jeremiah 5:31); *"Her priests have violated My law and profaned My holy things; they have not distinguished between the holy and unholy, nor have they made known the difference between the unclean and the clean; and they have hidden their eyes from My Sabbaths, so that I am profaned among them. Her princes in her midst are like wolves tearing the prey, to shed blood, to destroy people, and to get dishonest gain. Her prophets plastered them with untempered mortar, seeing false visions, and divining lies for them, saying, 'Thus says the Lord God,' when the Lord had not spoken"* (Ezekiel 22: 26-28).

Paul begins to challenge and encourage those he ministered to. They were to be truthful. *"So you, son of man: I have made you a watchman for the house of Israel; therefore you shall hear a word from My mouth and warn them for Me. When I say to the wicked, 'O wicked man, you shall surely die!' and you do not speak to warn the wicked from his way, that wicked man shall die in his iniquity; but his blood I will require at your hand. Nevertheless if you warn the wicked to turn from his way, and he does not turn from his way, he shall die in his iniquity; but you have delivered your soul."* (Ezekial 33:7-9). Effective ministry has many issues to deal with. From the writings of Richard Baxter, an English Puritan church leader, poet, & theologian. "Take heed to yourselves, lest you live in those sins which you preach against in others, and lest you be guilty of that which daily you condemn. Will you make it your work to magnify God, and, when you have done, dishonor him as much as others? Will you proclaim Christ's governing power? And condemn it, and rebel yourselves? Will you preach His laws, and willfully break them? If sin be evil why do you live in it? If it be not, why do you dissuade men from it? If it be dangerous how dare you venture on it? If it be not, why do you tell men so? If God's threatenings be true why do you not fear them? If they be false, why do needlessly trouble men with them, and put them into such frights without a cause? Do you know the 'judgment of God that they who commit such things are worthy of death'; and yet will you do them? Thou that sayest a man shall not commit adultery, or be drunk, nor covetous, art thou such thyself? ... O brethren, it is easier to chide at sin, than to overcome it."[74]

These words of Baxter could not be clearer and they are most needed. *"For our boasting is this: the testimony of our conscience that we conducted ourselves in the world in simplicity and godly sincerity, not with fleshly wisdom but by the grace of God, and more abundantly toward you"* (2 Corinthians 1:12).

The spiritual care of the flock is a metaphor referring to the shepherd's relationship to his congregation. The Scriptures often describes Israel and the church as a flock. *"You led Your people like a flock By the hand of Moses and Aaron"* (Psalms 77:20); *"But He made His own people go forth like sheep, And guided them in the wilderness like a flock"* (78:52); *"Therefore thus says the* LORD *God of Israel against the shepherds who feed My people: "You have scattered My flock, driven them away, and not attended to them. Behold, I will attend to you for the evil of your doings," says the* LORD. *"But I will gather the remnant of My flock out of all countries where I have driven them, and bring them back to their folds; and they shall be fruitful and increase"* (Jeremiah 23:2-3); *"I will surely assemble all of you, O Jacob, I will surely gather the remnant of Israel; I will put them together like sheep of the fold, Like a flock in the midst of their pasture; They shall make a loud noise because of so many people"* (Micah 2:12); *"The elders who are among you I exhort, I who am a fellow elder and a witness of the sufferings of Christ, and also a partaker of the glory that will be revealed: Shepherd the flock of God which is among you, serving as overseers, not by compulsion but willingly, not for dishonest gain but eagerly; nor as being lords over those entrusted to you, but being examples to the flock; and when the Chief Shepherd appears, you will receive the crown of glory that does not fade away"* (1 Peter 5:1-4). The major responsibility of a Pastor/Shepherd is to feed the flock. Those who are faithfully leading the church are to be given double honor. *"Let the elders who rule well be counted worthy of double honor, especially those who labor in the word and doctrine"* (1 Timothy 5:17). You see, the church is not the pastor's. The church belongs to God. *"Husbands, love your wives, just as Christ also loved the church and gave Himself for her, that He might sanctify and cleanse her with the washing of water by the word, that He might present her to Himself a glorious church, not having spot or wrinkle or any such thing, but that she should be holy and without blemish"* (Ephesians 5:25-27).

The leader of a congregation needs to protect the flock from false teachers. False teachers may be in the church or they may try to come from outside of the church. Paul spent three years giving it his all. Yet there were those who raised up that were false teachers. *"As I urged you when I went into Macedonia—remain in Ephesus that you may charge some that they teach no other doctrine, nor give heed to fables and endless genealogies, which cause disputes rather than godly edification which is in faith. Now the purpose of the commandment is love from a pure heart, from a good conscience, and from sincere faith, from which some, having strayed, have turned aside to idle talk, desiring to be teachers of the law, understanding neither what they say nor the things which they affirm"* (1 Timothy 1:3-7); *" ... of whom are Hymenaeus and Alexander, whom I delivered to Satan that they may learn not to blaspheme"* (1:20). "Many a minister fails as a pastor because he is not vigilant. He allows his church to be torn to pieces because he is half asleep. He took it for granted that there were no words, no birds of prey, no robbers, and while he was drowsing the enemy arrived. False ideas, destructive interpretations, demoralizing teachings came into his group, and he never knew it. He was interested, perhaps, in literary ; he was absorbed in the discussion contained in the last theological quarterly, and did not know what his young people were reading or what strange ideas had been lodged in the heads of a group of his leading members. There are errors which are as fierce as wolves and pitiless as hyenas; they tear faith and hope and love to pieces and leave churches once prosperous, mangled and half dead."[75]

The leader needs to study and pray. I pastored for 40 years. I religiously set time aside to spend with God and also for sermon preparation. There was no doubt this became some of the sweetest time of any given week. Prayer and time with God through the Word of God goes hand in hand together.

The book of Acts is full of times of prayer for God's people. For the spiritual leader, prayer and the study of God's Word is their primary responsibility.

Paul finishes the chapter by emphasizing the need to put the work of God first over the self-interests of the preacher. The indication of this is when the leader learns to give and not live to get. *"No one can serve two masters; for either he will hate the one and love the other, or else he will be loyal to the one and despise the other. You cannot serve God and mammon"* (Matthew 6:24); *"Let your conduct be without covetousness; be content with such things as you have. For He Himself has said, "I will never leave you nor forsake you"* (Hebrews 13:5). Paul received compensation at times yet did ministry with no expectations. Perhaps 2 Corinthians 9:18 best describes his ministry. *"Let your conduct be without covetousness; be content with such things as you have. For He Himself has said, "I will never leave you nor forsake you"* (2 Corinthians 9:18).

"It is more blessed to give than to receive" (Acts 20:35). This was a quote of Jesus known by the early apostles. There is no record in the gospel of this quote. *"And truly Jesus did many other signs in the presence of His disciples, which are not written in this book; but these are written that you may believe that Jesus is the Christ, the Son of God, and that believing you may have life in His name"* (John 20:30-31); *"And there are also many other things that Jesus did, which if they were written one by one, I suppose that even the world itself could not contain the books that would be written. Amen"* (John 21:25).

Paul kneels and prays with his friends. There is great weeping and grieving that this may be the last time they see the apostle. What a beautiful scene of the love the apostle and these leaders had with each other!

Questions

1. What are the two key and primary responsibilities for a spiritual leader?
2. What did Paul mean by his quote, *"It is more blessed to give than receive"* when the statement is not found in the gospel accounts?
3. What was Paul's major responsibility?

For Discussion

1. What is a biblical definition of humility? How do you experience humility in your life? What are the characteristics in others that portray humility?

24

The Story of Christianity
A Leader's Need to Be Courageous
When Misunderstood

(Acts 21:1-40)

*And it came to pass, that after we were gotten from them,
and had launched, we came with a straight course unto
Coos, and the day following unto Rhodes, and from thence
unto Patara: And finding a ship sailing over unto Phenicia,
we went aboard, and set forth. Now when we had discovered
Cyprus, we left it on the left hand, and sailed into Syria,
and landed at Tyre: for there the ship was to unlade her
burden. And finding disciples, we tarried there seven days:
who said to Paul through the Spirit, that he should not go
up to Jerusalem. And when we had accomplished those
days, we departed and went our way; and they all brought
us on our way, with wives and children, till we were out of
the city: and we kneeled down on the shore, and prayed. And
when we had taken our leave one of another, we took ship;
and they returned home again. And when we had finished
our course from Tyre, we came to Ptolemais, and saluted
the brethren, and abode with them one day. And the next
day we that were of Paul's company departed, and came
unto Caesarea: and we entered into the house of Philip the*

evangelist, which was one of the seven; and abode with him. And the same man had four daughters, virgins, which did prophesy. And as we tarried there many days, there came down from Judaea a certain prophet, named Agabus. And when he was come unto us, he took Paul's girdle, and bound his own hands and feet, and said, Thus saith the Holy Ghost, So shall the Jews at Jerusalem bind the man that owneth this girdle, and shall deliver him into the hands of the Gentiles. And when we heard these things, both we, and they of that place, besought him not to go up to Jerusalem. Then Paul answered, What mean ye to weep and to break mine heart? for I am ready not to be bound only, but also to die at Jerusalem for the name of the Lord Jesus. And when he would not be persuaded, we ceased, saying, The will of the Lord be done. And after those days we took up our carriages, and went up to Jerusalem. There went with us also certain of the disciples of Caesarea, and brought with them one Mnason of Cyprus, an old disciple, with whom we should lodge. And when we were come to Jerusalem, the brethren received us gladly. And the day following Paul went in with us unto James; and all the elders were present. And when he had saluted them, he declared particularly what things God had wrought among the Gentiles by his ministry. And when they heard it, they glorified the Lord, and said unto him, Thou seest, brother, how many thousands of Jews there are which believe; and they are all zealous of the law: And they are informed of thee, that thou teachest all the Jews which are among the Gentiles to forsake Moses, saying that they ought not to circumcise their children, neither to walk after the customs. What is it therefore? the multitude must needs come together: for they will hear that thou art come. Do therefore this that we say to thee: We have four men which have a vow on them; Them take, and purify thyself with them, and be at charges with them, that they may shave their heads: and all may know that those things, whereof they were informed concerning thee, are nothing; but that thou thyself also walkest orderly, and keepest the law. As touching the Gentiles which believe, we have written and concluded that they observe no such thing, save only that they keep themselves from things offered to idols, and from blood, and from strangled, and from fornication. Then Paul took the men, and the next day purifying himself with them entered into the temple, to signify the accomplishment of the days of purification, until that an offering should be offered for every one of them. And when the seven days were almost ended, the Jews which were of Asia, when they saw him in the temple, stirred up all the people, and laid hands on him, Crying out, Men of Israel, help: This is the man, that teacheth all men every where against the people, and the law, and this place: and further brought Greeks also into the temple, and hath polluted this holy place. (For they had seen before with him in the city Trophimus an Ephesian, whom they supposed that Paul had brought into the temple.) And all the city was moved, and the people ran together: and they took Paul, and drew him out of the temple: and forthwith the doors were shut. And as they went about to kill him, tidings came unto the chief captain of the band, that all Jerusalem was in an uproar. Who immediately took soldiers and centurions, and ran down unto them: and when they saw the chief captain and the soldiers, they left beating of Paul. Then the chief captain came near, and took him, and commanded him to be bound with two chains; and demanded who he was, and what he had done. And some cried one thing, some another, among the multitude: and when he could not know the certainty for the tumult, he commanded him to be carried into the castle. And when he came upon the stairs, so it was, that he was borne of the soldiers for the violence of the people. For the multitude of the people followed after, crying, Away with him. And as Paul was to be led into the castle, he said unto the chief captain, May I speak unto thee? Who said, Canst thou speak Greek? Art not thou that Egyptian, which before these days madest an uproar, and leddest out into the wilderness four thousand men that were murderers? But Paul said, I am a man which am a Jew of Tarsus, a city in Cilicia, a citizen of no mean city: and, I beseech thee, suffer me to speak unto the people. And when he had given him licence, Paul stood on the stairs, and beckoned with the hand unto the people. And when there was made a great silence, he spake unto them in the Hebrew tongue, saying, (Acts 21:1-40 KJV).

"**I**s it so bad, then, to be misunderstood?" asked Ralph Waldo Emerson. "Pythagoras was misunderstood, and Socrates, and Jesus, and Luther, and Copernicus, and Galileo and Newton … to be great is to be misunderstood."[76]

Emerson's observation appears to be on target. Strong leaders follow their convictions and there are occasions when they are misunderstood. As the apostle Paul continued on his missionary journey there were occasions when he had to stand true to his convictions and even his closest associates disagreed and did not understand his decisions.

A brief overview of men and women in Scripture reveals this fact about leaders. Joseph, despite being misunderstood by his own family and boss, courageously followed God's direction into Egypt and through strong management provided food during the famine. The spies, Joshua and Caleb, requested an immediate invasion despite giants in the land. The rest of the spies said no. Deborah urged Barak to lead the Israelites against Sisera and the Caanannite armies. David took on Goliath. Daniel, Shadrach, Meschech, and Abed-nego put their lives on the line to do the right thing as it is recorded in the book of Daniel. Joseph, the husband of Mary, the mother of our Lord, took the trip to Egypt. Such is the life of a leader.

As we approach Acts 21, the situation in Jerusalem is that the people are in need of basic resources. Paul's goal was to meet the basic needs.

Paul's Friends Offer Advice   (Acts 21:1-17)

Paul goes on a ship and leaves for Miletus. He goes straight to Cos, the capital city of the island, then on to Rhodes. The Colossus of Rhodes was one of the Seven Wonders of the World. Then he goes on to Patera. Ships did not go out at night because of the ocean breeze. Patera was on the mainland of Asia Minor at the mouth of the Xanthus River. They would then go on the Mediterranean Sea and on to Phoenicia, Cyprus and Tyre. The apostles goal was to get to Jerusalem on the Day of Pentecost. At this time there was a consistent issue with division amongst the believers. Jewish extremists, known as Judaizers desired the Gentiles live Jewish and accept the traditions and customs of Moses. Paul's desire was that the offering he received would show his love and care for the people, and that it had a way of giving evidence of the unity there can be in Christ. The disciples at Tyre were insistent that he not go to Jerusalem. In fact, they told Paul "through the Spirit" not to go. It is fascinating in these journeys to notice how the people loved, cared, and prayed for the apostle.

The deacon and evangelist, Philip, welcomed the entourage to Caesarea. Philip came here (Acts 8:40) after leading the Ethiopian Eunuch to Christ. It appears he lived in Caesarea going on forty years. Philip was one of the original deacons. He knew the first martyr, Stephen. It would be interesting to have listened to conversation between Paul and Philip.

The Prophet Agabus again appears. It is the same man who warned of a famine, and the apostle worked with him on a relief program (Acts 11:27-30). Agabus does a dramatic presentation. He binds his hands and feet with Paul's girdle and told the apostle he would be bound (imprisoned) in Jerusalem. The girdle was a large belt men wore. Agabus did this to reveal the severity and seriousness of the warning. "Surely the men chosen by the churches could deliver the love offering to James and the Jerusalem elders, and it would not be necessary for Paul to go personally."[77] Paul appreciated the concern but made it clear that he would not only be willing to be bound, but die if God so willed it.

In noticing Paul's issue, here are several observations where he was warned. It could have been the Holy Spirit saying "Prepare for what lies ahead" instead of "You must not go."Agabus did not forbid him to go. He was warning him about what to expect. When he went to Jerusalem he was taking his life in his own hands. There were still issues at Jerusalem between the legalistic Pharisees and the grace-minded Gentiles. Although the Jerusalem Council solved some of the issues, there was still trouble. Paul felt he was part of the solution and needed to personally go.

I have been in Christian leadership for over fifty years. There are occasions when there is an issue to solve and I am aware I must do it. It can't be farmed out.

So Paul takes a company of believers and travels the sixty-five miles to Jerusalem. This took probably around three days. The city would be overrun with those coming for the day of Pentecost. Paul goes to a man's home who is a young convert. His name was Mnason. Mnason enjoys providing hospitality. This man was very important at this strategic point in Paul's life.

There was an initial meeting and the "brethren received us gladly". There is no detail given on this initial meeting. There was no word about the offering. Perhaps this was a time to relax and prepare for the next day.

On the next day Paul told the wonderful story of how the Gentiles were accepting Christ. The disciple's response is that many Jews, too, have accepted the Lord and they are zealous of the law. The accusation against Paul is that the Jewish believers were led to believe that Paul taught the Gentiles to forsake Moses. It is important to be reminded of the admiration and love that the Jewish people had for Moses. Philip Yancey in his book, The Bible Jesus read quotes from Jewish writer Elie Wiesel on how Moses' contribution was revered.

Moses, "the most solitary and powerful hero in Biblical history. The immensity of his task and the scope of his experience command our admiration, our reverence, our awe. Moses, the man who changed the course of history all by himself; his emergence became the decisive turning point. After him nothing was the same again. It is not surprising that he occupies a special phase in Jewish tradition. His passion for social justice, his struggle for national liberation, his triumphs and disappointments, his poetic inspiration, his gifts as a strategist and his organizational genius, his complex relationship with God and His people, his relationship with God and His people, his requirements and promises, his condemnations and blessings, his bursts of anger, his silences, his efforts to reconcile the law with compassion, authority with integrity-no individual ever, anywhere, accomplished so much for so many people in so many different domains. His influence is boundless, it reverberates beyond time. The Law bears his name, the Talmud is but its commentary and Kabbula communicates only its silence."[78]

Wiesel captures the Jewish view of Moses. The author of Hebrews teaches us that Jesus is better than all who come previously. It is difficult to think of someone who is esteemed as highly as Moses to have a superior one. These Jewish believers accepted the resurrection, the work of the Holy Spirit, but struggled when it came to Moses.

A Meeting Gone Bad   (Acts 21: 18-40)

It is concluded that the assembly will meet and hear what the apostle has to say. It is also suggested that Paul demonstrate in a public way his love, respect, and affection given to the Jewish law. He is asked to connect and identify with four men who are following the Nazarite law (Numbers 6). The suggestion is that he pay for their sacrifices and attend their time of purification in the temple. Paul reports to the priest the next day. He does not take vows. They need to wait seven days to offer the sacrifices. Paul will show allegiance to the law by his participation. Sometimes the best laid plans go in reverse. This was the case.

"No foreigner may enter within the barricade which surrounds the sanctuary and enclosure. Anyone who is caught so doing will have himself to blame for his ensuring death." This was a sign in the temple on the wall where Gentiles were not allowed to go. The court of the Gentiles was separate from the rest of the Temple. Jewish religious leaders had requested from the Romans the right to exercise execution.

Asian Jews saw Paul in the temple. Immediately they concluded that Paul had desecrated by going beyond the wall. They assumed he was a Gentile. The assumption is that where Paul went his Gentile friends followed. Paul was seized and his life was now on the line. The Roman guards intervened. The charges against Paul were without merit. One charge against Paul was that he brought Trophimus, a Gentile, into the area where Gentiles were not permitted. To do so would bring the death sentence on Trophimus.

The temple guards shoved the people outside in order that Paul's death would not defile the temple. "And Jehoiada the priest commanded the captains of the hundreds, the officers of the army, and said to them, 'Take her outside under guard, and slay with the sword whoever follows her.'" For the priest had said, 'Do not let her be killed in the house of the LORD'"(2 Kings 11:15). The goal for the uncontrolled mob was to beat Paul to death. The Roman soldiers stopped the proceedings.

This mob scene is a reminder of the scene our Lord experienced. As they seized Paul, at least 1,000 soldiers were positioned at the Antonia Fortress which is located at the northwest section of the temple area. As with our Lord's trial the people are crying out "Away with him!" As the apostle is led into the barracks, Paul asks a question of the Centurion. In the Greek language he requests to speak. The centurion asks Paul concerning his identity. The question concerns an Egyptian who led an insurrection. The Egyptian disciples were known as Assassins. They were strong Jewish nationalists. Their nationalism made them bitter enemies of both Jewish and Roman leaders. They were vicious. Mingling with the crowd they stabbed their victims. They would either melt away into the crowd or brazenly join the mourners to escape detection. The Assassins were especially active during the Jewish festivals, such as Pentecost. The commander assumed the mob captured an Assassin.

Paul identifies himself. He is a Jew with every right to be where he is. He is a citizen of Tarsus in Cilicia. Now the apostle portrays a courage that is needed for the Law. He requests to speak. Paul is in chains, beaten and wounded. Paul is given permission to speak. He waves his arm, a hush sweeps over the vicious crowd, and the apostle begins to speak. He speaks in Hebrew. In a carefully thought out procedure he lays out a defense that will be a sermon for the ages.

Questions

1. Why did Paul agree to the Jewish customs in this chapter?
2. What was the charge brought against Paul?
3. Who did the commander think Paul was?

For Discussion

1. What lessons can we learn from Paul's reactions to a meeting that went bad?
2. What experiences have you had in your life when a meeting went bad: How was it handled? What was the result?

25

The Story of Christianity
Paul's Defense

(Acts 22)

Men, brethren, and fathers, hear ye my defence which I make now unto you. (And when they heard that he spake in the Hebrew tongue to them, they kept the more silence: and he saith,) I am verily a man which am a Jew, born in Tarsus, a city in Cilicia, yet brought up in this city at the feet of Gamaliel, and taught according to the perfect manner of the law of the fathers, and was zealous toward God, as ye all are this day. And I persecuted this way unto the death, binding and delivering into prisons both men and women. As also the high priest doth bear me witness, and all the estate of the elders: from whom also I received letters unto the brethren, and went to Damascus, to bring them which were there bound unto Jerusalem, for to be punished. And it came to pass, that, as I made my journey, and was come nigh unto Damascus about noon, suddenly there shone from heaven a great light round about me. And I fell unto the ground, and heard a voice saying unto me, Saul, Saul, why persecutest thou me? And I answered, Who art thou, Lord? And he said unto me, I am Jesus of Nazareth, whom thou persecutest. And they that were with me saw indeed the light, and were afraid; but they heard not the voice of him that spake to me. And

I said, What shall I do, Lord? And the Lord said unto me, Arise, and go into Damascus; and there it shall be told thee of all things which are appointed for thee to do. And when I could not see for the glory of that light, being led by the hand of them that were with me, I came into Damascus. And one Ananias, a devout man according to the law, having a good report of all the Jews which dwelt there, Came unto me, and stood, and said unto me, Brother Saul, receive thy sight. And the same hour I looked up upon him. And he said, The God of our fathers hath chosen thee, that thou shouldest know his will, and see that Just One, and shouldest hear the voice of his mouth. For thou shalt be his witness unto all men of what thou hast seen and heard. And now why tarriest thou? arise, and be baptized, and wash away thy sins, calling on the name of the Lord. And it came to pass, that, when I was come again to Jerusalem, even while I prayed in the temple, I was in a trance; And saw him saying unto me, Make haste, and get thee quickly out of Jerusalem: for they will not receive thy testimony concerning me. And I said, Lord, they know that I imprisoned and beat in every synagogue them that believed on thee: And when the blood of thy martyr Stephen was shed, I also was standing by, and consenting unto his death, and kept the raiment of them that slew him. And he said unto me, Depart: for I will send thee far hence unto the Gentiles. And they gave him audience unto this word, and then lifted up their voices, and said, Away with such a fellow from the earth: for it is not fit that he should live. And as they cried out, and cast off their clothes, and threw dust into the air, The chief captain commanded him to be brought into the castle, and bade that he should be examined by scourging; that he might know wherefore they cried so against him. And as they bound him with thongs, Paul said unto the centurion that stood by, Is it lawful for you to scourge a man that is a Roman, and uncondemned? When the centurion heard that, he went and told the chief captain, saying, Take heed what thou doest: for this man is a Roman. Then the chief captain came, and said unto him, Tell me, art thou a Roman? He said, Yea. And the chief captain answered, With a great sum obtained I this freedom. And Paul said, But I was free born. Then straightway they departed from him which should have examined him: and the chief captain also was afraid, after he knew that he was a Roman, and because he had bound him. On the morrow, because he would have known the certainty wherefore he was accused of the Jews, he loosed him from his bands, and commanded the chief priests and all their council to appear, and brought Paul down, and set him before them. (Acts 22:1-30 KJV).

P aul presents his defense. The charge that he opposes the Jews is full of emptiness. He clearly states that he is a Jew. He was raised in Jerusalem and educated under the most respected, revered, and greatest of the rabbis, Gamaliel. His education was according to the law. He was a Pharisee. He was a Pharisee who was blameless. " ... *circumcised the eighth day, of the stock of Israel, of the tribe of Benjamin, a Hebrew of the Hebrews; concerning the law, a Pharisee; concerning zeal, persecuting the church; concerning the righteousness which is in the law, blameless"* (Philippians 3:5-6).

His History   (Acts 22:1-5)

Paul was not just a student for academic reasons. He was zealous for God. The word zealous speaks of an uncompromising desire to accomplish the intended goal. It speaks of an eagerness. Paul was feared by the Christian community. He was considered a terrorist against the faith. He was a feared persecutor. From Stephen's martyrdom to his conversion he was feared. *"For you have heard of my former conduct in Judaism, how I persecuted the church of God beyond measure and tried to destroy it"* (Galatians 1:13). His statement in verse four declared his zeal. "I persecuted The Way to the death." It was not only improbable, it was impossible to question his zeal for the Law. He could quickly bring high priests and councils of the elders to testify of his dedication to the law.

His Testimony   (Acts 22:6-16)

Paul begins to speak of his conversion and uses an apologetic form by speaking of those who were with him on the Damascus Road where he was converted. When Paul heard the voice from heaven and was blinded by the light, his comrades saw the light and heard the sound of the voice of Jesus. Paul realized that this was Jesus. *"And the men who journeyed with him stood speechless, hearing a voice but seeing no one"* (Acts 9:7); *"Then he said, 'The God of our fathers has chosen you that you should know His will, and see the Just One, and hear the voice of His mouth'"* (22:14); *"But rise and stand on your feet; for I have appeared to you for this purpose, to make you a minister and a witness both of the things which you have seen and of the things which I will yet reveal to you"* (26:16); *"Am I not an apostle? Am I not free? Have I not seen Jesus Christ our Lord? Are you not my work in the Lord"* (1 Corinthians 9:1). Paul has the familiar conversation with Jesus (Acts 22: 7-10) and is told to go to Damascus. It is there that he meets Ananias. It is interesting that Paul speaks highly of Ananias' devotion to the law even though he is a Christian.

Paul describes his time with Ananias. Through Ananias' ministry the apostle receives his sight. He baptizes Paul, then reminds the apostle that God has chosen him for a very specific purpose. Paul will be the witness to many. Some have interpreted verse 15 to defend baptismal regeneration. *"But what does it say? "The word is near you, in your mouth and in your heart"* (that is, the word of faith which we preach): *that if you confess with your mouth the Lord Jesus and believe in your heart that God has raised Him from the dead, you will be saved. For with the heart one believes unto righteousness, and with the mouth confession is made unto salvation"* (Romans 10: 8-10). *"And as Moses lifted up the serpent in the wilderness, even so must the Son of Man be lifted up, that whoever believes in Him should not perish but have eternal life. For God so loved the world that He gave His only begotten Son, that whoever believes in Him should not perish but have everlasting life"* (John 3:14-16). Baptism always follows salvation and it is a declaration of a conversion. Going into the water pictures Christ's death, the moment in the water his burial, and coming out of the water his resurrection.

Paul declares he is acting in submission to God. He in a sense lays on the mob the fact that he is obeying the God that is sovereign of the ages.

His Experience   (Acts 22:17-21)

Paul had a brief ministry while he was in Damascus. He spent three years after that in Nabataeon Arabia. " ... *nor did I go up to Jerusalem to those who were apostles before me; but I went to Arabia, and returned again to Damascus. Then after three years I went up to Jerusalem to see Peter, and remained with him fifteen days"* (Galatians 1: 17-18). Paul returned to Jerusalem. He was praying in the temple and fell into a trance. A trance "denotes ... a condition in which ordinary consciousness and the perception of natural circumstances were withheld, and the soul was susceptible only to the vision imported by God."[79] The word is used when Peter had his vision in Joppa. *"then he became very hungry and wanted to eat; but while they made ready, he fell into a trance"* (Acts 10:10); *"And as I began to speak, the Holy Spirit fell upon them, as upon us at the beginning"* (11:15). When Ananias told Paul that he would "be a witness to all men" it was as it were a commission of the apostle to the Gentiles. Paul senses his speech is without folly, but the response is just the opposite.

The People React   (Acts 22:22-23)

The issue of a Gentiles salvation that bypassed them becoming Jewish proselytes was unthinkable to the crowd. This would bring Jews and Gentiles together as one. In their minds this could not be tolerated. The crowd goes berserk. They throw off their cloaks. They toss dust into the air. They consider Paul's statement to be blasphemous. Racial prejudice has been a struggle throughout the history of the world. The goal here is to kill Paul.

The Commander Acts   (Acts 22:24-29)

The commander decides to examine Paul through the process of scourging. The scourging was with a wooden handle. Leather thongs had bits of metal and bone. It was call a flagellum. Many died from such a beating. Infection would often set in or a loss of blood would cause the victim to die.

Paul was a Roman citizen. Roman citizens were exempted from such a beating. Paul explains his rights as a Roman citizen. The centurion who was to inflict the punishment goes to the commander to explain that Paul is a Roman citizen. The commander's military career could have ended and he may have lost his life to proceed with the flagellation.

The brief conversation in verse 28 is one for the ages. The commander questions Paul about his citizenship and then says he purchased his citizenship. In this era citizenship could be obtained by bribing corrupt officials. The statement to Paul seems to indicate that the commander bought his citizenship but it also indicates his assumption that this is how Paul became a citizen. Paul's calm yet forceful statement would possibly put chills up the spine of the commander. "But I was born a citizen."

The commander is now frightened. He has bound Paul. The next day began a time that would become very intriguing, enlightening, and frightening.

Questions

1. How was Paul both Jewish and Roman citizen?
2. Why did Paul rehearse his testimony to the mob?

For Discussion

1. How did Paul use his circumstances to provide an opportunity?
2. What do you feel Paul's attitude was during this experience?

CHAPTER

26

The Story of Christianity
God's Protection

Acts 23

And Paul, earnestly beholding the council, said, Men and brethren, I have lived in all good conscience before God until this day. And the high priest Ananias commanded them that stood by him to smite him on the mouth. Then said Paul unto him, God shall smite thee, thou whited wall: for sittest thou to judge me after the law, and commandest me to be smitten contrary to the law? And they that stood by said, Revilest thou God's high priest? Then said Paul, I wist not, brethren, that he was the high priest: for it is written, Thou shalt not speak evil of the ruler of thy people. But when Paul perceived that the one part were Sadducees, and the other Pharisees, he cried out in the council, Men and brethren, I am a Pharisee, the son of a Pharisee: of the hope and resurrection of the dead I am called in question. And when he had so said, there arose a dissension between the Pharisees and the Sadducees: and the multitude was divided. For the Sadducees say that there is no resurrection, neither angel, nor spirit: but the Pharisees confess both. And there arose a great cry: and the scribes that were of the Pharisees' part arose, and strove, saying, We find no evil in this man: but if a spirit or an angel hath spoken to him,

~ 247 ~

let us not fight against God. And when there arose a great dissension, the chief captain, fearing lest Paul should have been pulled in pieces of them, commanded the soldiers to go down, and to take him by force from among them, and to bring him into the castle. And the night following the Lord stood by him, and said, Be of good cheer, Paul: for as thou hast testified of me in Jerusalem, so must thou bear witness also at Rome. And when it was day, certain of the Jews banded together, and bound themselves under a curse, saying that they would neither eat nor drink till they had killed Paul. And they were more than forty which had made this conspiracy. And they came to the chief priests and elders, and said, We have bound ourselves under a great curse, that we will eat nothing until we have slain Paul. Now therefore ye with the council signify to the chief captain that he bring him down unto you to morrow, as though ye would enquire something more perfectly concerning him: and we, or ever he come near, are ready to kill him. And when Paul's sister's son heard of their lying in wait, he went and entered into the castle, and told Paul. Then Paul called one of the centurions unto him, and said, Bring this young man unto the chief captain: for he hath a certain thing to tell him. So he took him, and brought him to the chief captain, and said, Paul the prisoner called me unto him, and prayed me to bring this young man unto thee, who hath something to say unto thee. Then the chief captain took him by the hand, and went with him aside privately, and asked him, What is that thou hast to tell me? And he said, The Jews have agreed to desire thee that thou wouldest bring down Paul to morrow into the council, as though they would enquire somewhat of him more perfectly. But do not thou yield unto them: for there lie in wait for him of them more than forty men, which have bound themselves with an oath, that they will neither eat nor drink till they have killed him: and now are they ready, looking for a promise from thee. So the chief captain then let the young man depart, and charged him, See thou tell no man that thou hast shewed these things to me. And he called unto him two centurions, saying, Make ready two hundred soldiers to go to Caesarea, and horsemen threescore and ten, and spearmen two hundred, at the third hour of the night; And provide them beasts, that they may set Paul on, and bring him safe unto Felix the governor. And he wrote a letter after this manner: Claudius Lysias unto the most excellent governor Felix sendeth greeting. This man was taken of the Jews, and should have been killed of them: then came I with an army, and rescued him, having understood that he was a Roman. And when I would have known the cause wherefore they accused him, I brought him forth into their council: Whom I perceived to be accused of questions of their law, but to have nothing laid to his charge worthy of death or of bonds. And when it was told me how that the Jews laid wait for the man, I sent straightway to thee, and gave commandment to his accusers also to say before thee what they had against him. Farewell. Then the soldiers, as it was commanded them, took Paul, and brought him by night to Antipatris. On the morrow they left the horsemen to go with him, and returned to the castle: Who, when they came to Caesarea and delivered the epistle to the governor, presented Paul also before him. And when the governor had read the letter, he asked of what province he was. And when he understood that he was of Cilicia; I will hear thee, said he, when thine accusers are also come. And he commanded him to be kept in Herod's judgment hall (Acts 23 KJV).

Throughout the book of Acts we noted two important themes. The resurrection of Jesus Christ is the life changing event and the permanent arrival of God the Holy Spirit indwelling and filling believers. The message of the cross and the resurrection are turning many to Jesus Christ. In the midst of the message there arose huge opposition. Religious leaders began to promote Jewish antagonism against the apostles. This chapter springboards huge opposition. Several events led to the episode in this chapter reflecting the opposition was now out of hand. This opposition began on the day of Pentecost. "*Others mocking said, "They are full of new wine*" (Acts 2:13). It continued following the healing of a lame man in Acts 3. The disciples were told by the Sanhedrin not to speak in the name of Jesus. "*So they called them and commanded them not to speak at all nor teach in the name of Jesus"* (Acts 4:18). The persecution continues and seems to crescendo in this chapter.

Paul has been attacked in the temple area by a Jewish mob and viciously beaten. The commander of the Roman forces was unable to find what the charge was against the apostle. As Paul delivers a message before the mob on the step of the Antonian fortress he is taken and beaten because of his adding the Gentiles into the family of God.

The plan was to imprison Paul and bring him to the Sanhedrin the following morning. "Paul's appearance before the Sanhedrin marks the fifth (and last) time that body was called upon to evaluate the claims of Christ. The first was when Jesus himself stood before it. (Mark 14:34-65); the second involved Peter and John (Acts 4:5-22); the third followed the arrest of the apostles (5:21 ff); and the fourth was the trial of Stephen. (Acts 6: 12 ff)."[80]

There were three main groups that were members of this council. They were the High Priests, the Elders, and the Scribes. The two religious groups that made up the largest part of the Sanhedrin were the Pharisees and Sadducees. Other than capital punishment they were a powerful force that oversaw and executed Jewish law with punishment afflicted when necessary.

Paul makes an interesting statement about his conscience. *"Then Paul, looking earnestly at the council, said, 'Men and brethren, I have lived in all good conscience before God until this day'"* (Acts 23:1). No one could deny his commitment to God! The Greek word for conscience is *suneidesis*. It speaks of a witness to conduct. It is through conscience we understand the will of God, the sense of guilt, or a judgment of good and bad in our lives. Individuals often act a certain way because conscience requires it. Paul uses the word twenty-one times in his letters.

Scripture often speaks of conscience. A weak conscience is mentioned in 1 Corinthians 8: 7, 10. *"However, there is not in everyone that knowledge; for some, with consciousness of the idol, until now eat it as a thing offered to an idol; and their conscience, being weak, is defiled"; "For if anyone sees you who have knowledge eating in an idol's temple, will not the conscience of him who is weak be emboldened to eat those things offered to idols"* (1 Corinthians 8: 7, 10). The Scripture also speaks of a wounded conscience. *"To the pure all things are pure, but to those who are defiled and unbelieving nothing is pure; but even their mind and conscience are defiled"* (Titus 1:15). There is an evil conscience. *" … let us draw near with a true heart in full assurance of faith, having our hearts sprinkled from an evil conscience and our bodies* washed with pure water" (Hebrews 10:22). There is a seared conscience. " ... speaking lies in hypocrisy, having their own conscience seared with a hot iron" (1Timothy 4:2).

The Scripture teaches here, as in other passages, about a good conscience. "Pray for us; for we are confident that we have a good conscience, in all things desiring to live honorably" (Hebrews 13:18); " ... having a good conscience, that when they defame you as evildoers, those who revile your good conduct in Christ may be ashamed"; "There is also an antitype which now saves us—baptism (not the removal of the filth of the flesh, but the answer of a good conscience toward God), through the resurrection of Jesus Christ" (1 Peter 3:16, 21); "I thank God, whom I serve with a pure conscience, as my forefathers did, as without ceasing I remember you in my prayers night and day" (2 Timothy 1:3).

The high priest who is next to Paul is engaged in listening to Paul and when he hears Paul's statement, he ordered those around Paul to strike him. Paul's reaction is very vocal. Jesus said a similar statement. "Woe to you, scribes and Pharisees, hypocrites! For you are like whitewashed tombs which indeed appear beautiful outwardly, but inside are full of dead men's bones and all uncleanness " (Matthew 23:27). The prophet Ezekiel's statement to false teachers is also similar. "Because, indeed, because they have seduced My people, saying, 'Peace!' when there is no peace—and one builds a wall, and they plaster it with untempered mortar, that it will fall. There will be flooding rain, and you, O great hailstones, shall fall; and a stormy wind shall tear it down. Surely, when the wall has fallen, will it not be said to you, 'Where is the mortar with which you plastered it?' "Therefore thus says the Lord GOD: "I will cause a stormy wind to break forth in My fury; and there shall be a flooding rain in My anger, and great hailstones in fury to consume it. So I will break down the wall you have plastered with untampered mortar, and bring it down to the ground, so that its foundation will be uncovered; it will fall, and you shall be consumed in the midst of it. Then you shall know that I am the LORD. "Thus will I accomplish My wrath on the wall and on those who have plastered it with untempered mortar; and I will say to you, 'The wall is no more, nor those who plastered it, that is, the prophets of Israel who prophesy concerning Jerusalem, and who see visions of peace for her when there is no peace'" says the Lord GOD" (Ezekiel 13:10-16). Paul uses the law to declare his independence. As a Roman he should not be struck! The term "white wall" refers to the issue that the man was a hypocrite.

It is important to realize this Ananias is not the Annas referred to in Luke 3:2. " ... *while Annas and Caiaphas were high priests, the word of God came to John the son of Zacharias in the wilderness* " (Luke 3:2). This Ananias is considered one of the most evil and corrupt high priests in the history of the office. He had numerous enemies.

Those nearby were shocked at Paul's words against the high priest. They condemned him for reviling the high priest. The word revile refers to abusing or insulting Ananias. The high priest was an evil man, yet he had the position of authority. *"If a matter arises which is too hard for you to judge, between degrees of guilt for bloodshed, between one judgment or another, or between one punishment or another, matters of controversy within your gates, then you shall arise and go up to the place which the* LORD *your God chooses. And you shall come to the priests, the Levites, and to the judge there in those days, and inquire of them; they shall pronounce upon you the sentence of judgment. You shall do according to the sentence which they pronounce upon you in that place which the* LORD *chooses. And you shall be careful to do according to all that they order you. According to the sentence of the law in which they instruct you, according to the judgment which they tell you, you shall do; you shall not turn aside to the right hand or to the left from the sentence which they pronounce upon you. Now the man who acts presumptuously and will not heed the priest who stands to minister there before the* LORD *your God, or the judge, that man shall die. So you shall put away the evil from Israel"* (Deuteronomy 17:8-12). Paul responds appropriately and declares his innocence of awareness that this was the high priest. He admits that his outburst was against God's prohibition of demeaning a ruler. *"You shall not revile God, nor curse a ruler of your people"* (Exodus 22:28). Paul had not been in Jerusalem over several years and did not realize this was the high priest. Paul, in the midst of huge personal horror portrays a humble attitude in this crisis.

The Pharisees and Sadducees had huge disagreements. They had major theological differences plus a variety of political disagreements. Paul appeals to the fact that he is a Pharisee. Paul's goal was to end the hearing and trust that the Roman soldiers would protect him.

Here again the issue is the core doctrine of the Christian faith – the resurrection! This is the heart of the witness of Acts. *"You shall not revile God, nor curse a ruler of your people* (Acts 1:22); *This Jesus God has raised up, of which we are all witnesses"* (2:32); *" ... and killed the Prince of life, whom God raised from the dead, of which we are witnesses"* (3:15).

God's Protection of Paul   (Acts 23:12-35)

A plot is planned by a group who wanted Paul murdered. Outraged that the apostle escaped, they bound themselves under an oath to refuse food or drink until Paul was killed. Here is the apostle, guilty of no crime, about to be innocently murdered. Satan appeared to have a field day. Forty people planned the plot.

The fact that there were forty reflected the idea that the apostle was hated by this group. With more than forty conspirators no one individual would be blamed. They went to the Sanhedrin to request that they join in this madness. They request that the Sanhedrin notify the commander to bring him down for an investigation and while they were on the way Paul would be killed.

It is rather sad to see the Sanhedrin portrayal of corruption. It is always sad to see leadership turn to wicked devices and deceptive means. God places leadership in authority and when deception is from depraved planning, it is sometimes surprising, often alarming, and always disappointing.

The son of Paul's sister hears of the conspiracy. He goes to Paul to reveal the story. Paul, not charged with a crime, is in protective custody. Paul asks one of the centurions to take the lad to the commander. Upon hearing the report, the commander takes Paul's nephew by the hand and requests that he tell the report. The boy tells the story and urges the commander not to give in to the plot planned by the forty who are so serious they refuse to eat nor drink until this dastardly deal is done. The commander tells the boy to tell no one that he knows the plot.

The commander acts quickly. He tells the two centurions to get 200 soldiers and 70 horsemen, plus 200 spearmen. They will take Paul to Caesarea. He writes a letter to the governor Felix. The journey is around sixty-five miles. The formidable group put together by the commander leave at 9 PM and take the apostle to the governor. The letter was accurate with the content he revealed, yet to protect himself he does not mention the order to scourge Paul, nor that he mixed Paul up with another person from Egypt.

The entourage goes to Antipatris, then rest, and on to Caesarea. When Felix reads the letter, he then confirms the right to hear the case. Paul was from Celicia, a part of Syria. Felix had the authority to hear the case. Felix tells Paul he will give the apostle a hearing after the accusers arrive.

Paul would now begin a very grueling, yet rewarding time in his life. This would be the beginning of the Roman trials of the apostle.

Questions

1. List the summary from this chapter of God's protection on the apostle.
2. What were some good leadership principles found in the commander's decisions?
3. What were some poor leadership principles found in the commander's decisions?

For Discussion

1. Why does it seem that so many individuals struggle when placed in positions of authority with integrity and honesty issues?

CHAPTER

27

The Story of Christianity
Paul's Trial

(Acts 24:1-27)

And after five days Ananias the high priest descended with
the elders, and with a certain orator named Tertullus, who
informed the governor against Paul. And when he was
called forth, Tertullus began to accuse him, saying, Seeing
that by thee we enjoy great quietness, and that very worthy
deeds are done unto this nation by thy providence, We
accept it always, and in all places, most noble Felix, with
all thankfulness. Notwithstanding, that I be not further
tedious unto thee, I pray thee that thou wouldest hear us
of thy clemency a few words. For we have found this man
a pestilent fellow, and a mover of sedition among all the
Jews throughout the world, and a ringleader of the sect of
the Nazarenes: Who also hath gone about to profane the
temple: whom we took, and would have judged according
to our law. But the chief captain Lysias came upon us,
and with great violence took him away out of our hands,
Commanding his accusers to come unto thee: by examining
of whom thyself mayest take knowledge of all these things,
whereof we accuse him. And the Jews also assented, saying
that these things were so. Then Paul, after that the governor
had beckoned unto him to speak, answered, Forasmuch as

I know that thou hast been of many years a judge unto this nation, I do the more cheerfully answer for myself: Because that thou mayest understand, that there are yet but twelve days since I went up to Jerusalem for to worship. And they neither found me in the temple disputing with any man, neither raising up the people, neither in the synagogues, nor in the city: Neither can they prove the things whereof they now accuse me. But this I confess unto thee, that after the way which they call heresy, so worship I the God of my fathers, believing all things which are written in the law and in the prophets: And have hope toward God, which they themselves also allow, that there shall be a resurrection of the dead, both of the just and unjust. And herein do I exercise myself, to have always a conscience void to offence toward God, and toward men. Now after many years I came to bring alms to my nation, and offerings. Whereupon certain Jews from Asia found me purified in the temple, neither with multitude, nor with tumult. Who ought to have been here before thee, and object, if they had ought against me. Or else let these same here say, if they have found any evil doing in me, while I stood before the council, Except it be for this one voice, that I cried standing among them, Touching the resurrection of the dead I am called in question by you this day. And when Felix heard these things, having more perfect knowledge of that way, he deferred them, and said, When Lysias the chief captain shall come down, I will know the uttermost of your matter. And he commanded a centurion to keep Paul, and to let him have liberty, and that he should forbid none of his acquaintance to minister or come unto him. And after certain days, when Felix came with his wife Drusilla, which was a Jewess, he sent for Paul, and heard him concerning the faith in Christ. And as he reasoned of righteousness, temperance, and judgment to come, Felix trembled, and answered, Go thy way for this time; when I have a convenient season, I will call for thee. He hoped also that money should have been given him of Paul, that he might loose him: wherefore he sent for him the oftener, and communed with him. But after two years Porcius Festus came into Felix' room: and Felix, willing to shew the Jews a pleasure, left Paul bound. (Acts 24:1-27 KJV).

The Accusation   (Acts 24:1-9)

Ananias, the high priest arrives with some of his elders five days after Paul arrived in Caesarea. Joining them is the attorney, Tertullus. "Tertullus was a lawyer, who was employed by the Jews to state their case against Paul in the presence of Felix."[81] Tertullus begins the accusations by the customary words of flattery to bring Felix on his side. "Felix owed his position to the influence of his brother, Pollos, a favorite of Emperor Cluadius."[82] He exercised the power of a king with the mind of a slave. Nero removed Felix from office. He was a brutal man who caused the Jews many days of anguish. The flowery opening by the lawyer amounted to nonsense.

There are charges against Paul. The first is sedition. Sedition speaks to violations of Roman law. The issue is that Paul stirs up dissension. Pax Romona was the Roman concept of peace that existed between people groups in the empire of Rome. It began with Caesar Augustus and ended with Marcus Aurelius. Rome did not tolerate trouble makers. It is interesting to note that the Sanhedrin desired the overthrow of Rome and yet they are trying to indict Paul on this false charge.

Early Christians were not revolutionaries. They were not political insurrectionists. They had a truthful message. The Holy Spirit has come and Jesus of Nazareth had risen from the grave.

A second charge was that of heresy. Tertullus claims that Paul is the front runner of the Nazarenes. Using the term Nazarene was a put down to the followers of Christ. Although this term is not commonly mentioned, it was evidently known with no explanations forthcoming. The concept is that the early followers of Christ were a sect of Judaism that needed to be stopped for they were a detriment to Israel and Rome.

The third charge was the foolish inference that the apostle tried to desecrate the temple. The mob of a few days earlier had many charges against Paul but the Sanhedrin, in this public forum, stuck with one.

The commander in this narrative is Lysias. "Claudias Lysias is a figure mentioned in the New Testament book of the Acts of the Apostle ... Lusias was a Roman tribune and the commander (chiliarch) of the Roman garrison ("cohort" Acts 21:31) in Jerusalem."[83] The goal here seems to be to examine Lysias and not Paul to confirm these charges.

The Pretense   (Acts 24:10-21)

Paul has no lawyer. He defends himself.

Charge number one he quickly refutes. It is a foolish charge. He went to Jerusalem twelve days prior. Five of these days were in Caesarea. While in Jerusalem he was involved with days of purification. There was no time to cause a rebellion of insurrection. Then, the most serious charge is quickly dropped.

Secondly, he corrects Tertullus' decisive use of calling the followers of Christ, Nazarenes. He properly calls them members of The Way. " ... *and asked letters from him to the synagogues of Damascus, so that if he found any who were of the Way, whether men or women, he might bring them bound to Jerusalem"* (Acts 9:2); *"But when some were hardened and did not believe, but spoke evil of the Way before the multitude, he departed from them and withdrew the disciples, reasoning daily in the school of Tyrannus"* ... *"And about that time there arose a great commotion about the Way"* (19: 9, 23); *"But when Felix heard these things, having more accurate knowledge of the Way, he adjourned the proceedings and said, 'When Lysias the commander comes down, I will make a decision on your case'"* (24:22). He clearly proclaims that he serves the "God of our Fathers". Paul uniquely presents the concept that a devoted follower of Jesus the Messiah is a worshipper of the God of heaven. He accuses his detractors by stating that they were the ones not worshipping the true God. It is interesting to note that the Sadducees accepted the Pentateuch as divinely inspired while the Pharisees accepted the 39 books of the Old Covenant. Paul believed in all the Old Testament making him a follower of Jehovah God.

It is here that Paul emphasizes the resurrection of both saved and lost. He clearly declares this truth.

On the third charge Paul tells the listeners that he did not come to Jerusalem to start a rebellion, but to bring an offering that many had given sacrificially to. He reminds those present that he sponsored four Jewish Christians who were taking Nazarite vows.

Paul then speaks about those who came from the Roman province of Asia with false charges of him desecrating the temple. This too had no basis.

The summary is obvious. Paul was accused. He was accused of being anti-Jewish. He was accused of being against Pax Romana! (The peace that existed between nationalities and the Roman Empire.) Since there were no facts, the decision became one that involved circumstantial evidence.

The Decision   (24:22-27)

"If ever a man failed both personally and officially, that man was Felix, procurator of Judea. He certainly could not plead ignorance of the facts, because he was well acquainted with The Way. His wife, Drusilla, was a Jewess and perhaps kept him informed of activities among her people, and as a Roman official, he would carefully (if privately) investigate these things. He saw the light, but he preferred to live in darkness."[84]

Felix has a tough position he is in. There are no eye witnesses to verify the crimes. He put off making a decision. He says he needs further information from Lysias. Remember, Claudius Lysias has previously given a report. *"I found out that he was accused concerning questions of their law, but had nothing charged against him deserving of death or chains"* (Acts 23:29). He concluded Paul did not commit a crime. There is no scriptural support that Felix ever made contact with the governor. This appears to be a stall maneuver.

Paul was given freedom while in prison. Certainly Felix met with him about his faith in Jesus Christ. His wife, Drusilla had previous partners in marriage. There is some belief that the meeting with Paul was at Drusilla's request. This author is not sure of the reliability of this information.

Felix heard about righteousness, self-control, and the judgment to come (24:25). His statement is so sad, yet so typical. *"Go away for now; when I have a convenient time, I will call for you"* (24:25). Procrastination is a thief. *"For He says: "In an acceptable time I have heard you, And in the day of salvation I have helped you. "Behold, now is the accepted time; behold, now is the day of salvation"* (2 Corinthians 6:2); *"Truly, these times of ignorance God overlooked, but now commands all men everywhere to repent"* (Acts 17:30); *"A good name is to be chosen rather than great riches, Loving favor rather than silver and gold"* (Proverbs 22:1).

Felix desired money. Perhaps he thought he could get some of the funds from the offering Paul raised He may have had in mind that the Jewish Sanhedrin had some. Sadly, there is no indication Felix ever accepted the

Lord. He is replaced by Porcius Festus. He leaves Paul in prison thinking that the Jews will be pleased.

Questions

1. Why do you think Felix never came to Christ as his Savior?
2. Discuss the strength and weakness of the attorneys' charges against Paul.

For Discussion

1. Why do you think the resurrection did not change people's view of Jesus?

CHAPTER

28

The Story of Christianity
Another Trial

(Acts 25:1-27)

Now when Festus was come into the province, after three
days he ascended from Caesarea to Jerusalem. Then the
high priest and the chief of the Jews informed him against
Paul, and besought him, And desired favour against him,
that he would send for him to Jerusalem, laying wait in the
way to kill him. But Festus answered, that Paul should be
kept at Caesarea, and that he himself would depart shortly
thither. Let them therefore, said he, which among you are
able, go down with me, and accuse this man, if there be any
wickedness in him. And when he had tarried among them
more than ten days, he went down unto Caesarea; and the
next day sitting on the judgment seat commanded Paul to
be brought. And when he was come, the Jews which came
down from Jerusalem stood round about, and laid many
and grievous complaints against Paul, which they could not
prove. While he answered for himself, Neither against the
law of the Jews, neither against the temple, nor yet against
Caesar, have I offended any thing at all. But Festus, willing
to do the Jews a pleasure, answered Paul, and said, Wilt
thou go up to Jerusalem, and there be judged of these things
before me? Then said Paul, I stand at Caesar's judgment

seat, where I ought to be judged: to the Jews have I done no wrong, as thou very well knowest. For if I be an offender, or have committed any thing worthy of death, I refuse not to die: but if there be none of these things whereof these accuse me, no man may deliver me unto them. I appeal unto Caesar. Then Festus, when he had conferred with the council, answered, Hast thou appealed unto Caesar? unto Caesar shalt thou go. And after certain days king Agrippa and Bernice came unto Caesarea to salute Festus. And when they had been there many days, Festus declared Paul's cause unto the king, saying, There is a certain man left in bonds by Felix: About whom, when I was at Jerusalem, the chief priests and the elders of the Jews informed me, desiring to have judgment against him. To whom I answered, It is not the manner of the Romans to deliver any man to die, before that he which is accused have the accusers face to face, and have licence to answer for himself concerning the crime laid against him. Therefore, when they were come hither, without any delay on the morrow I sat on the judgment seat, and commanded the man to be brought forth. Against whom when the accusers stood up, they brought none accusation of such things as I supposed: But had certain questions against him of their own superstition, and of one Jesus, which was dead, whom Paul affirmed to be alive. And because I doubted of such manner of questions, I asked him whether he would go to Jerusalem, and there be judged of these matters. But when Paul had appealed to be reserved unto the hearing of Augustus, I commanded him to be kept till I might send him to Caesar. Then Agrippa said unto Festus, I would also hear the man myself. To morrow, said he, thou shalt hear him. And on the morrow, when Agrippa was come, and Bernice, with great pomp, and was entered into the place of hearing, with the chief captains, and principal men of the city, at Festus' commandment Paul was brought forth. And Festus said, King Agrippa, and all men which are here present with us, ye see this man, about whom all the multitude of the Jews have dealt with me, both at Jerusalem, and also here, crying that he ought not to live any longer.

But when I found that he had committed nothing worthy of death, and that he himself hath appealed to Augustus, I have determined to send him. Of whom I have no certain thing to write unto my lord. Wherefore I have brought him forth before you, and specially before thee, O king Agrippa, that, after examination had, I might have somewhat to write. For it seemeth to me unreasonable to send a prisoner, and not withal to signify the crimes laid against him (Acts 25:1-27 KJV).

The story of Christianity again gives credence to two thoughts that I have mentioned throughout this volume. There is the work of the Holy Spirit and the message of the resurrection. Although there are numerous other subjects, these two are pivotal. Paul's ministry at this juncture has the Holy Spirit all over it.

The previous governor, Felix, was a procrastinator, a man of little courage, and politically desiring personal gain. The new governor, Porcius Festus was a better man and immediately set out to address the issue of Paul. Jewish politics were challenging and the new governor shortly found that out. The Jews wanted to kill Paul. The Romans were not sure what to do with him. To release Paul would cause trouble and to keep Paul would leave the governor without an explanation. The governor knew it was important to act quickly.

As we approach this section I would like to have us visualize three scenes.

Scene One   Festus and the Jewish Leaders   (Acts 25: 1-12)

Recognizing the importance of a good relationship with the Jewish leader, Festus visits Jerusalem. The Jewish leaders immediately address the issue of Paul. "The new high priest was Ishmael; for he had replaced Jonathan who had been killed by Felix. Ishmael wanted to resurrect the plot of two years before and remove Paul once and for all."[85]

"And when it was day, some of the Jews banded together and bound themselves under an oath, saying that they would neither eat nor drink till they had killed Paul. Now there were more than forty who had formed this conspiracy. They came to the chief priests and elders, and said, 'We have bound ourselves under a great oath that we will eat nothing until we have

killed Paul. Now you, therefore, together with the council, suggest to the commander that he be brought down to you tomorrow, as though you were going to make further inquiries concerning him; but we are ready to kill him before he comes near'" (Acts 23:12-15). Whereas the original plot was a group that wanted Paul killed, now it was the members of the council.

Festus invites the leaders to accompany him to Caesarea. Another hearing took place. The same accusations are made. Paul stood firm denying any crime against Jewish law, or the sacred temple, or the Roman government. Festus asked Paul if he would go to Jerusalem to be tried. Paul wisely refused. A Roman judge did not have the authority to move a hearing to another court without agreement from the defendant. Paul wisely rejected the offer. So the governor agrees to send Paul to Nero.

Scene Two

Several days passed. Festus was in a quandary. How could he send this prisoner with such notoriety to the emperor with a list of charges? Herod Agrippa II and Herod's sister, Bernice, made a state visit to Festus. This king was the last son of the Herodians to rule. He was the great grandson of Herod who killed the Bethlehem babies. Additionally, he was the son of the Herod who killed the apostle James. There were rumors of incest because Bernice lived with Agrippa II. Jewish law condemned incest (Leviticus 18).

The issue with Paul was summed up accurately in Festus' mind. There were no civil issues. He surmised the issues had to do with the religious teachings of the Jews. Festus rehearses the issues with Agrippa and gives the impression that the Apostle Paul needs to go to Jerusalem to be tried because of the religious nature of the charges. He states the reason to go to Jerusalem is because Jewish people should settle the religious debate. His real reason was to please Jewish leaders.

Paul is clearly proclaiming the resurrection of Jesus Christ. Festus speaks rather flippantly of Jesus resurrection. *" … but had some questions against him about their own religion and about a certain Jesus, who had died, whom Paul affirmed to be alive"* (Acts 25:19).

The king was a student of Judaism. He would have deep interest in Paul who was known as the man who started the chaos in the temple.

The king requests to meet with Paul and arrangements are made for the next day. As the next day approaches, it is interesting to see the King and Bernice with regal, royal clothing, and great pomp as they enter the auditorium. This room was known as the audience room. The important military officers and soldiers also gathered. Paul's reputation had produced discussions that were embellished and rumors that were spread.

Festus begins with an over exaggerated explanation of the proceedings. He said "all … the Jews" had charges against the apostle. This was not the case. Festus presents a plan for the king to examine Paul. In a rather remarkable turnabout Paul becomes judge and jury and Agrippa and Bernice the defendants.

We come to the Third Scene.

CHAPTER

29

The Story of Christianity
The Third Scene
(Acts 26:1-32)

*Then Agrippa said unto Paul, Thou art permitted to speak
for thyself. Then Paul stretched forth the hand, and answered
for himself: I think myself happy, king Agrippa, because I
shall answer for myself this day before thee touching all the
things whereof I am accused of the Jews: Especially because
I know thee to be expert in all customs and questions which
are among the Jews: wherefore I beseech thee to hear me
patiently. My manner of life from my youth, which was at
the first among mine own nation at Jerusalem, know all the
Jews; Which knew me from the beginning, if they would
testify, that after the most straitest sect of our religion I lived
a Pharisee. And now I stand and am judged for the hope
of the promise made of God, unto our fathers: Unto which
promise our twelve tribes, instantly serving God day and
night, hope to come. For which hope's sake, king Agrippa,
I am accused of the Jews. Why should it be thought a thing
incredible with you, that God should raise the dead? I verily
thought with myself, that I ought to do many things contrary
to the name of Jesus of Nazareth. Which thing I also did in
Jerusalem: and many of the saints did I shut up in prison,
having received authority from the chief priests; and when*

they were put to death, I gave my voice against them. And I punished them oft in every synagogue, and compelled them to blaspheme; and being exceedingly mad against them, I persecuted them even unto strange cities. Whereupon as I went to Damascus with authority and commission from the chief priests, At midday, O king, I saw in the way a light from heaven, above the brightness of the sun, shining round about me and them which journeyed with me. And when we were all fallen to the earth, I heard a voice speaking unto me, and saying in the Hebrew tongue, Saul, Saul, why persecutest thou me? it is hard for thee to kick against the pricks. And I said, Who art thou, Lord? And he said, I am Jesus whom thou persecutest. But rise, and stand upon thy feet: for I have appeared unto thee for this purpose, to make thee a minister and a witness both of these things which thou hast seen, and of those things in the which I will appear unto thee; Delivering thee from the people, and from the Gentiles, unto whom now I send thee, To open their eyes, and to turn them from darkness to light, and from the power of Satan unto God, that they may receive forgiveness of sins, and inheritance among them which are sanctified by faith that is in me. Whereupon, O king Agrippa, I was not disobedient unto the heavenly vision: But shewed first unto them of Damascus, and at Jerusalem, and throughout all the coasts of Judaea, and then to the Gentiles, that they should repent and turn to God, and do works meet for repentance. For these causes the Jews caught me in the temple, and went about to kill me. Having therefore obtained help of God, I continue unto this day, witnessing both to small and great, saying none other things than those which the prophets and Moses did say should come: That Christ should suffer, and that he should be the first that should rise from the dead, and should shew light unto the people, and to the Gentiles. And as he thus spake for himself, Festus said with a loud voice, Paul, thou art beside thyself; much learning doth make thee mad. But he said, I am not mad, most noble Festus; but speak forth the words of truth and soberness. For the king knoweth of these things, before whom also I speak freely: for I am persuaded that none of these things are hidden from him; for this thing was not done in a corner. King Agrippa, believest thou the prophets? I know that thou believest. Then Agrippa said unto Paul, Almost thou persuadest me to be a Christian. And Paul said, I would to God, that not only thou, but also all that hear me this day, were both almost, and altogether such as I am, except these bonds. And when he had thus spoken, the king rose up, and the governor, and Bernice, and they that sat with them: And when they were gone aside, they talked between themselves, saying, This man doeth nothing worthy of death or of bonds. Then said Agrippa unto Festus, This man might have been set at liberty, if he had not appealed unto Caesar (Acts 26: 1-32 KJV).

King Agrippa gives permission for Paul to speak. The auditorium is anxious to hear the words of the defendant. This was a situation that could only be ordained and orchestrated by God. Paul is about to give his defense. Technically, this is his apologia.

There are five key thoughts that will characterize his defense in this third scene.

His Past (Acts 26: 4-11)

"But when Paul perceived that one part were Sadducees and the other Pharisees, he cried out in the council, "Men and brethren, I am a Pharisee, the son of a Pharisee; concerning the hope and resurrection of the dead I am being judge"" (Acts 23:6). He was devoted to the teaching of the Pharisees. He was a <u>zealot.</u> There were many who considered that Paul would become a very successful Pharisee. *"For you have heard of my former conduct in Judaism, how I persecuted the church of God beyond measure and tried to destroy it. And I advanced in Judaism beyond many of my contemporaries in my own nation, being more exceedingly zealous for the traditions of my fathers"* (Galatians 1:13-14). When his life was changed in his experience on the Damascus Road, his outlook changed based on his new recognized reality that Jesus Christ had risen from the grave. Because of this belief and his commitment to this truth, he was now a prisoner.

In his defense the apostle clearly expresses his loyalty to the strictest of Jewish traditions. In attendance are Pharisees, Sadducees, Romans, and Greeks. Paul's challenge to them surrounds the importance of the resurrection. *"Why should it be thought incredible by you that God raises the dead"* (Acts 26:8). In 1 Corinthians, the apostle clearly presents his position on the resurrection. Prior to his meeting Jesus on the Damascus road he gladly imprisoned and voted to kill the group called The Way who believed in the resurrected Lord. *"This I also did in Jerusalem, and many of the saints I shut up in prison, having received authority from the chief priests; and when they were put to death, I cast my vote against them"* (Acts 26:10). Paul would travel to synagogues and find the Jewish believers. Like a madman out of control, he did everything he could to rid the earth of them. *"This I also did in Jerusalem, and many of the saints I shut up in prison, having received authority from the chief priests; and when they were put to death, I cast my vote against them"* (Acts 26:11).

His Conversion   (Acts 26: 12-13)

Paul was a scholar and a Pharisee. His antagonism toward Christians continued as he went to other cities to promote his rather heart aching opposition. Paul had the great light shine from heaven. He was blinded for three days. He heard Jesus speak to him. His conversion is one of the most amazing in the foundational days of Christianity.

His Calling   (Acts 26:14-18)

Jesus spoke to Paul. Perhaps at the time this was the last person the apostle wanted to hear from. Paul rehearsed this recorded testimony as it is found in Acts 9. Paul is to be appointed as a minister (Acts 26:16) and a witness. The word minster is very unique. It is the Greek word *huperetes* meaning an under-rower, a seaman. It refers to acting under another's direction. He will now be under the direction of the one he persecuted the most ... The Lord Jesus Christ! He would eventually be sent to the Gentiles. Although the apostle had a huge love for his Jewish people (Romans 1:13-16; 9-13) he would be the leader in expanding the gospel to the lost. The spiritual plight is clearly mentioned in Acts 26:18) " ... to open their eyes, in order to turn them from darkness to light, and from the power of Satan to God, that they may receive forgiveness of sins and an inheritance among those who are sanctified by faith in Me" (Acts 26:18).

~ 269 ~

Other Scripture proclaims this truth. *"Then the eyes of the blind shall be opened, And the ears of the deaf shall be unstopped"* (Isaiah 35:5; *"The Spirit of the Lord GOD is upon Me, Because the LORD has anointed Me To preach good tidings to the poor; He has sent Me to heal the brokenhearted, To proclaim liberty to the captives, And the opening of the prison to those who are bound"* (Isaiah 61:1). Trusting Jesus fully and only will bring salvation.

His Mission   (Acts 26:19-21)

Paul now explains what happened in the controversial Temple experience. Paul was declaring the message of Jesus who rose from the grave, and this was the Messiah to Israel, but also the Savior to the Gentile world. The religious Israelites, concerned about losing their positions and watering down Moses teaching did not want any part of this.

His Faithful Witness   (Acts 26:22-32)

Paul had an incredible beginning in his Jewish faith. He faithfully proclaimed the truth as he understood it. He positions himself with the prophets and Moses declaring they looked forward to the coming of Jesus who would suffer, rise from the dead and that his message would go out to both Jewish and Gentile people. It is interesting that the message of the resurrection was presented over and over again. This was the heart of the issue. Every generation is found with the same question ... Who is Jesus Christ? ... Did He really rise from the grave? Paul would stake his life on it.

As Paul completed some of his thoughtful apologia, two issues caused consternation with the listeners. The first was the resurrection of Jesus. The second is that this salvation was as much for the Gentiles as it was for the Jews. Festus, always trying to please the crowd, accused Paul of being mad. The Greek word is maria. It speaks of madness or a mad man. He has lost his common sense. The accusation is that Paul has studied so much he has lost his ability to have clear understanding. He is a maniac in Festus' view. Remember, Paul is speaking directly to King Agrippa. Now he speaks to the governor, but then addresses the thoughts back to the King. He reminds them that these events about Jesus Christ's life were not done in quiet but that Agrippa, a student of Judaism, knew about Jesus. Paul brings to a decision his defense. *"The Spirit of the Lord God is upon Me, Because the Lord has anointed Me To preach good tidings to the poor; He has sent Me to heal the brokenhearted, to proclaim liberty to the captives, And the opening of the prison to those who are bound"* (Acts 26:27). The meaning of these words are. "Do you think that in such a short time, with such few words, you can persuade me to become a Christian? Perhaps he spoke with a smirk on his face and a "sneer in his voice."[86] "Paul's defense was not just for the others, but to the Christian faith."[87] The primary goal of "Paul's defense was not just for the others, but to convert Agrippa to the Christian faith".[88] "The primary goal of Paul's testimony was not to exonerate himself, but to convert Agrippa."[89] Paul with passion challenges Agrippa to become a follower of Jesus. *"And Paul said, 'I would to God that not only you, but also all who hear me today, might become both almost and altogether such as I am, except for these chains'"* (Acts 26:29).

The King stands up. The hearing is concluded. Paul is declared innocent of any crime that would be capital in nature to bring about death. Over and over again in various trials Paul is declared innocent. *"And when it was day, the magistrates sent the officers, saying, 'Let those men go. Now therefore depart, and go in peace.'" But Paul said to them, 'They have beaten us openly uncondemned Romans, and have thrown us into prison. And now do they put us out secretly? No indeed! Let them come themselves and get us out.'" And the officers told these words to the magistrates, and they were afraid when they heard that they were Romans. Then they came and pleaded with them and brought them out, and asked them to depart from the city. So they went out of the prison and entered the house of Lydia; and when they had seen the brethren, they encouraged them and departed"* (Acts 16:35-40); *"When Gallio was proconsul of Achaia, the Jews with one accord rose up against Paul and brought him to the judgment seat, saying, 'This fellow persuades men to worship God contrary to the law.'" "And when Paul was about to open his mouth, Gallio said to the Jews, 'If it were a matter of wrongdoing or wicked crimes, O Jews, there would be reason why I should bear with you. But if it is a question of words and names and your own law, look to it yourselves; for I do not want to be a judge of such matters.'" And he drove them from the judgment seat. Then all the Greeks took Sosthenes, the ruler of the synagogue, and beat him before the judgment seat. But Gallio took no notice of these things"* (Acts 18:12-17).; *'I found out that he was accused concerning questions of their law, but had nothing charged against him deserving of death or chains'"* (Acts 23:29); *'But when I found that he had committed nothing deserving of death, and that he himself had appealed to Augustus, I decided to send him'"* (Acts 25:25).

Paul turned the tables here. With these five thoughts he brought the case to Agrippa and Festus. What will they do with Jesus has greater consequences than what they would do with Paul. These five thoughts at the end of the third scene are a classic example of the proclamation of the resurrection of Jesus Christ through the ministry of the Apostle Paul.

Questions

1. How did Paul turn the tables on his accusers?
2. Explain how Paul was a citizen both of Rome and Israel?

For Discussion

1. What do you think Paul's motive was in his defense?

30

The Story of Christianity
An Interlude

In 2001 I set out to preach through the book of Acts. In September I arrive at Acts 27. That week the unthinkable occurred. Four coordinated terrorists attack by al-Qaeda, an Islamic terrorist group occurred. 2,996 people were killed with another 6,000 being injured. There was around $10 billion loss in property damage. Four passenger airliners with United Airlines and American Airlines were hijacked by 19 al-Qaeda terrorists. Additional individuals died of cancer and respiratory disease shortly after the attacks due to their being in or near the World Trade Center, New York City or Pentagon in Washington DC. Our country would never be the same again.

On September 10, 2001 I had the privilege of speaking in the evening session for the American Association of Christian Schools at their annual meeting In Washington D.C. The next day our group of educators and pastors were going to the White House for a briefing. The morning was beautiful. On the way to the meeting the Association president said that a plane had hit the world Trade Center. I remember thinking that the plane did not get high enough. Assuming it was a small plane, I thought this was a major mistake. We arrived at the White House and I was walking toward a private entrance with my colleagues. A woman came from the building crying frantically. Shortly after a guard came out with what looked like an old fashioned Walky-talky. Someone was speaking to him on the machine. Then he said to us, "A plane is coming full throttle toward the White House." I thought he then said "Run to J Street". I found later he said 'G

Street'. I knew what run meant and led the pack. I arrived at G. Street, then I saw the Pentagon in smoke. The plane that appeared to be heading to the White House went over the president's quarters and into the Pentagon.

Upon returning home (at that time I lived in Florida) the next five weeks our church joined thousands of others with an attendance far larger than normal. The attendance stayed larger for five weeks. Then things went back to normal. As we have been studying the book of Acts, I would suggest that the resurrection of Jesus Christ was an event that did turn the world upside down for good. 9/11 was a tragic time in American history. Yet good came out of it. I remember how proud I was of our president George W. Bush leading the country with a pastoral type direction. The American flags were on our cars. We united together.

As we come to the last two chapters of the book of Acts, it would be my desire for all of us to unite together, as Americans did, with the greatest of all causes. The proclamation of the resurrection of Jesus Christ. He and He alone is the only Savior of the world! Also, say a prayer for those who lost loved ones in the tragedy of 9/11.

CHAPTER

31

The Story of Christianity
Paul's Journey to Rome
(Acts 27: 1-44)

And when it was determined that we should sail into Italy,
they delivered Paul and certain other prisoners unto one
named Julius, a centurion of Augustus' band. And entering
into a ship of Adramyttium, we launched, meaning to sail
by the coasts of Asia; one Aristarchus, a Macedonian of
Thessalonica, being with us. And the next day we touched
at Sidon. And Julius courteously entreated Paul, and
gave him liberty to go unto his friends to refresh himself.
And when we had launched from thence, we sailed under
Cyprus, because the winds were contrary. And when we
had sailed over the sea of Cilicia and Pamphylia, we came
to Myra, a city of Lycia. And there the centurion found a
ship of Alexandria sailing into Italy; and he put us therein.
And when we had sailed slowly many days, and scarce
were come over against Cnidus, the wind not suffering us,
we sailed under Crete, over against Salmone; And, hardly
passing it, came unto a place which is called The fair
havens; nigh whereunto was the city of Lasea. Now when
much time was spent, and when sailing was now dangerous,
because the fast was now already past, Paul admonished
them, And said unto them, Sirs, I perceive that this voyage

will be with hurt and much damage, not only of the lading and ship, but also of our lives. Nevertheless the centurion believed the master and the owner of the ship, more than those things which were spoken by Paul. And because the haven was not commodious to winter in, the more part advised to depart thence also, if by any means they might attain to Phenice, and there to winter; which is an haven of Crete, and lieth toward the south west and north west. And when the south wind blew softly, supposing that they had obtained their purpose, loosing thence, they sailed close by Crete. But not long after there arose against it a tempestuous wind, called Euroclydon. And when the ship was caught, and could not bear up into the wind, we let her drive. And running under a certain island which is called Clauda, we had much work to come by the boat: Which when they had taken up, they used helps, undergirding the ship; and, fearing lest they should fall into the quicksands, strake sail, and so were driven. And we being exceedingly tossed with a tempest, the next day they lightened the ship; And the third day we cast out with our own hands the tackling of the ship. And when neither sun nor stars in many days appeared, and no small tempest lay on us, all hope that we should be saved was then taken away. But after long abstinence Paul stood forth in the midst of them, and said, Sirs, ye should have hearkened unto me, and not have loosed from Crete, and to have gained this harm and loss. And now I exhort you to be of good cheer: for there shall be no loss of any man's life among you, but of the ship. For there stood by me this night the angel of God, whose I am, and whom I serve, Saying, Fear not, Paul; thou must be brought before Caesar: and, lo, God hath given thee all them that sail with thee. Wherefore, sirs, be of good cheer: for I believe God, that it shall be even as it was told me. Howbeit we must be cast upon a certain island. But when the fourteenth night was come, as we were driven up and down in Adria, about midnight the shipmen deemed that they drew near to some country; And sounded, and found it twenty fathoms: and when they had gone a little further, they sounded again, and found it fifteen fathoms. Then fearing lest we should have fallen upon rocks, they cast four anchors out of the stern, and wished for the day. And as the shipmen were about to flee out of the ship, when they had let down the boat into the sea, under colour as though they would have cast anchors out of the foreship, Paul said to the centurion and to the soldiers, Except these abide in the ship, ye cannot be saved. Then the soldiers cut off the ropes of the boat, and let her fall off. And while the day was coming on, Paul besought them all to take meat, saying, This day is the fourteenth day that ye have tarried and continued fasting, having taken nothing. Wherefore I pray you to take some meat: for this is for your health: for there shall not an hair fall from the head of any of you. And when he had thus spoken, he took bread, and gave thanks to God in presence of them all: and when he had broken it, he began to eat. Then were they all of good cheer, and they also took some meat. And we were in all in the ship two hundred threescore and sixteen souls. And when they had eaten enough, they lightened the ship, and cast out the wheat into the sea. And when it was day, they knew not the land: but they discovered a certain creek with a shore, into the which they were minded, if it were possible, to thrust in the ship. And when they had taken up the anchors, they committed themselves unto the sea, and loosed the rudder bands, and hoised up the mainsail to the wind, and made toward shore. And falling into a place where two seas met, they ran the ship aground; and the forepart stuck fast, and remained unmoveable, but the hinder part was broken with the violence of the waves. And the soldiers' counsel was to kill the prisoners, lest any of them should swim out, and escape. But the centurion, willing to save Paul, kept them from their purpose; and commanded that they which could swim should cast themselves first into the sea, and get to land: And the rest, some on boards, and some on broken pieces of the ship. And so it came to pass, that they escaped all safe to land (Acts 27: 1-44 KJV).

As of this writing I have made five trips to Italy. Being an Italian has always produced a tug in my heart to see homeland. On four occasions I flew to Rome. One occasion was a flight to Florence. Paul the apostle planned to go to Rome. It is interesting his trip was as a prisoner.

In every organization there is a need for leadership. Families need leadership. Throughout the book of Acts we see the leadership of several individuals such as Peter, Stephen, Philip, James, Festus, Agrippa, and many others. This chapter is the story of a voyage, storm, and shipwreck. One of the keys to the story is the leadership of the apostle Paul. As we approach this chapter we will view two characteristics of the leading of Paul's leadership through a storm.

The Wisdom of Paul   (27:1-20)

Paul is a prisoner on a ship. There are other prisoners on board. Julius is the centurion. A centurion had a group of one hundred Roman soldiers. The centurion finds a coastal ship and the boat leaves Caesarea and goes eighty miles to Sidon in one day. Paul visits some friends then reboards the ship and goes to Myra. There the 276 passengers onboard. The ship goes from Myra to Cnidus, then Crete off Salmone and eventually arrives in Fair Haven. A decision is to be made. Should they winter in Fair Haven or try to go to Phoenix? The storm that was brewing could be deadly. Paul has experienced storms and shipwrecks. (2 Corinthians 11:25).

It is interesting to think through the thoughts of the centurion. Fair Haven was not known as a place to settle because it was susceptible to winter storms with little shelter. Phoenix was a sheltered harbor. The master owner recommended that the ship go to Phoenix or at least go as far as they could. Forty miles is not a long journey. With expert advice they set sail. As they leave the wind dies down. The word tempestuous in Acts 27:14 is the Greek *tuphonikus* which means typoon. The term that was used by the sailors is *Euroclydon* which means northeaster.

The ship drifted twenty-three miles to the island of Clauda. As the storm intensified they wrapped ropes around the hull and took down sails. Then on the second day they threw some of the wheat overboard and the following day did the same with furnishings.

Paul had warned them not to move ahead, but the ship-leaders did not listen. The Centurion had the responsibilities. Paul was guided by the

Lord. Paul showed wisdom. *"For the Lord gives wisdom, from His mouth come knowledge and understanding."* (Proverbs 2:6). The Greek word for wisdom is *Sophia*. Knowledge is to know what God says in His Word. Wisdom is the application. In this section of Scripture Paul shows great wisdom based on what he has learned through experience.

The Encouragement of Paul   (27:21-44)

Crisis and trouble come to all of us. A crisis shows what a person has in them and it will reveal what they are made of. Leadership is revealed during crisis. Paul, with humility, reminds the ship's leadership they should have listened to him.

Paul begins his encouragement with relating how the angel of God assured him he would stand before Caesar. He tells the leadership to have courage. This is God's will. Thus they should be encouraged.

For two weeks they had been at sea and the ship was driven off course for several hundred miles. The Adrian Sea (Ionian today), was getting shallow. Paul had told the people to stay on board, but some had abandoned the boat. The soldiers also cut the boat free.

Paul then took bread and said the blessing. The food refreshed the people. When daylight came the pilot saw the futility of the occasion. Passengers jumped into the water to head for land. The soldiers were concerned about losing the prisoners. Paul assured them if they would listen, all would be right.

Questions

1. Who can you think of in Scripture who tried to escape God when trouble came?
2. What is revealed in a person's life when storms come?

For Discussion

1. Tell of an example you may know of when someone used wisdom and leadership during a crisis.

CHAPTER

32

The Story of Christianity
Paul's Arrival in Rome

(Acts 28:1-31)

And when they were escaped, then they knew that the island was called Melita. And the barbarous people shewed us no little kindness: for they kindled a fire, and received us every one, because of the present rain, and because of the cold. And when Paul had gathered a bundle of sticks, and laid them on the fire, there came a viper out of the heat, and fastened on his hand. And when the barbarians saw the venomous beast hang on his hand, they said among themselves, No doubt this man is a murderer, whom, though he hath escaped the sea, yet vengeance suffereth not to live. And he shook off the beast into the fire, and felt no harm. Howbeit they looked when he should have swollen, or fallen down dead suddenly: but after they had looked a great while, and saw no harm come to him, they changed their minds, and said that he was a god. In the same quarters were possessions of the chief man of the island, whose name was Publius; who received us, and lodged us three days courteously. And it came to pass, that the father of Publius lay sick of a fever and of a bloody flux: to whom Paul entered in, and prayed, and laid his hands on him, and healed him. So when this was done, others also, which had diseases in the island, came, and were healed: Who also honoured us with many honours; and when we departed, they laded us with such things as were necessary. And after three months we departed in a ship of Alexandria, which had wintered in the isle, whose sign was Castor and Pollux. And landing at Syracuse, we tarried there three days. And from thence we fetched a compass, and came to Rhegium: and after one day the south wind blew, and we came the next day to Puteoli: Where we found brethren, and were desired to tarry with them seven days: and so we went toward Rome. And from thence, when the brethren heard of us, they came to meet us as far as Appii forum, and The three taverns: whom when Paul saw, he thanked God, and took courage. And when we came to Rome, the centurion delivered the prisoners to the captain of the guard: but Paul was suffered to dwell by himself with a soldier that kept him. And it came to pass, that after three days Paul called the chief of the Jews together: and when they were come together, he said unto them, Men and brethren, though I have committed nothing against the people, or customs of our fathers, yet was I delivered prisoner from Jerusalem into the hands of the Romans. Who, when they had examined me, would have let me go, because there was no cause of death in me. But when the Jews spake against it, I was constrained to appeal unto Caesar; not that I had ought to accuse my nation of. For this cause therefore have I called for you, to see you, and to speak with you: because that for the hope of Israel I am bound with this chain. And they said unto him, We neither received letters out of Judaea concerning thee, neither any of the brethren that came shewed or spake any harm of thee. But we desire to hear of thee what thou thinkest: for as concerning this sect, we know that every where it is spoken against. And when they had appointed him a day, there came many to him into his lodging; to whom he expounded and testified the kingdom of God, persuading them concerning Jesus, both out of the law of Moses, and out of the prophets, from morning till evening. And some believed the things which *were spoken, and some believed not. And when they agreed not among themselves, they departed, after that Paul had spoken one word, Well spake the Holy Ghost by Esaias the prophet unto our fathers, Saying, Go unto this people, and say, Hearing ye shall hear, and shall not understand; and seeing ye shall see, and not perceive: For the heart of this people is waxed gross, and their ears are dull of hearing, and their eyes have they closed; lest they should see with their eyes, and hear with their ears, and understand with their heart, and should be converted, and I should heal them. Be it known therefore unto you, that the salvation of God is sent unto the Gentiles, and that they will hear it. And when he had said these words, the Jews departed, and had great reasoning among themselves. And Paul dwelt two whole years in his own hired house, and received all that came in unto him, Preaching the kingdom of God, and teaching those things which concern the Lord Jesus Christ, with all confidence, no man forbidding him* (Acts 28:1-31 KJV).

The group arrived at the Isle of Malta. Malta means refuge and it would appear this is how the 276 people viewed Malta. The natives were hospitable in welcoming the newcomers. The word native is interesting. "The primary meaning of the Greek word is 'people who speak in a foreign tongue', i.e. non-Greeks."[90]

Paul was a beautiful example of being a servant. He was gathering a bundle of sticks when a viper fastened on his hand. The snake was poisonous and the natives expected Paul to die. The word for creature is *thesion.* Every people group has a sense of right and wrong and justice. Assumptions were that Paul had a criminal record and the viper was judgment.

Of all God's creatures. I must confess that the snake is one I loathe. My father took me fishing years ago in the Tioughnioga River near Marathon, New York. It is a 34 plus mile long tributary of the Chenango River in Central New York. We both had waders on. As I went out I saw something coming at me on the top of the water. It was a snake about two feet long. It went down between my waders and as a young 10-12 year old, I was petrified the creature was in my boot. Of course, it wasn't. I threw my pole into the air and ran towards shore. My father, probably 20 yards away in the river, laughed until he was dark red in the face. As he turned around there was a snake on a tree branch at his head. He did the same thing I just did. I then laughed as I was ridding myself of the waders. Since that day snakes and I have no friendship!

Paul's calmness in this episode is to be admired. The natives thought Paul might fall down dead. When Paul shook the creature off and did not swell up, the people thought he was a god. When he was fine it quickly gave him great credence with those natives.

For three months the people were treated kindly by the natives. Paul's example was the impetus that helped the passengers. Having lost all, they were treated with gifts and dignity.

Paul's Ministry

The book of Acts winds down with a new ship secured and Paul heading towards Rome. It was 80 miles for them to travel to Syracuse, then another seventy to Rhegium. On then to the Port of Naples named Puteoli. Julius allowed Paul, some prisoners, and guards to take a week for rest and relaxation.

Word has traveled to Rome that Paul was coming. There is no indication in the sacred writings how people knew. Julius took the Appian Way and traveled to Rome. About forty-three miles from Rome is the Forum of Appii. A group of Christians met Paul there. A second group met him at a place called Three Taverns, ten miles from Rome. Paul's goal was to meet with Caesar.

"On the day appointed, Paul spent "from morning till evening" explaining the Scriptures and revealing Christ in the Law and the Prophets. He had 'dialogued' this way with the Jews in one synagogue after another, and now he was sharing the Word with the leaders of many synagogue in Rome ... The result? Some were persuaded and some were not. When the Jewish leaders left Paul's house, they were still arguing among themselves. But Paul had faithfully given his witness to the Jews in Rome, and now he would turn to the Gentiles."[91]

These Jewish leaders, students of God's word, had become dull of hearing God's Word. " ... *of whom we have much to say, and hard to explain, since you have become dull of hearing*" (Hebrews 5:11). The word dull is the Greek word *nothros* meaning slow, sluggish, or slow of heart. Someone is not hearing when they are dull spiritually. The gospel went from Jerusalem to the Jews and through Paul's ministry, it would come to Rome to the Gentiles. This chapter is key to understanding the process and progress of the gospel.

Here is Paul ... chained to a guard ... House open ... why? Bible Study! Some were saved. Paul spent much of his time writing. He wrote Ephesians, Philippians, Colossians, and Galatians. He expects to be released. *"For I am hard-pressed between the two, having a desire to depart and be with Christ, which is far better. Nevertheless to remain in the flesh is more needful for you. And being confident of this, I know that I shall remain and continue with you all for your progress and joy of faith, that your rejoicing for me may be more abundant in Jesus Christ by my coming to you again. Only let your conduct be worthy of the gospel of Christ, so that whether I come and see you or am absent, I may hear of your affairs, that you stand fast in one spirit, with one mind striving together for the faith of the gospel"* (Philippians 1:23-27). Timothy is with him. *"Paul and Timothy, bondservants of Jesus Christ, To all the saints in Christ Jesus who are in Philippi, with the bishops and deacons"* (Philippians 1:1); *"Paul, an apostle of Jesus Christ by the will of God, and Timothy our brother"* (Colossians 1:1). He also has John Mark, Demas, Justus, Luke, Epaphras, pastor of Colossae. He leads the runaway slave, Onesimus, to Christ. Epaphroditus is a friend of Paul's. He brings a gift. Paul heard he was sick and almost dies. *"Yet I considered it necessary to send to you Epaphroditus, my brother, fellow worker, and fellow soldier, but your messenger and the one who ministered to my need; since he was longing for you all, and was distressed because you had heard that he was sick. For indeed he was sick almost unto death; but God had mercy on him, and not only on him but on me also, lest I should have sorrow upon sorrow. Therefore I sent him the more eagerly, that when you see him again you may rejoice, and I may be less sorrowful. Receive him therefore in the Lord with all gladness, and hold such men in esteem; because for the work of Christ he came close to death, not regarding his life, to supply what was lacking in your service toward me"* (Philippians 2:25-30); *"Indeed I have all and abound. I am full, having received from Epaphroditus the things sent from you, a sweet-smelling aroma, an acceptable sacrifice, well pleasing to God"* (4:18).

I wish the case before Caesar was written here. It appears that Paul was released and he continued his ministry. The voyage to arrive is " ... the remarkable account of ancient sea navigation in the annals of history."[92]

The case before Caesar is not detailed by Luke. Some contend that Paul never appeared before Caesar. This is possible if the accusers never came with their case. This does not seem plausible since the angel of the Lord was very clear. " ... *saying, 'Do not be afraid, Paul; you must be brought before Caesar; and indeed God has granted you all those who sail with you"* (Acts 27:24).

One thing we do know. The Bible is the very inspired Word of God. The course of events to the Biblical revelation of redemption is what really matters. Those are the words God has decided to give the inspired writers.

Some added thoughts are these. Paul was known among the whole palace guards. These palace guards were known as praetorian guards. They were a group of 10,000 guards. These were very powerful people who had many special privileges. Emperors wanted their respect and favor. The apostle's influence went beyond the group to emperor's palace. *"All the saints greet you, but especially those who are of Caesar's household"* (Philippians 4:22).

Paul, after his release, would go to Spain. " ... *whenever I journey to Spain, I shall come to you. For I hope to see you on my journey, and to be helped on my way there by you, if first I may enjoy your company for a while"* (Romans 15:24). He would write the pastoral epistles to Titus and Timothy. He has as his goal the winning of Jews and Gentile to Jesus.

Paul's life would become challenging. He was arrested again. He was treated as a criminal. *"However, for this reason I obtained mercy, that in me first Jesus Christ might show all longsuffering, as a pattern to those who are going to believe on Him for everlasting life* (1 Tim. 1:16); " ... *in like manner also, that the women adorn themselves in modest apparel, with propriety and moderation, not with braided hair or gold or pearls or costly clothing"* (2:9). Many believers sadly forsook him. Here is the apostle that gave all he had to God's work only to be abandoned by the people he was a blessing to. Some wanted to stay away from him because they did not want to identify with him as a prisoner. Tradition teaches he was beheaded somewhere between 60 and 69 AD.

Paul was a hero. Would to God more of us would be like him and Peter.

Questions

1. What did Paul do when he arrived in Rome?

2. What was it about Paul's character that allowed so many people to treat him kindly?

For Discussion

1. Why do you think there is no mention of his meetings with Caesar?
2. Do you think there was a meeting?

CHAPTER

33

The Story of Christianity Conclusions

The following are 50 lessons that are taken from the book of Acts. The lessons are given based upon the narrative of the Acts document. It is not the intention to rehash the story line or theology we found in the exposition. The purpose is to list 50 lessons that one takes away which will encourage the reader. Each lesson will be listed with a few comments. Preachers and teachers of God's Word can take these lessons and develop them into very helpful sermons, Bible Studies, discussions, and lessons.

The Lessons

1. Acts is a book that presents the early history of the story of Christianity. How did Christianity begin? Here is the story. Remarkably, it is estimated that one third of the world's population has an affinity with the faith that Jesus Christ established. His followers were amazing in their loyalty and allegiance. Across the world there are many spiritually hungry followers of Jesus.

2. The two themes of the Acts are the resurrection of Jesus Christ and the work of the Holy Spirit. Jesus' resurrection changed lives. The evidence is clear in the lives of the apostles and early followers of Jesus. The book of Acts makes it clear that Jesus of Nazareth is the Messiah of Israel. When the Holy Spirit came

as a permanently indwelling presence, 3,000 Jews recognized Jesus for who He was on the day of Pentecost.

3. Believers in Acts 2 were Old Testament followers of God who now realized that Jesus Christ is the Messiah of Israel and that they received the Holy Spirit, thus preparing them to follow Jesus.

4. The early church's structure is listed in Acts 2:41-47. The structure included preaching (both proclamation and evangelization) and teaching of the Word of God, baptism, community, prayer, fear (the awe of God; respect of God) producing worship, giving, and witnessing as evidenced by changed lives.

5. The qualifications to be an apostle are founded on the basis that they should have seen Jesus and been with Him in order to proclaim the resurrection. (John 15:27; Acts 1:21-22; 1 Corinthians 9:1; Acts 22:14-15).

6. Preaching was primary in the Book of Acts. The early Christians preached and the followers anxiously and faithfully listened. It may be estimated that twenty-five percent of the Acts is dedicated to preaching. Every generation needs Biblical preaching.

7. The keys given to Peter as recorded in Matthew 16:16-20 are the keys to the kingdom of heaven and not keys to heaven. A key was a sign of authority (Luke 11:52). They were used to open doors. Peter used the keys to open the door of the gospel to the Jews on the day of Pentecost. (Acts 2). He also did this after the preaching of Philip in Samaria. (Acts 8: 14-17). He then finished this by going to the house of Cornelius. (Acts 10). The early apostles were given authority to 'bind' and 'loose'. This spoke of the rabbis who had authority to forbid and permit various practices. The Holy Spirit was now within them. This fulfills the great commission by taking the gospel to the world. (Acts 1:8; Jerusalem, Judea, Samaria and the uttermost part of the world). Once this was accomplished, the keys belong to Jesus. (Revelation 1:18; 9:1).

8. A name is often given to a baby with a belief that their character would be revealed. Many Jewish mothers to this day continue this practice.

9. People need to be saved because of one reason. They are lost, in sin, and in need of a Savior (following the preaching of the early apostles).

10. The evidence that one has been with Jesus is the evidence of their lifestyle. (Acts 4:13).

11. A person's giving is dependent on their heart to give. (Acts 20:35).

12. A Christian's worth is based on the provision of Jesus Christ. The Christian life is impossible to live unless Christ is living His life through believers. (Ephesians 1-3).

13. Although there are many men and women who have a special place in the story of the Book of Acts, two men are the key leaders. First, there is Peter. Secondly, is Paul. Although Peter took the message of the resurrection to Cornelius, an Italian Gentile and not a Jew, the apostle was primarily the apostle to the Jews. Paul, who also ministered to the Jews, became however, the apostle to the Gentiles.

14. The Book of Acts tells us numerous stories of how God has the right people, in the right place, at the right time. For example, in Acts 3, there is a crippled man and Peter and John show up. Philip goes to the Ethiopian Eunuch from Samaria. This is often true in our lives.

15. Although evangelism is a primary way for Christianity to grow; greater growth is often accomplished through persecution. The Word of God spread ... Why? Because of persecution. All apostles except John were mentored.

16. All Christians have a place in God's kingdom. Acts is full of names, not well known, that made a major impact on the gospel. (Matthias, Nicanor, Nicolas; and many more).

17. The laying on of hands symbolizes a conferral of authority which include both responsibility and obligation. There is a load of responsibility that includes obligation. (Acts 8:17; 6:6; 13:3). The Old Testament teaches that this was a method for future ministry (Numbers 8:10; 27:18).

18. Religion is a detriment to Christianity. Religion is a belief in a supernatural being. True Christianity is more than a belief in a supernatural being, it's a belief in a personal relationship

with Jesus Christ through the sacred writings of the Scriptures. The Book of Acts endorses this reality. (Note in Acts 9).

19. Not all preachers are members of modern day clergy. Stephen is an example.

20. The quotations in Acts from the Old Covenant condensed the divinely inspired Scriptures of both Testaments. (Joel 2:25-31; cf Acts 2:16-21 is an example).

21. Never give up on someone in regards to their salvation. The Apostle Paul is a powerful example.

22. The main thing of the Christian faith is to teach people about the message of the death and resurrection of Jesus.

23. One's appearance means little in comparison to the anointing of God on a life. One example is Paul who many believed to be rather short and not attractive.

24. There were many 'lords' in the days of the book of Acts. Jesus is proclaimed in Acts to be the Lord. (Acts 9).

25. The story of God's preparation to bring people to Jesus floods the book of Acts. In Acts 2 the Holy Spirit arrives on the day of Pentecost. Jerusalem is flooded with visitors. In Acts 10 Cornelius is seeking God and brings his family and friends to hear Peter. These are just 2 examples.

26. The Great commission has several aspects. In Matthew the emphasis is on *discipleship*; Mark … *preaching*; in Luke … going, and in John one on one connection. In Acts the focus is on the Holy Spirit and location.

27. The speaking in tongues in Acts were languages that people heard in their own dialect.

28. The work of providing for our salvation is finished. Jesus did that through his death, burial, and resurrection. The work of evangelism continues.

29. Christians were known as members of the Way. They were first called Christians in Acts 11. The nonbelieving Jews looked at Jesus' followers as a sect of Judaism. One thing they knew, regardless of what they were called, they were changed by Jesus; the Son of God.

30. The Grace of God is at the heart of the Christian faith.

31. The atonement and resurrection of Jesus Christ is what sets Christianity apart from religion.

32. Prayer was the greatest discipline and practiced by the early church. (Acts 1:13-15; 3:1-5).
33. There are two spiritual kingdoms … the kingdom of God and the kingdom of the devil.
34. Christians have disagreements. Acts 15 is a good example of solving them with conviction and compromise.
35. Missions was a key part of the early church. (Note the 3 missionary journeys of Paul).
36. A question that needs regular discussion is this. Is the modern, contemporary church following the example of the Book of Acts?
37. The Book of Acts teaches the importance of doing what is necessary in order to reach people.
38. Everyone needs community. Other than family, the church should be the key community for Christians.
39. The life of a spiritual leader includes protecting his followers from evil and false teaching.
40. In the speeches that Paul gave to defend his faith, his goal was to communicate clearly the resurrection.
41. Peter and Paul were vocal, yet wise leaders.
42. Success is the accomplishment of a worthy goal. Despite persecution and jail time, Paul kept his focus on going to Rome.
43. Strong political leaders who are unregenerate are no match for a well-taught man of God. Notice that fact in Paul's apologia messages.
44. God prepares the way for the unbelievable. The exposition for Acts gives numerous such examples.
45. The body of Christ is open to everyone.
46. Jesus Christ is the Messiah of Israel!
47. The Book of Acts does not record Paul's meeting with Caesar. Yet it teaches that Paul arrived in Rome. Paul spends two years preaching the Word of God as a prisoner without restraint. It is a reminder that the Scriptures are always accurate, but the theme is the redemptive story. No details at Paul's meeting with Caesar seems anticlimactic. The Bible is a book of redemption. Not all details are necessary or needed. The story of redemption is mandatory.

48. The Great Commission commands are fulfilled as evidences by the following list of conversions in the Book of Acts.
Conversion of the 3,000 (Acts 2:22-47)
Conversion of the Samaritans (Acts 8:5-15)
Conversion of the Ethiopian Eunuch (Acts 8:26-38)
Conversion of Saul/Paul (Acts 9:1-18; 22:6-15)
Conversion of Cornelius (Acts 10:30-48)
Conversion of the Proconsul (Acts 13:12)
Conversion of Lydia (Acts 16:13-16)
Conversion of the Jailer (Acts 16:26-31)
Conversion of Dionysius, Damaris (Acts 17:34)
Conversion of Crispus (Acts 18:8)
Conversion of Apollas (Acts 18:24-26)
Conversion of 25 disciples of John (Acts 19:1-4)

49. Baptism is the public expression of faith in Jesus Christ. The word baptism is found 16 times in the gospel accounts, but 19 times in the Book of Acts. (Acts 2:37-41; 8:5-13, 36, 38; 9:10-12,17-19; 10:47-48; 16:13-15, 27-34; 18:5-8; 19:1-5; 22:14-17).
In almost every case, believers were baptized immediately after salvation, highlighting the importance of the act. It portrays the death, burial, and resurrection of Jesus Christ and the desire to follow the Savior. In the book of Acts, baptism was the identification, publically, of ones' faith in Christ.

50. So there you have it. The amazing story of the beginning of Christianity! The fact is the God of the Christian has always been.

The Book of Acts is the forty-fourth book of the Holy Bible. The first verse of the Bible begins with "In the beginning God created the heavens and the earth." There was a beginning and God created everything. Questions abound. For example, how long ago did God create? What method did God use? How did He do this? What did God do? He created. What did He create? The heavens. The heavens include the galaxies. There are probably more than 170 billion galaxies in the universe. It is estimated that there are between 200-400 billion stars in the Milky Way (our galaxy).

The fact is, God has always been. Note the following:

> *"In the beginning"* – Time   *"God created the*
> *heavens"* – Space   *"and the earth"* – Solid

This is who our God is! He is the beginning and all space and solid are from His creation.

The Bible ends with the words *"The grace of our Lord Jesus Christ be with you all. Amen."* (Revelation 22:21).

This wonderful God who spoke all into existence has given us His grace. Grace is that unmerited favor He has promised to all who come to Christ because His grace pulls us.

So here, in the Book of Acts we are told the story of the God of the Universe who sent His only Son to be the Savior through the process of the death, burial and resurrection. The early days of the Christian Faith are chronicled in the Book of Acts. The Christian's foundation is through God's working in the lives of men and women. He continues in this work today.

Endnotes

1. Baker Evangelical Dictionary of Biblical Theology. R. David Rightmire 1996 Baker
2. Theophilus (biblical), https://wikipedia.org/wiki/Theophilus_(biblical), date accessed January 10, 2019.
3. Alfred Edersheim, Sketches of Jewish Social Life. the Life and Times of Jesus the Messiah Hendrickson Publisher, 1984, p. 17.
4. 22 Study Sources: Charts and Outlines. Probable occasion when each Psalm was written 1044 B.C. https://www.blueletterbible.org/study/parallel/parall8.cfm, date accessed January 10, 2019.
5. Elmer Towns, Did Jesus Preach to Angels in Hell, Bible Sprout https://www.biblesprout.com/articles/jesus-christ/preach-angels-hell-spirits-prison/, date accessed January 10, 2019.
6. W. Edward Bedore, Th. D. Hell, Sheol, Hades, Paradise, and the Grave, Berean Bible Institute P.O. Box 587, Slinger, WI. Berean Bible Studies, https://www.beranbible institute.org/files/articles-devotions/HellSheolHadesParadiseandthegrave.pdf, date accessed January 10, 2019.
7. Warren Wiersbe, The Bible Exposition Commentary New Testament, Volume 1 2001 409
8. Thomas Thigpen, True Grace Missions, The Biblical Doctrine of Hell, 1855 PT. 2
9. Paul Summers, The Two Lords, www.hebrew-streams.org/works/hebrew/2-lords.html, date accessed January 10, 2019.
10. Erika Strassburger, Family Share, Translation and adaptation of the original article, "50 names biblicas poderosos para for a seu Bebe – suns origins a significados" – published on familia.com.br. March 15, 2017
11. 951 Names and Title of God: Alphabetical list of names, https://christiananswers.net/dictionary/namesofgod.html, date accessed January 10, 2019.
12. Josephus Antiquities 1.20. Chapter 8, Section 7, quoted from Got Questions
13. Orbin Root; Acts (Cincinnati, Ohio Standard Publishing Company, 1966) 23

14. Horatio Spafford, It is well with my soul, https://en.wikipedia.org/wiki/
It_Is_Well_with_My_Soul, Date Accessed January 10, 2019.

15. Tertullian, The Apology of Tertullian for the Christians, 197 A.D. 143

16. Mark the cousin of Barnabas, https://en.wikipedia.org/wiki/
Mark_the_cousin_of_Barnabas, date accessed January 10, 2019.

17. The History and Pathology of Crucifixion. S\S Afr Mead 2003 Dec 93
(12) 938

18. Kaufman Kohler, Emil G. Hirsch. Crucifixion Jewish Encyclopedia. The
unedited full text of the 1906 Jewish Encyclopedia 11 221

19. Seven Deacons, https://en.wikipedia.org/wiki/Seven_Deacons, date accessed
January 10, 2019.

20. Bill Mounce, Is Waiting on Tables A Ministry? May 16, 2004, https://www.
billmounce.com/monday-with-mounce/waiting-tables-ministry-acts-6-2,
date accessed January 10, 2019.

21. Ellicott's Commentary for English Readers, Zondervan 1954 116

22. Josephus, Antiquities XIX 7, ,2 Paraphrase from Ellicott

23. Charles Ryrie, Ryrie Study Bible, 1738; 1986

24. A.T. Robertson, Robertson's Word Pictures of the New Testament, Acts
7:54,55 1958

25. Marshall. Acts: An Introduction and Commentary, Vol. 5 Tyndale New
Testament Commentaries 158

26. Kevin Kruse, Employee Engagement 2.0, Employment Engagement, 2012

27. Albert Barnes, Commentary on Acts 8:4. "Barnes Notes on the New
Testament" https//www.Study Light.org/commentaries/bnb/Acts 8
html.1870, date accessed January 10, 2019.

28. Charles Ryrie, Ryrie Study Bible Moody,, Moody,1986 1743

29. Numbers and their meanings –Crystalinks www.crystalinks.
com – Numberology

30. Charles Ryrie Study Bible, NASB, Moody, 1747 Comment on Acts 10:24

31. Samuel John Stone, The Church's One Foundation. https://hymnary.org/
text/the_churchs_one_foundation, date accessed January 10, 2019.

32. Samuel John Stone, (1866-01-01) Lyra Fidelion

33. Christian population growth, https://en.wikipedia.org/wiki/
Christian_population_growth, date accessed January 10, 2019.

34. Ibid.

35. David B. Barrett: George Thomas Kurion: Todd M. Johnson, eds. February
15,2001

36. World Christian Encyclopedia 360 Oxford University Press USA

37. Were those who believed in God during Old Testament times
saved through Christ? Billy Graham Answers, Billy Graham
Evangelistic Associates, June 1, 2004, https://billygraham.org/answer/

were-those-who-believed-in-god-during-old-testament-times-saved-through-christ/, date accessed January 10, 2019.

38. Tertullian Apologeticus, Chapter 50, Autumn 197 AD
39. The Famine of Acts 11, http://www.biblehistory.net/newsletter/acts11_famine.htm, date accessed January 10, 2019
40. F. Josephus, & Whiston, W. (1987). The works of Josephus: complete and unabridged, Peabody: Hendrickson. 95
41. Charles Ryrie, Ryrie Study Bible, NASB, 1920, Footnotes
42. Charles Ryrie. Ibid
43. Unleavened Bread, https://en.wikipedia.org/wiki/Unleavened_bread, date accessed January 14, 2019.
44. Hebrews Roots/Holy Days of Week of Unleavened Bread, https://en.wikibooks.org/wiki/Hebrew_Roots/Holy_Days/Week_of_Unleavened_Bread, date accessed January 10, 2019.
45. 40. F. Josephus, & Whiston, W. (1987). The works of Josephus: complete and unabridged, Peabody: Hendrickson, 434
46. Charles Ryrie's Study Bible, Moody Publishers 1751 1990 Update
47. All the Women of the Bible, Chapter 2 Alphabetical Exposition of Named Bible Women. M – Mary, mother of John Mark, Zondervan, All Rights Reserved
48. I. Howard Marshall, Acts, Tyndale New Testament Commentaries (Grand Rapids, MI. Eerdmans 1980), 214 quoted from Grace Communion International.
49. Charles Ryrie, The Ryrie Study Bible, Moody Press, 1753, ASV 1995 Update
50. Charles Ryrie, The Ryrie Study Bible, Moody Press, 287 1995 Update
51. Got Questions? What is the Gospel? https://thewordknust.wordpress.com/2018/05/30/got-questions-what-is-the-gospel/, date accessed January 10, 2019.
52. Charles Ryrie, The Ryrie Study Bible, Moody Press 1755, RSV 1995 Update
53. JVP New Testament Commentaries Acts 14 – Exegesis Intervarsity Press, View Acts 14:1-7 1994
54. Oxford University Press Classical Mytheology. Michael Sham. Ovid. The Story of Lycon Website.
55. John McArthur, The McArthur New Testament Commentary, 1996; 61 Moody Press
56. Charles Ryrie, The Ryrie Study Bible, Moody Press Updated 1996 1757
57. R.C.H. Lenski. The Interpretation of the Acts of the Apostles [Minneapolis: Augsburg, 1961] 43 563
58. Charles Ryrie. The Ryrie Study Bible, Moody Press Updated 1996 1757
59. Wikipedia, Gamaliel the Elder edited by Maczkopeti

60. John MacArthur. The McArthur's New Testament Commentary 1996 96 Moody Press

61. John B. Pothill, The New American Commentary; Acts [Nashville: Broadman 1992] 351

62. Everitt F. Harrison, Taken from Interpreting Acts. The Expanding Church. [Grand Rapids. Zondervan 1986] 292

63. G. Campbell Morgan, The Acts of the Apostles [Revell, 1924], 405-6)

64. Charles Ryrie, Ryrie Study Bible, Moody Press, 1995 1764

65. Hendrickson, New International Biblical Commentary: Acts [Peabody, MA: Hendrickson 1990] 329

66. John MacArthur, MacArthur New Testament Commentary, Volume 2, Moody Press 1996, 166

67. The Book of Acts, The New International Commentary on the New Testament [Grand Rapids: Eerdmans, 1971] 388-389

68. John MacArthur, MacArthur New Testament Commentary, Volume 2 Moody Press 1996 177

69. John MacArthur, MacArthur New Testament Commentary, Volume 2 Moody Press 1996 200

70. Epistle to the Magnesians IX; the Ante-Nicene Fathers [reprint; Grand Rapids; Eerdmans, 1973] 163

71. Charles Ryrie, Ryrie Study Bible, Moody Press, 1995 1768

72. John MacArthur, MacArthur New Testament Commentary, Volume 2 Moody Press 1996 210

73. The Reformed Pastor [Edinburgh Banner of Truth, 1979] 67-68

74. The Minister as Shepherd [Hong Kong Living Books for All, 1980] 41-42, 43-44

75. Warren Wiersbe, The Bible Exposition Commentary. New Testament, Volume 1. 2001 Cook Press 488

76. Warren Wiersbe, The Bible Exposition Commentary. New Testament Volume 1. 2001 Cook Press 489

77. E.M. Blaiklock and R.K. Harrison, eds, The New International Dictionary of Biblical Archeology [Grand Rapids Zondervan, 1983], 389

78. Philip Yancy, The Bible Jesus Read, Zondervan Publishing House, 1999, 100; from Messengers of God. Elie Wiesel

79. John MacArthur, The MacArthur New Testament Commentary, Vol 2 Moody Press; 1996 278

80. John MacArthur, New Testament Commentary, Vol 2 Moody Press 1996 278

81. John MacArthur, New Testament Commentary, Vol 2 Moody Press 1996 303

82. FF Bruce, Paul, Apostle of a Heart Set Free [Grand Rapids: Eerdmans 1977] 355

83. Claudius Lysias, https://en.wikipedia.org/wiki/Claudius_Lysias, date accessed January 10, 2019.

84. Warren Wiersbe, The Bible Exposition Commentary New Testament, Part 1, 2001 Cook Press 501

85. Warren Wiersbe, The Bible Exposition Commentary New Testament, Part 1, 2001 Cook Press 503

86. Warren Wiersbe, The Bible Exposition Commentary New Testament, Part 1, 2001 Cook Press 503

87. Warren Wiersbe, The Bible Exposition Commentary New Testament Part 1, 2001 Cook Press 1996 507

88. John MacArthur, The MacArthur New Testament Commentary, Volume 2, Moody Press 1995 332

89. Charles Ryrie, The Ryrie's Study Bible, Moody Press 1995 1698

90. A. T. Robertson, Word Pictures in the New Testament, Grand Rapids: Bakers reprint of the 1930 edition, 3 749

91. Wayne Jackson, Christian Courier "Paul's Two-Year Prison Imprisonment" Access Date August 27, 2018

CPSIA information can be obtained
at www.ICGtesting.com
Printed in the USA
FFHW022155210619
53160944-58815FF